920
HoL

Telephone : 01 - 340 3343

Reserve Stock

HIGHGATE LITERARY & SCIENTIFIC INSTITUTION
II, SOUTH GROVE, N.6

——

Time allowed FOURTEEN Days

TURN ON THE FOUNTAINS

Dean Hole by Charles Furse, A.R.A.

TURN ON THE FOUNTAINS

A Life of Dean Hole

by

BETTY MASSINGHAM

———————

LONDON
VICTOR GOLLANCZ LTD
1974

© Betty Massingham 1974

ISBN 0 575 01817 8

14264
———
920

PRINTED IN GREAT BRITAIN
BY EBENEZER BAYLIS AND SON LTD
THE TRINITY PRESS, WORCESTER, AND LONDON

To Persis

The Duke of Rutland told the Dean that he could go over the gardens of Belvoir Castle whenever he wished. Arriving one day unannounced, the Dean asked the head gardener for permission to look round. The head gardener readily agreed and began to conduct the Dean round himself. They got on famously. After a time, realizing that his visitor was a knowledgeable gardener as well as a dignitary of the Church, the man asked the Dean to whom he might have the pleasure of showing the gardens. "The Dean of Rochester, Dean Hole," came the reply. Upon which the gardener cupped his hands over his mouth and shouted down the gardens to various under-gardeners working there: "Turn on the fountains! Turn on the fountains!"

Recalled by Dame Sybil Thorndike

"He who would have beautiful roses in his garden must have beautiful roses *in his heart*. He must love them well and always."

S. Reynolds Hole, *A Book About Roses*

CONTENTS

LIST OF ILLUSTRATIONS

COLOUR PLATES

ACKNOWLEDGEMENTS

I have to make many acknowledgements.

First I recall with gratitude and pleasure the time spared to me so willingly and the kindness and unfailing help and encouragement given to me by the late Lady Tallents, grand-daughter of Dean Hole. I must also especially thank her family who have reflected her good taste and good humour in all matters concerning this biography. Tim, Persis, Martin and Miranda—nothing has been too much trouble for them and their ready help has always been forthcoming. The copyright of all letters, articles and books written by the Dean has been allowed for my use with complete freedom of selection.

I wish to thank individually Cressida Pemberton Pigott for her photograph of her sister Halcyon in their great-great-grandmother's archery dress: Halcyon for modelling the dress with such grace, Viola for her interest throughout.

Mrs John Hole, MBE, has made available for my perusal many family papers, records, diaries and the visitors' book and made contacts for me with people locally who could be of help. I appreciate her permission to allow me to quote from the diaries of both the Dean's mother and his wife. Mrs Hole introduced me to the Dean's nephew, Mr William Francklin, who lived at the Deanery from about the age of eleven until he was nineteen and who kindly related to me his memories of those days. (He has recently died at the age of ninety-two.)

Dame Sybil Thorndike, DBE, also had childhood recollections of the Deanery and of visiting "granfer" as the Thorndike family called Dean Hole. (Her father was an hon. canon of Rochester and in The Archives of the Dean and Chapter of Rochester there is this note: "Special Chapter holden on Thursday, twenty 2nd. day of September, 1887: Resolved that the Revd A. J. W. Thorndike be informed that the Dean and Chapter consent to his removing into the house . . . lately occupied by the Revd J. Hamblin Smith . . .") Dame Sybil remembered the Dean as "a darling man", and they always revelled in the atmosphere of fun and amusing nonsense which prevailed when they went to see him. I am most grateful for the precious time she spared to talk to me.

Among those I wish to thank for permission to quote from books, articles or letters, are: Mr A. V. Caudery, Director of *Punch*, for many excerpts from the Henry Silver Diaries and Miss Jane Haughton, librarian, for her help; Lord David Cecil; Mrs Edward Norman-Butler, first for her kind encouragement and second for generously allowing the publication of two letters from Anne Thackeray to Reynolds Hole (and reproduction of part of one of them) together with passages from letters of Anne Thackeray Ritchie already published and edited by her daughter; *The Cornhill Magazine*, pub. John Murray, for a poem in the March number 1860, and especially Mrs Osyth Leeston for additional help over other copyright; Mrs B. Coxon for allowing the use of an unpublished letter from the Baroness Burdett-Coutts; Mrs Vivian Noakes for advice in connection with an Edward Lear letter; Mrs George Bambridge for most kindly allowing the use of two long unpublished letters from Kipling, and Mrs Frances Trueman of A. P. Watt & Son for her help in the matter; Mrs Alexandra Ingram of the Rights and Permissions Department of Messrs Oliver & Boyd, and Peter Hutchison for putting me in touch with them in connection with letters from Dr John Brown of Edinburgh; The Provost and Fellows of Eton College and also the Assistant Keeper of College Collections, Mr Patrick Devlin; Mr Ian Herbert, general editor, Sir Isaac Pitman and Sons Limited; Miss J. M. Peggs, Principal Administrative Assistant, Charing Cross Hospital, for quotations from *Art For Love*; and the Trustees of Miss Gertrude Jekyll.

I offer my warm thanks to Mr John Hamer, MBE, BA, of the Royal Horticultural Society for permission to photograph rose prints in the Library and to Mr P. S. M. Stageman, Chief Librarian for his kind co-operation and also to Miss Elspeth Napier; to Mr C. Brickell, and also Miss M. H. Granger, for allowing us to photograph the "Gloire de Dijon" rose on Battleston Hill in The Royal Horticultural Society's Gardens at Wisley; to Mr Leonard Hollis (Vice-President) and to Mr L. G. Turner (Secretary), of The Royal National Rose Society and to Mr J. L. Harkness, Editor, *The Rose Bulletin*, for obtaining a print of the Dean as a young man, and other help; to Mr E. L. Crowson, FRPS, AIIP, photographer to The Royal National Rose Society; to John Miller for his excellent photographs taken for the cover, frontispiece and colour illustrations.

Many people have kindly given permission for the use of illustrations and they are acknowledged individually on pages 11 and 12.

For help in various ways I must thank the following: Melanie Anderson; Christine Baker; Stephanie Bellairs; Ralph Boot; Miriam Hodgson; Mr Derrick Cornish; my aunts, Miss Gosselin and Sister Eileen; Bobby Holmes; Mrs H. Hyde-Parker; Virginia Hutchison; Alison Hutchison; Gillian Lawson; Alan Maclean; Adam Massingham (my son); Mrs Hugh Meredith; Nicholas Petsalis-Diomedes; Dr T. Taylor-Jones; Laura Thoresby; Mr Graham Watson; Mr Charles Westley; The Right Rev. the Bishop of Taunton and the Rev. G. Neville; The Right Rev. S. W. Betts, Dean of Rochester; The Archdeacon of Maidstone, the Ven. N. K. Nye; Canon Paul A. Welsby, Ph.D., Librarian of Rochester Cathedral Library; Dr Francis Hull, Kent County Archivist; Sir Ralph Millais; Mr John Davies, ALA, Librarian, The University of Nottingham; Mr Paul Sykes, DMA, FLA, City Librarian, City of Nottingham Public Libraries and Mrs Cook, Chief Librarian, The City Archives and Local Studies Division; Mr Norman Tomlinson, FLA, Borough Librarian, Borough of Gillingham Public Libraries; Mr Sydney G. Poock, contributor to *The Rose Annual*; Mr W. Heath, The Nottingham Rose Society (programme secretary); Mr G. Greenfield, ALA, Librarian, Newark Public Libraries (and his staff); Mr R. F. Songhurst, News Editor, *Kent Life*. I owe especially most sincere thanks to the staff of the London Library.

There is some material for which I have been unable to obtain permission; the copyright holders are either unknown or have long since disappeared. In such cases I wish to make a general acknowledgement.

With reference to the Nottingham Rose Show on p. 45 I have permission from the Nottingham Rose Society, formerly the St Ann's Rose Society, to say that although varying dates for the early shows have been given in good faith by the Hon. Sec. of the Society, these cannot, unfortunately, be confirmed categorically owing to the loss of many of the early documents of the Society.

My profound gratitude is due to Miles Hadfield who has read and corrected the proofs; to Diana Cookson who typed the script with a pleasure that was heart-warming; to June Smith whose secretarial work is combined with much kindness and encouragement. I owe a great deal to Peter Day for his skill and care in editing the book.

B.M.

TURN ON THE FOUNTAINS

AUTHOR'S NOTE

Reynolds Hole, Dean of Rochester, is known widely as a rosarian and as the Founder of the National Rose Show. By a few people still alive who recall his work at Rochester, he is remembered with respect and affection. But as an author of several books, a preacher and a friend of men and women working under the difficult and often disgraceful conditions of the nineteenth century, he is little known; in the felicity of his home life he is even less remembered. With regard to the latter aspect of a biography, Lord David Cecil, speaking on Jane Austen in one of the Leslie Stephen Lectures given at Cambridge 1935, said: "A man's relation to his wife and children is at least as important a part of his life as his relation to his beliefs and career; and reveals him as fundamentally. Indeed it reveals his moral side more fundamentally. If you want to know about a man's talents you should see him in society, if you want to know about his temper you should see him at home."

It is, therefore, the object of this biography to try to show Dean Hole in the general circumstances of his life, as a person, not only in his connection with the rose world, but also to see his work in the light of the times.

BETTY MASSINGHAM

BIDDENDEN KENT
January 1974

1

"Enter a man . . ."

1819–1840

"Enter a man swimming for his life"[1]—line one of scene one of the first act of a drama written by Reynolds Hole at the age of eight. He writes some years later:

> With a remarkable anticipation and prescience of the sensational incidents which would be most acceptable to the popular taste, I did not weary my audience with preliminary explanations and dull details, but I conducted them at once to scenes of wild excitement, and to situations of terrible distress.[2]

This sense of the dramatic served him well throughout his long life and perhaps best of all in the pulpit. He never spoke of anything of which he had not had personal experience, he never had resource to padding or repetition, he went straight to the point, he knew what he was talking about and felt deeply what he was saying. He leant over the edge of the pulpit and talked to his congregation, laughing with them if he had introduced a joke, or crying with them if his subject was a sad one.

But he also asked something of his congregations, as indeed he asked of the actors in his drama.

> . . . if any of my readers will place themselves on a carpet, as in the act of natation, and endeavour to propel themselves along the floor, they will give me credit for courage which was ready, like Cassius, to "leap into the angry flood and swim to yonder point" the point being an armchair . . . representing the welcome shore.[3]

> . . . unemployment, low wages and starvation were periodic among the industrialists of Nottinghamshire, Yorkshire and Lancashire, partly owing to the first effects of new machinery.[4]

England was worn out and exhausted by years of warfare, taxes were high as also was the price of bread. In what proved to be a vain endeavour to strengthen the supply of homegrown wheat a new Corn Law was passed preventing the buying of foreign wheat until the cost had reached £4 a quarter. This meant that many factory workers were near to starvation, being unable to pay such high prices. Riots broke out, and one of the most disastrous of these took place in 1819, when a mass meeting of reformers marched to a waste area known as St Peter's Field, Manchester. They were brutally dispersed with subsequent loss of life by a charge of yeomen and the event became known as "Peterloo". After this tragedy it was realized that a peacetime police force was necessary and in 1829 the blue-uniformed corps was established, not a minute too soon.

1829, too, saw the birth at Nottingham of William Booth, later General Booth, the founder of the Salvation Army. In the preface to his book *In Darkest England And The Way Out* he describes his childhood memories of conditions in Nottingham:

When but a mere child the degradation and helpless misery of the poor Stockingers of my native town, wandering gaunt and hunger-stricken through the streets, droning out their melancholy ditties, crowding the Union or toiling like galley slaves on relief works for a bare subsistence, kindled in my heart yearnings to help the poor which have continued to this day and which have had a powerful influence on my whole life. . . .

The commiseration then awakened by the misery of this class has been an impelling force which has never ceased to make itself felt during forty years of active service in the salvation of men.[5]

Nottingham, like the other industrial areas, had much to answer for. A Bill was under discussion in the House of Lords to punish severely those workers who were smashing the machinery which was robbing them of their chances of livelihood. Another well-known resident of the area became involved in the cause of the "frame-breakers":

During his stay at Newstead, Byron had seen some of these things for himself. The manufacturers round Nottingham had been installing new stocking-frames which enabled one man to take the place of seven. The workless had come into contact with the cavalry, and the Government had had to send down two additional regiments to Nottingham. They wanted to apply the death penalty to the "frame-breakers". Byron had seen these poor creatures with his own eyes, and realized their honesty of purpose. He decided to speak.[6]

The conditions for the lace-makers were not dissimilar but it was in their long hours of employment rather than the introduction of machinery that their chief tragedy lay. Perhaps this may have been due to the fact that the "new lace machine was heavier, more costly and not so adaptable to domestic use".[7]

The conditions for the employment of children were the most shameful of all:

The physical appearance and condition of all the children employed in the lace trade is in general far below the average of factory children: stunted in growth, sometimes deformed, weak and sickly and usually susceptible of disease which they have no strength to resist. Lace children look victims to excessive constitutional debility. The children were often sent for at 1, 2, 3 or 4 a.m., after working till midnight. There was no instance of beds being provided at the factory. The children would sleep on the floor or under a table or perhaps on carriage boxes or men's old jackets.... The heat and bad ventilation of workrooms made them susceptible to cold and irregularity of meals and want of rest destroyed their physical resistance.[8]

Lord Althorp's Factory Act of 1833 tried to ameliorate the conditions under which children worked and appointed factory inspectors whose job it was to visit and enquire into such conditions. Some employers welcomed the Act but others—and this often included parents—resisted any attempts to curtail child labour.

Samuel Hole, Reynolds's grandfather, farmed from a leasehold property, Caunton Grange, near Newark, Nottinghamshire. He had fifteen children. Such a large family led to financial embarrassment and some had to fend for themselves. Reynolds's father, Samuel, who was born in 1778, went with his younger brother, Richard, to Manchester about 1812, the time of his marriage to Mary Cooke, to make his fortune amongst "those dark Satanic mills". It is said in the family that they did so by "putting the spots into cotton".

Caunton Manor was built about 1800 and had gone through the hands of three different families by 1819, the year that Reynolds was born. He was the third child, having two elder sisters, and was brought to Caunton Manor when a few months old. It was here that his sister, Sara, was born in 1821. The house had not been well cared for and did not, at the time when the Holes took possession, aspire to its later establishment as a fine country house. However, it did have a fair

amount of pastureland and some good trees. A large beech still stands
in grass outside the front door, a weeping beech on the left inside the
main gates, and a rustle of bamboos on the right. The house is on the
outskirts of the small village, which comprises of a few cottages close
to the church. Through the churchyard, where it is now bordered on
one steep bank by willows, flows the Caunton Beck. It is willowed,
too, as it idles its way through the manor land where, at every turn,
there are pools suitable to attract a good fat trout. In some places it
backs on to kitchen gardens, in others it is thickly wooded where it
traverses park and gardens landscaped by Capability Brown.

It is an undulating countryside, studded with tall elms, with fields
for pasture and fields for corn, with curving roadways, sometimes
bordered by hedgerows and sometimes having extensive views. When
writing as an old man of his childhood memories, Reynolds Hole
mentions the ancient law which had enforced the cutting back on both
sides of all highways any trees or tall shrubs for a distance of 200 feet,
to ensure safety from robbers, assassins or other villains. However, this
law had long ago fallen into abeyance in Nottinghamshire as everywhere else, and he recalls especially:

A mile from my home there was an umbrageous curve in the road
which was known as the "Dark Turn", and there dwelt, as we
children believed, a mixed company of ogres, demons, bandits, snakes
and hyaenas, prowling the darkness to devour their prey. Whenever
in our walks . . . we came in sight of the Dark Turn, we were seized
with a sudden weariness, a yearning for home, a presentiment of
drenching rains.[9]

He was ten years old before the first railway for passengers was
opened in England, and so communications during his early years were
dependent on horse-driven vehicles. What was going on in Nottingham
might not even be known in Newark, twenty miles away, still less in
a small village such as Caunton. Roads were gradually being
"macadamized"—in the Bristol area this was accomplished as early
as 1816—but there were still many hazards in the outlying countryside.
Again remembering his childhood he writes:

I have never forgotten a striking incident which occurred in a long
and heavy fall of snow, when the Scotch mail being unable to
proceed, the coachman and the guard put saddles on two of the
horses and rode on with the bags. The horse ridden by the coachman was exhausted, stumbled and fell, and being lame when
he rose, was with great difficulty led back to the inn. His rider before

leaving his companion besought him to give up the hopeless endeavour to proceed, but the guard replied that he must do his best to reach a post office, which was only three miles away. He never came, and when a search was made the bags were found suspended on the branch of a tree which grew over the road, his last effort in the work committed to his charge. He may have had a presentiment that the end was near and not many yards from the tree he fell with his horse down a steep bank into a great drift of snow, and there they lay dead together.[10]

In such a small community there was almost a family feeling about the village. There was general interest towards one's neighbours, concern if things were not going well as in illness or bereavement, deliveries of hot soup and home-made dandelion wine, and readiness to saddle a horse to fetch the doctor or the squire or the vicar if they were from home and there was an emergency. Reynolds Hole recalled a catastrophe in which he was involved when quite a young boy; his father being away at the time. The village shop kept a small store of medicines and on this occasion the owner gave a bottle of laudanum by mistake to a neighbour who had come for tincture of rhubarb for her sick husband. As a result, he died, and his widow declared that she would seek revenge. Her only son was a farm labourer, "of weak intellect",[11] whom she urged to carry out the dastardly deed and one night, on his return from a circus at Newark—flushed, no doubt, with the excitement of the bright lights and hurdy-gurdy and perhaps combined with the stimulation of alcohol—he left his friends, broke into the shop-keeper's house and strangled her in her bed.

Hole wrote many years later: "I shall never forget seeing her next morning, for my father was from home, and, though I was but fourteen, I was sent for as his representative, turned a crowd of gossips out of the house, and despatched a messenger for the police."[12]

All requests for help were not as urgent or dramatic as that one, but the nearest medical man would have been at Newark or Southwell, and it would have taken time to reach him. Southwell could, perhaps, be described as within bee-flying distance of Caunton. (There was one known instance of a gardener working at the manor, worried by innumerable wasps. Taking out his bicycle he set off down the road to Southwell in search of a nest, eventually tracking it down well in sight of the Minster.) One of the hay-makers putting a pitch-fork through his foot, or a child trapping its fingers in the schoolroom door would be the kind of examples where someone would come rushing to the manor for help.

One of his first recorded recollections of childhood was connected with painting, when he was presented with a sixpenny box of paints and later admonished for using them to decorate himself and his clothes. This small setback seemed to discourage his artistic ideas and he turned towards archery which became a keen interest in his life. He recalls practising with his father at the targets and later, as an adult, becoming a member of the Royal Sherwood Archers.

Another account of his childhood reports that he was "systematically spoiled and trained to be a nuisance".[13] He relates the story of a famous painter whose child, from lack of discipline, "gave way from time to time to paroxysms of violent and vindictive rage, and that in one of these furious moods he kicked and spat at his father."[14] Later, full of remorse and wishing for forgiveness, he came to apologize: "Father", he said, "the devil told me to kick you; the spitting was my own idea."[15]

At the age of four Reynolds Hole rode a pony, at the age of eight he wrote a tragedy and at ten years he began to write poetry, most of it scribbled down during the rather dull and incomprehensible sermons preached by an aged vicar, not only well above his head but also delivered so indistinctly as to produce a soporific wandering of attention amongst his hearers. The epic was entitled *The Battle of Waterloo* and opens dramatically with the line: "We heard the rambling of Great Gallia's drum, . . ." His next poetic production was published in *The Nottingham Journal* and dealt with *The Death of William the Fourth*. To be in print while still a schoolboy must have been an experience to be remembered with understandable pride.

He recalls an early love of wild flowers and also of collecting plants for the garden.

And then the first plant which I could call my own, the salvia, which I bought for sixpence from the nurseries near to our school! I have grown and shown a multitude of specimens in the greenhouse and the stove since then; I have won prizes of gold and cups of silver, but I have never exhibited nor seen others exhibit anything half so precious as that . . . no colour which could compare with its splendid crimson flowers.[16]

But there was a natural lapse during his later schooldays when other interests came along—"the busy occupations of our manhood, and the dazzling attractions of the world".[17]

But before he reached these dizzy heights of "manhood" his education must be attempted and he was sent to Mrs Gilbey's school at Newark. Here one of his most cherished memories was of food. "I recall the days as if they were yesterday," said Hole on one occasion,

. . . though it is sixty years since, when I sat next to Mr Gilbey, joint overseer, at breakfast, and saw him with yearning eyes take every morning frizzled bacon—and I thought at the time in my little mind that if ever I had a sufficient income to justify me in having frizzled bacon, there would be little left in this world to wish for.[18]

He excelled in naughtiness at Mrs Gilbey's and for his sins was one day locked in the cellar. "After I had been there a short time I went to the top of the steps and shouted through the keyhole, 'You can do what you like about letting me out but I've turned the tap of the beer barrel.' "[19]

When he was old enough he was transferred to Newark Grammar School, "up the street some few hundred yards away".[20] Some of his education was supplied by Dickens whose *Pickwick* was coming out in parts at this time "and he managed to save a shilling [5p] a month—fifty per cent of his monthly income—to buy it; (and this in spite of an infinite appreciation of cheese-cakes). Dickens, hearing long afterwards of this, said that it was one of the best compliments ever paid him."[21] He recalled the smoking of his first cigar "at the corner of Kirkgate"[22] and the rambles round the countryside surrounding Newark. "I think I have been over almost every hedge and over or into every ditch about the place."[23]

Soon after Hole's arrival at the Grammar School, William Ewart Gladstone (ten years his senior) had received the invitation to stand as a Conservative candidate for the ancient borough of Newark-upon-Trent. The Reform Bill had become law on 7 June 1832, giving the vote to wider sections of the community and thus readjusting the parliamentary representation so that large towns such as Leeds, Manchester and Birmingham, previously unrepresented, now had two members each. (In the past somewhere like Old Sarum, a fortress in Wiltshire, deserted since the thirteenth century, had returned two members.) Gladstone, now aged twenty-three, was to stand for election in the reformed parliament.

Born at 62 Rodney Street, Liverpool, on 29 December 1809—the same year as Tennyson and Darwin—Gladstone was educated at Eton and Christ Church, Oxford. One of the Cambridge visitors to an important debate at the Oxford Union in November 1829, Monckton Milnes, wrote afterwards to his mother: "The man that *took* me most was the youngest Gladstone of Liverpool—I am sure, a very superior person."

Gladstone's brilliant and enquiring mind led him to visit dissenting chapels—on one occasion to hear Rowland Hill preach—to attend Dr Pusey's lectures on Hebrew, and Burton's on Divinity. It was while still at Oxford that he found a sobbing young woman leaning over a bridge about to throw herself into the river below. He quietly and sympathetically questioned her about the reason for her obvious distress and slowly the facts emerged—that she was an orphan who, having failed in an attempt to become an actress, and being hungry and in need of money and shelter, had resorted to prostitution.

From this meeting stemmed a strange, unforeseen succession of events. Gladstone was able to help her through the kindness of Mrs Tennant, widow of a clergyman who lived at Clewer near Windsor and who took her in. He later supported Dr Pusey in founding an English Sisterhood (see p. 35, ch. 2) and helped Mrs Tennant when she started the first Home of Mercy at Clewer.

Following Oxford, he spent the summer of 1832 in Italy, falling in love with Rome, and wondering about going into the Church. At home the Reform Bill had ploughed its stormy way through both Houses and had become law. With it came the new Parliamentary system, and, subsequently, a special invitation to Gladstone to play his part.

In a letter to an old Newark supporter written in 1875 and quoted by Robbins in *The Early Public Life of William Ewart Gladstone* he wrote:

I remember, as if it were yesterday, my first arrival in the place, at midnight, by the Highflyer coach, in August or September 1832, after a journey of forty hours from Torquay, of which we thought nothing in those days. Next morning at eight o'clock we sallied forth from the Clinton Arms to begin a canvass, on which I now look back as the most exciting period of my life. I never worked harder or slept so badly, that is to say, so little.[24]

His first speech was given on 8 October,

and on the following morning he issued to the constituency from the Tory headquarters his second address ... Of this Mr Gladstone long afterwards wrote to the historian of Newark that it "certainly justified criticism. It was that of a warm and loyal Tory, who was quite unaware that it contained in it the seeds of change to come. ..."[25]

The return of Mr Gladstone as Member for Newark was described years later by Reynolds Hole. He

related how, when the adherents of the defeated candidate, Sergent Wilde, paraded the town at night with music and torches, the boys at the grammar school threw open the windows of their dormitories and shouted "Red for ever", an injudicious manifestation of political opinion which was followed by the instant breaking of the windows by a volley of stones from "the Blues".[26]

Towards the end of his life, Hole was remarking to the Bishop of Rochester, Dr Thorold, that he had seen Mr Gladstone canvassing before he got his seat in the House.

"That is strange," said the bishop, "I saw him chaired after election." And when I enquired how he came to be there he [the bishop] replied that his home in Lincolnshire was no great distance from Newark, and that he was sent there to a school which was kept by Mrs Gilbey. As the older boy, I had left her tutelage when Master Thorold came, but I had only moved up the street to the Grammar School, some hundred yards away, and it was a curious coincidence that we should meet again in such close association, after a severance of so many years . . .[27]

Fortunately the headmaster of the Grammar School and Mrs Gilbey gave their pupils a holiday to "celebrate the election of 'young Mr Gladstone' as the Conservative member for Newark"[28] and even as a schoolboy, Reynolds Hole was struck by "his gentle manners and . . . his kind, thoughtful, intellectual face".[29] He writes: "From that day, and for more than half a century, he was of all public men the one whom I most admired and revered."[30]

Industrial problems were not the only ones facing the government of the day, for, whilst Mr Gladstone was travelling by Highflyer coach from Torquay to Newark, John Brown of Edinburgh, a future friend of Reynolds Hole, but then a young medical student spending two years as assistant to a doctor in Chatham before returning to Edinburgh to get his degree in 1833, was sailing down the Medway to attend a case of cholera. The calls nearly always came about midnight or in the very early morning, the times when the disease struck most frequently, and on one occasion Reynolds Hole describes how: "They rowed in silence down the dark stream, passing the huge hulks which were then on the Medway, and hearing the restless convicts turning in their beds and their chains. The men rowed with all their might and in silence: they had too many dying or dead at home to have any heart for conversation."[31]

Another schoolboy memory for Reynolds Hole is of Archbishop Harcourt Vernon, who took his confirmation service at Newark—"a tall, aristocratic man in a wig, which became him well". He goes on:

There was in those days a scant administration and a large abuse of the Apostolic ordinance. Seldom offered, and only in cities and towns, the ceremony was attended by crowds ... who behaved with much irreverence and levity within the church and outside as though at a fair. From a parish adjoining my own the candidates went in a waggon, and gave a fiddler half a crown to play them merry tunes on their journey![32]

The success of his earlier poetry was followed by another literary achievement at the age of eighteen, when he was still at Newark school, supposedly working at his studies. However, as he remarks in his *Memories*: "Then I became an editor. The *Newark Bee* was issued monthly, by the same firm which had published for Byron, and was as precious in the estimation of its contributors as the Hours of Idleness."[33] It is reported that Byron wrote *The Hours of Idleness* in what is now the Newark Labour Exchange. (Reynolds Hole would have been a child of four or five when Byron's body was brought home from Greece, unloaded at London Docks and the funeral procession formed to set out for Nottingham, and the little church of Hucknall Torkard.) "Why Hucknall Torkard should have been selected [for the Byron Vault] is a matter for conjecture, for although Bulwell Wood Hall, one of the family seats was in that parish, Newstead Abbey ... was at some little distance."[34]

The Newark Bee was published in March 1838, and the price was 2d (1p). It lasted until February 1839, the last two numbers being larger and published at 4d (1½p).

About a month after the final instalment of *The Newark Bee*, a letter, dated 30 March 1839, from Gonalston, Nottingham, was written by John Francklin shortly after his marriage to Miss Edgell. Had they lived they would have been Reynolds's parents-in-law, for their eldest child, Caroline, was to be his wife twenty-two years later. Its interest lies also in the manner of writing, in vogue shortly before the introduction of the penny post by Rowland Hill in 1840.

At that time a single sheet of paper, not exceeding an ounce in weight, varied in price from 4d to 1s 6d according to the distance it was carried; if it exceeded an ounce it was charged fourfold. .... Letters in those days consisted only of a single sheet without an envelope, which was formed by the last page of the sheet itself being folded over and fastened by a wafer.[35]

As it was the recipient who paid for the letter and not the sender it was expedient to get as much writing into as little space as possible; and so gave rise to a particular form of eye-torture of lines written across lines. It is just such a torture which evokes our sympathy for Emma in dreading the reading by Miss Bates of a letter from Jane Fairfax. As Miss Bates explains on one of these occasions: "I really must, in justice to Jane, apologize for her writing so short a letter—only two pages, you see, hardly two, and in general she fills the whole paper and crosses half."[36]

John Francklin had much to say so that most of the letter resembles a Chinese puzzle; but it is possible to decipher a line or two here and there. "I should like very much to give you", he writes, "a long account of our matrimonial proceedings and relate how I bear the fetters of married life, but really I do not know where to begin, or beginning where I shd stop. . . ." He contrives to convey various aspects of marriage, however, such as that of carrying a shopping basket on his arm through the streets of Nottingham "much to the delight and amusement of my old batchelor companions who witness my *slavery* with suspicious glances". However, through a maze of criss-crossed lines and some thicknesses of the pen in letters with loops, one discovers that "She is uncommonly well and I am more fond than ever of her which is extraordinary as courtship and matrimony are so different". He ends on the rather cosy note that "We are uncommonly comfortable and really are so steady that we quite dread the idea of leaving 'HOME' ".

In 1839 came the move from Newark to Brasenose College, Oxford, from discipline to freedom, from being a teenager to being a young man. "There is a delightful fascination in our new experience of comparative independence, possession and authority."[37] There were the beauties of Magdalen Bridge, "the High", the various colleges and schools, the quadrangles, chapels and the Botanic Gardens; as well as the late-night discussions, hours spent on the river, theatricals, mad schemes for racing:

At Brasenose we invented "The Grind", though I am unable to explain the origin or meaning of the word. It was applied to a small company of undergraduates, meeting, after lectures at a rendezvous outside of Oxford, mounted on the ordinary hack, selecting some building or plantation two or three miles away, and racing towards it as our winning post. The excitements of the contest were heightened by the incapacity of the steeds, and by the appearance of some furious farmer encouraging his men to pursue and capture [them].[38]

2

Oxford Days
1839–1844

IN A LETTER from Buckingham Palace dated 18 June 1844, Queen Victoria acknowledges her relief to her uncle, the King of the Belgians, that the "Government obtained a majority".

> I can write to you with a light heart, thank goodness, today . . . we were generally in the greatest *possible* danger of having a resignation of the Government *without knowing to whom to turn*, and this from the recklessness of a handful of foolish *half* "Puseyite" half "Young England" people![1]

Looking back it would hardly have seemed possible at that time that any religious sect or party could have influenced a government majority; indeed that religious thought in this country was vital enough to be dangerous to any reform or school of ideas whatever. Certainly it was prophesied that Dr Arnold, appointed to the headmastership of Rugby in 1828, would introduce a new aspect to education by combining the intellectual and the moral life. Certainly there were people in the Church like Charles Kingsley's father at St Luke's, Chelsea; and Dr Whateley's name was closely connected with *Letters of an Episcopalian*, published in 1826. But generally it could not be assumed that the spirit of zeal was abroad in religious matters in this country.

We have only to turn to the pages of Jane Austen to read of the indifference felt towards the Church—where we find Mrs Dashwood advising Edward on the benefits and interest resulting from the study of a profession. "I do assure you," he replied,

> that I have long thought on this point as you think now . . . but unfortunately my own nicety and the nicety of my friends, have made me what I am, an idle, helpless being. We never could agree in our choice of a profession. I always preferred the church, as I still do. But that was not smart enough for my family. They recommended

the army. That was a great deal too smart for me . . . and, at length, as there was no necessity for my having any profession at all . . . idleness was pronounced on the whole to be the most advantageous and honourable . . . I was therefore entered at Oxford, and have been properly idle ever since.[2]

Again, as Miss Crawford expresses her surprise when she hears that Edmund is to be ordained, he replies: "Why should it surprise you? You must suppose me designed for some profession, and might perceive that I am neither a lawyer, nor a soldier, nor a sailor."[3] After some discussion Miss Crawford settles the point. "Men love to distinguish themselves, and in either of the other lines distinction may be gained, but not in the church. A clergyman is nothing."[4] As far as his hopes with Miss Crawford were concerned it was Edmund's profession that had cooked his goose.

Although much of Miss Austen's work was written in the early years of the century before Hole was born, the same attitude must have prevailed, at any rate in country parishes, into his period as a curate. In an opening paragraph on this subject he writes many years later:

I remember a remark made by the late Bishop of London (Dr Jackson) that when he recalled the sad condition of apathy, indolence and disobedience into which the Church of England had fallen, it seemed marvellous to him that it continued to exist. . . .

My first memory ecclesiastical is of a time in which we never saw or heard of our vicar . . . our curate, who lived five miles away, rode over for one dreary service on the Sunday, dined, and we saw him no more during the week. He was much occupied in the pursuit of the fox, which, it is charitable to suppose, he mistook for a wolf, and like a good shepherd was anxious to destroy. The service was literally a duet between the parson and the clerk, except when old John Manners, the bricklayer, gave the keynote for the hymn from his bassoon, a sound which might have been uttered by an elephant in distress, and we sang—"O turn my pi—— O turn my pi—— O turn my pious soul to Thee;" . . .

The altar was represented by a small rickety deal table, with a scanty covering of faded and patched green baize, on which were placed the overcoat, hat, and riding-whip of the officiating minister, who, sitting there in a huge surplice, had a conversation with the sexton before the service began, and looked as though he were about to have his hair cut. The font was filled with coffin-ropes, tinder-box and brimstone matches, candle-ends, etc. It was never used for baptism.[5]

He recalls elsewhere in his writings that for this particular sacrament of the Church the pudding basin was frequently brought into use.

Born in the same year as Reynolds Hole, George Eliot makes a similar comment on the "duties" of a vicar in her first published short story, "The Sad Fortunes of the Rev. Amos Barton", worthy of note not only for its perfection but because its success led her on the path to fiction. She takes the trouble to make this particular ecclesiastical situation clear:

You are not imagining, I hope, that Amos Barton was the incumbent of Shepperton. He was no such thing. Those were days when a man could hold three small livings, starve a curate a-piece on two of them, and live badly himself on the third. It was so with the vicar of Shepperton; a vicar given to bricks and mortar, and thereby running into debt far away in a northern county—who executed his vicarial functions towards Shepperton by pocketing the sum of thirty-five pounds ten per annum [£35.50], the net surplus remaining to him from the proceeds of that living, after the disbursement of eighty pounds as the annual stipend of his curate. . . . This was the position of the Rev. Amos Barton, as curate of Shepperton rather more than twenty years ago.[6]

Published later with this story was *Janet's Repentance* from which come these further comments:

Even the Dissent in Milby was then of a lax and indifferent kind. The doctrine of adult baptism, struggling under a heavy load of debt, had let off half its chapel area as a ribbon-shop; and Methodism was only to be detected, as you detect curious larvae, by diligent search in dirty corners. The Independents were the only Dissenters of whose existence Milby gentility was at all conscious. . . .[7]

Who, then, were the "Puseyites" to whom Queen Victoria referred in her letter of June 1844, how could they shake a government election, from where did they operate, and what had they to say? In his *Memories* Dean Hole writes of his undergraduate days.

I was greatly impressed as an undergraduate by Dr Pusey's preaching, as afterwards by his published writings, by his saintly life, and his loyal love, faithful unto death, for the Church, in which he received from those in authority so much opposition and distrust. His manner was in itself a sermon, and he went up to preach with a

EARLY IN MARCH, 1838,

No. 1,

PRICE TWOPENCE,

OF THE

NEWARK BEE:

A PERIODICAL,

TO BE CONTINUED MONTHLY.

THE pages of the NEWARK BEE will be devoted to original Essays, Translations, Tales, and Poetry, with occasional Notices of the Literature of the day. The Conductors will ever bear in mind the admirable Horatian precept, 'omne tulit punctum, qui miscuit utile dulci.'

This Work is not the offspring of that insatiable love of writing,—that 'scribendi cacoethes,' which only defeats its own purpose—but of an earnest desire to promote literary efforts, and to amuse without relaxing the understanding of the reader.

All communications to be addressed to the Editors, at Messrs. Ridge's—post paid.

S. AND C. RIDGE, PRINTERS, NEWARK.

"The Newark Bee was issued monthly, by the same firm which had published for Byron, and was as precious in the estimation of its contributors as the Hours of Idleness."

"Modest beginnings of the vast Boot enterprise were laid by John Boot, the labourer who opened a tiny herbalist shop in Goose Gate. He died in 1860, leaving his wife and Jesse, aged ten, to carry on the business." (*Victorian Nottingham, 1815–1900* by R. A. Church, F. Cass & Co.)

Letter dated 30 March 1839, from Reynolds Hole's future father-in-law, John Francklin, shortly after his marriage to Miss Edgell, showing the crossed writing used at this time.

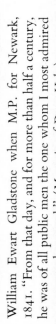

William Ewart Gladstone when M.P. for Newark, 1841. "From that day, and for more than half a century, he was of all public men the one whom I most admired

manifest humility, which no hypocrite could assume, and no actor copy.[8]

For this was, of course, the time of the Oxford Movement, a revolution within the English Church which spanned a period of twelve years from 1833 to 1845.

Started by Oxford men, promoted and discussed and forwarded on its way by its leaders such as John Keble (1792–1866), John Henry Newman (1801–1890), Richard Hurrell Froude (1803–1836) and Edward Bouverie Pusey (1800–1882), it formed the most conspicuous part of a religious revival long overdue throughout the land. And the fact that it was associated with Oxford may have given it a special appeal. The Sunday afternoon sermons at the University Church of St Mary the Virgin were nearly always given by Dr Newman week by week, month by month.

> Those who never heard him might fancy that his sermons would . . . be about apostolical succession, or rights of the Church, or against Dissenters. Nothing of the kind. . . . His power showed itself chiefly in the new and unlooked-for way in which he touched into life old truths, moral or spiritual, which all Christians acknowledge, but most have ceased to feel. . . . After hearing these sermons you might come away still not believing the tenets peculiar to the High Church system; but you would be harder than most men, if you did not feel more than ever ashamed of coarseness, selfishness, worldliness, if you did not feel the things of faith brought closer to the soul.[9]

On the few occasions when Dr Pusey took Dr Newman's place it is reported that he preached much longer sermons, thereby making some of the undergraduates late for their College dinners which usually meant that the food, instead of being reasonably hot was unattractively cold. Perhaps for this reason his sermons were sometimes described by a contemporary as "dull and tedious".

Reynolds Hole also regarded Dr Newman as a "far more attractive preacher".[10] Writing years later, he described why he felt this:

> There was such a pathetic tone in his utterance, of that which the French describe as "tears in the voice", such a tender appeal of plaintive sweetness that I remember to this day the first words of the first sermon I heard from his lips—"Sheep are defenceless creatures, wolves are strong and fierce!"[11]

To enter the church of St Mary the Virgin today is to feel the strange and moving events which have taken place within its walls, many of which relate to the preaching which not only stirred those present at the time but had far-reaching effects throughout the whole country. The undergraduates of today stand where John Wesley preached for the last time within the Church of England, and the present pulpit, dating from 1827, is the one from which John Keble preached the initiating sermon of the Oxford Movement on 14 July 1833, and from which Dr Newman preached his many Sunday afternoon sermons, including his last before joining the Church of Rome. It must, of course, have been in this church that Dean Hole heard the sermon opening with the text of the sheep and the wolves just quoted. But although he felt drawn towards Dr Newman—as most churchmen did who heard him take a service or knew him as a close friend—he never understood why the University should wish to have a statue of him as a Cardinal of Rome. "I can understand the gratitude and respect which built a college in honour of Keble, and a 'house' in remembrance of Pusey . . ."[12] he wrote.

It was to Dr Pusey to whom he gave his chief loyalty; and as it is at Dr Pusey's door that we can lay some of the credit for awakening the fervour and sincerity of Hole's work in the Church, perhaps we should see how much the Oxford Movement meant to him.

Reynolds Hole went up to Oxford with his head full of horses, hunting, archery, charades, pretty girls and cricket. He was a great lover of the country and of country things and people. This was all very right and proper but it does not appear that his scholastic aptitude had any great expectation and he seems, according to family legend, to have taken more interest in collecting waistcoats than in collecting books. But he was drawn to the Sunday afternoon services at St Mary's—and he must have gone to many of these—and during the time he spent at Brasenose the Oxford Movement, though well established, was going through some of the most critical years in its history. Among the undergraduates the Movement, and especially its leaders, must have been one of the chief subjects for discussion and argument. It had, by now, gone far beyond the boundaries of Oxford city and Dr Pusey was, for various reasons, as we have seen from Queen Victoria's letter, a name to be reckoned with and to be trusted in the outside world.

The early days of the Movement had gathered together a band of enthusiasts, most of them Oriel men. Joining their ranks in the mid 1830s came Dr Pusey. Writing in his *Apologia* Dr Newman gave him credit for stabilizing the whole situation. "Dr Pusey", he writes,

gave us at once a position and a name. Without him we should have had no chance especially at the early date of 1834, of making any serious resistance to the Liberal aggression. But Dr Pusey was a Professor and Canon of Christ Church; he had a vast influence in consequence of his deep religious seriousness, the munificence of his charities, his Professorship, his family connexions and his easy relations with the University authorities.

Such a comment from Dr Newman could not be taken lightly and as Dean Church, sometime Dean of St Paul's, remarks:

> Dr Pusey became, as it were, its official chief in the eyes of the world. He became also in a remarkable degree, a guarantee for its stability and steadiness: a guarantee that its chiefs knew what they were about, and meant nothing but what was for the benefit of the English Church. . . .
> His position, his dignified office, his learning, his solidity and seriousness of character, his high standard of religious life, the charm of his charity, and the sweetness of his temper naturally gave him the first place in the movement in Oxford and the world.[13]

Reynolds Hole, writing with appreciation of the Newman sermons, was nevertheless certain that the

> . . . undergraduates were more permanently impressed by the sermons of Dr Pusey. We understood them more readily, and while they aroused an anxious fear, they were bright with the consolations of hope. The rainbow was always on the cloud. Newman was too severe for us. In the days when we were, it may be, too scrupulous as to the cut and colour of our raiment—we did not seem quite to grasp the idea of sackcloth and ashes. Or, again, when we were all of us in a sweet agony of love with "the face that was the fairest that e'er the sun shone on", we were altogether powerless to understand the meaning of a celibate life.[14]

Emphasis has been given to the work of Dr Pusey because it was he, as we have seen, who, through his ideas and his person, exercised most influence on the young Reynolds Hole.* But this is not to belittle the other schools of thought which made up the Oxford Movement or the men behind the ideas. Dean Church, in his preface to *The Oxford Movement 1833-45*, writes of them in this way:

* Only a year after he came down from Oxford in 1844, we find that "the first English Sisterhood since the Reformation was established by Dr Pusey, with the support of Gladstone".[15] Thus the two people who, more than any others, had cast their spells on him, first as a pupil, and secondly as an undergraduate, are here found working together.

For their time and opportunities the men of the movement, with all their imperfect equipment and their mistakes, still seem to me the salt of their generation . . . I wish to leave behind me a record that one who lived with them, and lived long beyond most of them, believed in the reality of their goodness and height of character, and still looks back with deepest reverence to those forgotten men as the companions to whose teaching and example he owes an infinite debt, and not he only but religious society in England of all kinds.[16]

In his mother's diary for 1844—the year in which Queen Victoria wrote the letter to her uncle quoted at the beginning of this chapter— there are entries which cover Reynolds Hole's last terms at Brasenose, his graduation, ordination and his first weeks in his new appointment as curate at Caunton. Perhaps we shall see whether the influence of Dr Pusey shone through his work in these early days.

1844.
2nd January. Tuesday.
A walk—Distributed part of Lady Alicia's gift to the poor. Wrote to Lady Alicia.
24th January. Wednesday.
Reynolds took leave of me before leaving for Oxford.
9th February. Friday.
George, Sara and Annie went to an evening party at Mrs Tallents. Amused with Miss Edgeworth's Tale.
20th February. Tuesday.
Letter from my dear Reynolds, and Floss. Wrote to S.R.H. A drive to Kelham and then took up Sara dear.
A short turn in the garden.
29th February. Thursday.
Sara better. Fine soft day.
I in the garden nearly an hour.
Papa to call on Dr Wilkins.
Mr Anders.
1st March. Friday.
Not quite so well. Beautiful day. In the garden nearly an hour. Sara a very long walk.
Papa rabbit shooting.
11th March. Monday.
Letter from dear Reynolds.
Very stormy, preventing Sara going to Southwell.
Expecting Mr Bristowe, who did not come owing to a severe cold.

Cut out, and began of six chemises for myself. Finished "Amy Herbert".

15th March. Friday.

Not so well as usual, owing to half a preserved apricot. Wrote to Aunt Anne. Letters from her and my dear Reynolds. Very wet morning but clearing off at noon. Mr Anders called. Has had a fall and much bruised.

6th May. Monday.

Letters from our dear Reynolds who took his Bachelor's Degree on Saturday. [*sic*] Dear Annie came to see us. A drive with Pip round by Newark Bridge.

15th May. Wednesday.

My dear Reynolds came home in the evening, very well, and not at all the worse of his reading to prepare for his Degree of B.A. which he took very honourably on Friday *the 3rd.* [*sic*]

24th May. Friday.

Wrote to S.R.H. with his Testament that young Antelope having left it with me. He set forth early to Oxford to don his B.A.'s gown. Mr Anders.

27th May. Monday.

Dear Annie and George with the Darlints arrived to spend a week with Granma—all in high health and beauty. Dr Cooke spent the day and gave the Club of the Friendly Society a most excellent sermon.

Wrote to my absentees.

28th May. Tuesday.

Gents to Newark Fair. We a walk.

Letter from dear Sara.

26th June. Wednesday.

Mr Hole to the Book Club Dinner.

Sister and I two walks.

The air quite cold, but bracing.

1st July. Monday.

Note from George with the delightful news of Annie having a little Boy at ½ past 11. She had been to Evening Service previously and took them quite by surprise. I a drive with Pip, and stroll afterwards.

7th July. Sunday.

Sweet, soft air, though no sun.

Dr Cooke and Sam here. A drive and long stroll. Feel really better, and more hopeful again.

11th July. Thursday.

Beautiful day for the Archery Meeting.

Wrote to Lil.

Sara, Reynolds, G. Hutton, George Marsland the party from here. A drive with Pip and stroll in the garden.

14th July. Sunday.

Dr Cooke as usual.

Rain in the morning and a delightful evening. A long out in the garden.

17th July. Wednesday.

Mama and Sara drove over to see Annie, and had the pleasure of finding her very well. Took her into the garden. The Babe a beautifully healthy child. Stayed 7 hours with her. A very fine day, but a shower in the evening, just to satisfy St Swithin.

18th July. Thursday.

Fine morning. Busy with arrangements.

A drive and walk, as usual.

Violent thunderstorm in the afternoon.

21st July. Sunday.

Put on mourning for Mrs Richard Hole. Dr Cooke here. Beautiful day. To Church twice. Wrote a few lines to Pip, between services.

29th July. Monday.

Bettison begins to cut wheat, and several others.

Wrote to Miss Brown. Wrote to John with half-note.

A long beautiful, though cold, drive with Pip. Reynolds to the Southwell Cricket Club.

31st July. Wednesday.

Rather showery. Letter from Flossie. Wrote to Annie by Eddie's Basket. S.R.H. with Eddie to Newark on his way home. Note to John with 2nd Half of note.

5th August. Monday.

Left home for Blackpool.

8th August. Thursday.

An exceedingly high wind. Endeavoured to walk out but was glad to turn in again. Letter from dear Aunt Anne.

9th August. Friday.

Beautiful morning. Sara and I drove an hour on the sands. Lil and S.R.H. walking—out a long time.

12th August. Monday.

Beautiful day. All bathed, except S.R.H.—out of doors nearly all day.

13th August. Tuesday.

Very fine. Out all morning. I bathed. I a letter from dear Pip, Lil one from Annie. Wrote to Pip. A drive upon the sands after dinner.

15th August. Thursday.

Very fine sea and high wind. Bathed. Out all morning. A drive towards Lytham in the evening.

16th August. Friday.
A short walk. The girls bathed. Very wet. Disappointed of going to Lytham.

26th August. Monday.
Making the most of our last day at old Blackpool. Bathed, walked, strolled, drove with "Liverpool Jim", walked, etc., etc. Concert. Loafed. Shrimped.

27th August. Tuesday.
Up early, taking a farewell walk. . . .
Left dear old Blackpool at 12.
Last view of the beautiful sea and Tide just full in. . . .

29th August. Thursday.
Had a good journey home and found dear Pip quite well. Letters from Annie and Aunt Anne. The house a perfect picture of cleanliness and the abode of happiness.

30th August. Friday.
Very happy in looking about.
A walk with dear Pip in the evening.

5th September. Thursday.
Cold Shower. Bath. Wrote a long letter to sister Anne. Pip shooting. The young ones a drive. I a walk alone through many fields to Moor Lane, by the Brunk-Wood (?) and to Caunton Lodge—a good long step, reminding me of former strolls.

6th September. Friday.
Misty uncertain morning, but cleared at 10. o'clock. Mr Hole to shoot with G. Sutton at Holme, and dine. Sara to spend the day with Mrs Darwin and Reynolds to ditto with Mr Harrison of Elston. Rather fitful weather. A walk. Putting work, drawers, baskets, etc. tidy.

9th September. Monday.
George Hutton to breakfast. Bathed. Sara to spend a week at Beckingham. I a long stroll through Park Wood. Took a little relief to the poor old Atkinsons.

10th September. Tuesday.
Mr Hole shooting. Reynolds to luncheon with the Archdeacon to be introduced to the Bishop. I drove with him as far as I could walk back. We sent 30 boys and girls by H. Holt and John Wood's carts to be confirmed at Southwell. Gave them each a beer, wine and ale when they returned.

18th September. Wednesday.
Very pleasant morning. Our friends left us after luncheon. Pip to Newark. Sara and I a walk. Dear Reynolds went to Lincoln preparatory to his Ordination.

22nd September. Sunday.

Our dear son ordained at Lincoln. Mr Fletcher administered the Sacrament. . . .

29th September. Sunday.

Our dear son did the duty for the first time and got through it very well indeed. His sermon was excellent and very much liked. Dr Cooke assisted.

30th September. Monday.

Beautiful frosty morning. I called on Mrs Wilkins and Miss Barrow. Dear Lil and the chicks arrived, all well, in the evening. Harvest home and apple throwing.

4th October. Friday.

A walk. The Miss Darwins and Mr Harrison to dinner. Very nice girls. A very pleasant evening.

6th October. Sunday.

My dear son officiated in all the services of the day in a very excellent way—gave universal satisfaction.

13th October. Sunday.

Reynolds did the whole duty, most admirably for a man so young in the Church. The afternoon sermon very excellent.

20th October. Sunday.

Our dear young Minister the whole day's service, with a Churching and two christenings. Very cold. A walk at noon.

27th October. Sunday.

My dear son did the duty as usual. The sermons both upon the brevity of life.

3rd November. Sunday.

George took part of the duty with Reynolds. The new Altar-cloth and matting, very neat.

Very wet day.

10th November. Sunday.

Dear Reynolds as usual. The church very well filled.

17th November. Sunday.

Soft, fair day.

Reynolds as usual.

The chanting extremely good.

24th November. Sunday.

The Archdeacon. Reginald came to spend the day. The A. took an equal part of the duty with Reynolds. Mr Bristowe did not come as he had engaged to do.

1st December. Sunday.

Our dear Reynolds as usual.

Mr Anders over again to see Louis.

5th December. Thursday.

Dear Reyn's birthday. Wrote a long letter to Anne. Sara and Reynolds rode to Southwell. I walk to the second milestone. Mr Bristowe dropped in as we sat at dessert, and stayed the evening and night. Wrote note to Lil to go by nurse in the morning.

Letter from Lil.

6th December. Friday.

Beautiful frosty morning. Dear Louis and Nurse left. Mr Bristowe left at noon. Sara and Reyn a ride—I a walk to the second milestone again. Wrote a long letter to my dear sister Anne.

8th December. Sunday.

My dear son, as usual. In the afternoon his sermon, upon the Advent of our Saviour, the best he has written yet, of many good ones.

15th December. Sunday.

S.R.H. as usual.

Very cold, dark, foggy day. I could not venture to Church again in the afternoon.

25th December. Wednesday. 1844.

Reynolds took the Duty at Fenton.

Mr Fletcher administered the Sacrament here. 40 communicants. Mr F. and Miss Fanny left after . . . Dr Cooke, Anne, Sam, Matthew, James Hole to dinner. The singers as usual. A very merry, happy evening.

These diary excerpts, reflecting the day-to-day happenings of a family in a small Nottinghamshire village during the first half of the 19th century, might reasonably be compared with the general way of life described in Jane Austen's novels a few years earlier. Although Miss Austen died two years before Reynolds Hole was born and much of her work centres on the city of Bath, the seaside town of Lyme Regis or visits to London, life in a small village such as Longbourn in *Pride and Prejudice* or Barton in *Sense and Sensibility* would be less likely to alter in a matter of twenty-five years, and has much in common with Mrs Hole's diary from Caunton.

First, there is a keen appreciation of, and much discussion about, the weather and the quality of the air. Instead of taking a turn in the shrubbery like Fanny and Miss Crawford, or Emma with Mr Knightley, Mrs Hole took "a short turn in the garden" or was "in the garden nearly an hour" or had "a long out in the garden". She also mentions the air: "Sweet, soft air, though no sun". "The air quite cold but bracing", "Soft, fair day" and "Fine, soft day". Miss Austen makes Marianne Dashwood wait for "a soft, genial morning"[17] to go out after her serious illness, and the day that Fanny recommenced her riding was "a pleasant fresh-feeling morning".[18]

The mention of rain could be depended on to keep a conversation going for some time, as when Colonel Brandon and Lady Middleton found themselves at a loss, ". . . much was said on the subject of rain by both of them".[19] On holiday at Blackpool the Hole family bathed although it was "very wet" and they were "disappointed of going to Lytham". The rain brought mud on most of the roads and lanes at Caunton much as it did on the walk from Longbourn to Meryton "sometimes dirty and sometimes cold"[20] and previous to the Netherfield Ball "there was such a succession of rain as prevented" (the younger Miss Bennets) "walking to Meryton once".[21]

In the matter of letters or other communication there was much similarity. Notes were frequently sent by a visitor who happened to call or be staying in the house. Mrs Hole "wrote to Annie by Eddie's basket . . . S.R.H. with Eddie to Newark on his way home". A fall of snow made Emma "a most honourable prisoner. No intercourse with Harriet possible but by note".[22] Visitors came to call and stayed the night at Caunton Manor: "Mr Bristowe dropped in as we sat at dessert and stayed the evening and night"; and on the next day "Mr Bristowe left at noon". Elizabeth Bennet, paying her first visit to Mr and Mrs Collins after their marriage stayed six weeks. Lady Catherine De Bourgh was astonished. "I expected you to stay two months."[23] Longer journeys were undertaken by coach and shorter ones on horseback. Mr Bingley was frequently seen "to enter the paddock and ride towards the house"[24] at Longbourn and Mrs Hole notes: "Sara and Reynolds rode to Southwell" . . . "Sara and Reyn a ride".

3

Early Days with Roses and Rose Growers

1844–1858

Sauntering in the garden one summer's evening with cigar and book, and looking up from the latter during one of those vacant moods in which the mind, like the jolly young waterman, is absorbed in "thinking about nothing at all", my eyes rested on a rose.[1]

This reads as a simple statement made by a young man with an abundant source of leisure. As Mr George Dewar writes in his memoir of Reynolds Hole: "If we knew nothing of him save through his correspondence, we should hardly picture a great worker."[2] The same applies to much of his writing. He was careful not to put any emphasis on his own activities for other people and somehow contrived to give an impression of endless spare time. Even when he described some of the missions he undertook, usually lasting for ten days at a time and frequently beginning the day with a service of Holy Communion at 5.30 a.m., he never stressed the amount of work involved and seldom complained of tiredness. The other part of the statement—the fact that his eyes "rested on a rose"—is not as casual as it may at first appear.

The result of this chance encounter, enhanced as it was by "the splendour of the setting sun" meant not only that he never lost his first affection for rose d'Aguesseau (*gallica*) but that on the next evening walk into the garden a pencil took the place of his cigar, for making "careful" notes, and the book under his arm was *Rivers on the Rose*.[3] It was the initiation into his love of roses. The beauty of the rose caught in the radiant light of the sunset startled his imagination and the "dear little red book—this guide to amateurs, which has brought so much happiness . . . so much instruction to the learner, so many glad memories and genial sympathies to all rose-growers, quite completed my conversion".[4]

Until this moment he had, as he describes it, "wandered flowerless through a flowery world";[5] for his recreation he was more intent on riding his horse to hounds or trying his skill in archery than digging his garden. But this was the moment of conversion and he never forgot what he felt was his enormous debt to the author of that little book:

> Rivers, the Arch-Rosarian, said to me in my youth, "You may, you must, lose your present enjoyment of recreations, which require physical strength and power of endurance, but you will never lose your delight in the garden." I have fulfilled his prophecy and, more than that, I regard the success which I have had in my humble but hearty efforts to persuade others to believe in this doctrine, with a gratitude which I cannot express, as the best work which I have been permitted to do.[6]

The words "this doctrine" apply to his belief in gardening as an occupational therapy—a means of work and interest which can fully occupy a man's mind so that he does not have to depend on the beer-shops or gambling at the races for his pleasure.

> . . . Get a man . . . into the fresh pure air, interest him in the marvellous works of his God, instead of in the deformities of vice, give him an occupation which will add to his health and the comforts of his family, instead of destroying both, then build Revealed upon Natural Religion and hope to see him a Christian.

Like Miss Burdett-Coutts, who was doing such fine work to this end, he believed in societies for the improvement of cottage gardens, for the provision of window-boxes for town dwellings and, above all, in allotments. But we will return to this part of his belief later; for the present we must consider his conversion.

"And thus I became a rosarian."[7] He goes on to describe how his interest developed from complete ignorance to the first stages of a little knowledge.

> There was a time when, although I had taken the degree of Bachelor of Arts, if I had gone for an examination into a school of botany and had been requested to write a description of the distinctive features of the peony, the dahlia, and the rose, the most lenient examiner must inevitably have torn my paper into shreds; and yet as soon as I became overpowered by the conviction that the rose was the loveliest of all the flowers and had steadfastly resolved to devote myself to its

culture—from that time every effort which I made to acquire and apply information inspired me with a stronger determination and with a more confident hope.[8]

He realized very wisely that it was not just a case of sitting down and expecting knowledge to flow towards him, of crooning over rose catalogues (of which there were not many at this time) or sighing over a beautiful rose in someone else's garden. "I read every book I could find on the rose . . . if I heard of a garden in which roses were grown, I went to see—they were few and far between in those days, but I had youth and horses on my side and I drove any distance."[9]

It may have been about this time (see ack. p. 15) that another incentive came along, and before we follow him further in his search for knowledge and the friendships formed with the early rose-growers, this important incident should, I think, be recorded. Writing of the event in 1869, he begins, "Some years ago, one cold slate-coloured morning towards the end of March . . ." he received a note. His interest in roses must have already got around the country districts where he lived, and penetrated as far as Nottingham, about twenty-five miles distant, because the note invited him to judge a rose show to be held in Nottingham on the following Easter Monday. The writer was a mechanic and the exhibition was being put on by his fellow workmen. This fact also indicates that he was already thought of as a friend by these working men, and gives a foretaste of his love for them and his relationship with them throughout his long life. And so this unimportant-looking slip of paper seems to me to combine the two ways in which his service to his Maker were to be chiefly dedicated. He goes on: "Not having at the time a rose in my possession, although to my shame be it spoken, I had ample room and appliances . . . It never occurred to me that the tiny glasshouses which I had seen so often on the hills near to Nottingham, could be more honourably utilized . . ."; nor produced on Easter Monday; and the proximity of the date given to April Fools' Day made him suspicious. However, impressed by the "tone of genuine reality", he wrote off asking how roses could be achieved in Nottingham at such an early date, and nowhere else. "By return of post I was informed, with much more courtesy than I had any claim to, that the roses in question were grown under glass—*where* and *how*, the growers would be delighted to show me, if I would oblige them with my company."

Accordingly, on the Easter Monday in question, in typical English Easter weather "when spring and winter, sleet and sunshine were fighting round after round . . . I went to Nottingham. Again, as the hail beat upon the window of the rail conveyance, and I sat *dithering* in the eastern wind . . . a horrible dread of imposition vexed my unquiet soul."

Naturally enough, we should say. But his fears were dispelled after taking his hansom from the station to the General Cathcart Inn, when he was met by the landlord with a fine rose in his buttonhole, "which glowed among the gloom like the red light on a midnight train and (in my eyes, at any rate) made summer of that dark ungenial day."

There were many exhibitors some of whom sported a rose in their coat "and some without for the valid reason that they were in their shirt-sleeves, with no coats at all, just as you would see them at their daily work, and some of them only spared from it to cut and stage their flowers." The roses were on show upstairs and the contrast of the room, flooded with the colour and scent of roses when it was usually full of "cooked meats and steaming tumblers, heavy with the smoke and smell of tobacco" was almost unbelievable. The roses were exhibited in bottles, used to holding beer or other alcoholic liquids but now filled with water. Among their tea-roses were Adam (int. 1833), Devoniensis (1838), Madame Willermorz (1845), and Souvenir d'un Ami (1846)—these were given special mention by the two judges. (The other judge was a local nurseryman skilled in his growing of roses.)

After the judging was over the Rev. Reynolds Hole went with some of the men to look at their gardens. These turned out to be quite small allotments but they were in a good position just outside the town on a sunny slope. Hole gives in his book an enlightening quotation from the *Nottinghamshire Guardian* of 18 March 1867.

No town in England displays the gardening spirit more manifestly than "old Nottingham". Independently of gardens attached to residences, there are, we believe, nearly 10,000 allotments within a short distance of the town; and as many of these are divided, it is not too much to affirm that from 20,000 to 30,000 of the inhabitants, or nearly one half, take an active interest in the garden. And where will you see such roses as are produced upon the Hunger Hills by these amateurs—such cabbage and lettuce, rhubarb and celery?

A list of the various plants and shrubs grown there is given by him, showing the wide variety with which the men were successful: winter aconites, Christmas roses, laurustinus, variegated holly, winter jasmine and winter-flowering violets. In the spring these were followed by heathers, berberis, daphne, hepaticas, snowdrops, crocus and tulips and later on by lilacs, laburnum, philadelphus, flowering currant and wistaria and, of course, roses.

But on the occasion of this visit it was perhaps the "glasshouses" which most aroused the sympathy and admiration of their judge. They were so small that it was almost impossible to stand up in any of them or to enter others at all. Hole wrote: "That 'bit of glass' had been, nevertheless, as much a dream, and hope, and happiness to its owner as the Crystal Palace to Paxton." And it produced fine roses on an Easter Monday!

Much of this pioneer work amongst industrial labourers was carried out at some cost to themselves. When Reynolds Hole enquired from one of them how he afforded the expensive new varieties the answer came back quickly and to the point. "I'll tell you", he said, "how I managed to buy 'em—by keeping away from the beershops!" Another, whose garden was more than a mile away from his house, walked there and back often before work, in his dinner hour, and after work in the evening. And there is the story related by Hole of a lady visitor calling on the wife of one of these Nottingham enthusiasts during a cold winter spell. She noticed that there were few blankets on the bed, and enquired if they had no more. "Yes, ma'am, we've another", replied the housewife; "but . . ." and here she paused. "But what?" said her visitor. "It is not at home, ma'am; Tom has only just taken it; . . . he took it—took it to keep the frost out of the greenhouse; and we don't want it . . ."

Such devotion brought results and it is perhaps well to remember that these were some of the beginnings on which our contemporary rose shows were built up.

Certainly the event marked the beginning of Reynolds Hole's own collection of roses, for he ends his account by saying: ". . . nor did I quite regain my equanimity until, reaching home, I had written and posted an order for an assortment of *Roses in pots.*"

Having made the serious decision to become a rosarian, the Rev. Reynolds Hole had taken every possible step, it may be remembered, to acquaint himself with the rose either by reading books about it or by travelling to see it growing in other people's gardens. "Indeed", he writes, "these visits were only preliminary to the longer expeditions which I made soon after to the great rose nurseries and to our famous rosarians."[10] And as a result of these expeditions he came to know and to number amongst his closest friends some of the great nursery-garden names of the century.

Roses, however, were not the only flowers being collected or improved, for Hole knew personally the orchid displays of Mr Bull, the narcissi of Mr Barr, the begonias of Mr Laing, the rhododendrons of Mr Waterer, Mr Pearson and his pelargoniums, Mr Cannell with his dahlias and primulas and Mr Sutton with his cyclamen and gloxinias. The Barr family also successfully devoted their energies to the michaelmas daisy and Mr Bunyard at Maidstone to his magnificent apples. Glenny, writing in 1848, commented on the popularity of the fuchsia and the Clyde was famous not only for Paisley shawls but also for eighty varieties of Paisley laced pinks. (Loudon reported in 1828 that "their attention to raising flowers contributed to improve their genius for invention in elegant fancy muslins" in his *Encyclopaedia of Gardening*,[11] and in the new edition, published in 1878, Paisley is linked with Manchester in producing a pink "carried to a high degree of perfection".)

It is nevertheless rosarians with whom we are chiefly concerned and one of the grandees of rose-growing was without any doubt Thomas Rivers, to whom Loudon wrote with reference to his Rose Catalogue:

Bayswater, April 9th, 1836.

My dear Sir, Accept my best thanks for your very interesting communication. I wish you would only send me such articles more frequently. You must please to reccolect [sic] that you never finished your first Tour in Belgium.

It is singular that when I received your letter, I had just sent to the printers for the Art. Brit., a sort of synopsis of your Catalogue of Roses, which I hope will be gratifying to you, as well as be of service in a business point of view.

The only point that I have altered in your communication is respecting the [illegible] which bears abundance of seed in the neighbourhood of London in fine [illegible] from which many young plants have been raised.

I hope your father is in good health. Please to present my kindest respects to him. I remain My dear Sir, Yours very sincerely, J. C. Loudon.

Apr. 9th. The above was written last night, about 10 o'clock, soon after which the carrier's parcel arrived, bringing your letter of the 7th, in answer to which I shall be most happy to receive the continuation of your former paper, which you will see I allude to, in the beginning of this note. Your communications are so original and refreshing that I cannot have too many of them. J.C.L.

Referring to this Rose Catalogue, Reynolds Hole wrote that

foremost among these horticultural heroes I place that "grand old gardener", to whom I and all loyal subjects of the queen of flowers are so much indebted for his ROSE AMATEUR'S GUIDE (pub. 1837), Mr Rivers of Sawbridgeworth. . . . I went to see him in his pleasant

"29 September 1844. Sunday. Our dear son did the duty for the first time and got through it very well indeed. His sermon was excellent and very much liked. . . ."

Rosa Gallica
d'Aguesseau

"Sauntering in the garden one summer's evening with cigar and book, and looking up from the latter during one of those vacant moods in which the mind . . . is absorbed in 'thinking about nothing at all', my eyes rested on a rose." Reynolds Hole never lost his first affection for rose d'Aguesseau (*gallica*) as he saw it then in 'the splendour of the setting sun'. Plate from *The Rose Garden* by William Paul, 1848.

home. The house stood at the top of a bank, on which he had planted
and trained the Ayrshire roses, so that he looked out in the summer-
tide on a white cascade of flowers. . . . He was hale and handsome—
tall and erect as one of his own "standards", and with some of their
roseate hue on his kindly, clever face. A propos of standards he told
me that the Duke of Clarence paid a thousand pounds for the same
number of trees.[12]

Mr Rivers describes his bank of Ayrshires in his book the *Rose
Amateur's Guide*:

I have a steep bank of hard white clay, which owing to a cutting
made in the road became too steep for cultivation. About sixteen
years since, this was planted with Ayrshire roses; holes were made
in the hard soil with a pick two feet over and two feet deep; some
manure mixed with the clay, after it had lain exposed to the frost to
mellow it, and climbing roses planted. This bank is, when the roses
are in bloom, a mass of beauty.[13]

The first examples of this recent discovery to be grown in English
soil were imported by Mr Rivers from hedgerows in Hertfordshire—
not from abroad—and his foreman "protested in vain against Master
Tom planting 'those rubbishy brambles, instead of fruit trees', but they
proved to be more precious than golden pippins and every briar
was transformed into a magnum bonum."

Mr Wood of Maresfield was another well-known rosarian of the
time, having learnt his art in France, together with Mr Lane of Berkhampstead and Mr Adam Paul of Cheshunt. "These were the heroes of
my youth", Mr Hole writes, "and when I joined the service, a raw re-
cruit, in 1846, the four last-named—Rivers, Wood, Paul, Lane—were
its most distinguished chiefs." And then, continuing his reminiscences:

I like to think of Lee of Hammersmith complacently surveying those
standard rose-trees which he introduced from France in the year
1818, which were the first ever seen in England. . . . I like to imagine
the elder Rivers looking on a few years later, half pleased and half
perplexed, as Rivers the younger budded his first batch of briars. . . .
Then I wonder what those other heroes of the past, Wood of Maresfield, Paul of Cheshunt, and Lane of Berkhampstead, would say to
their sons and grandsons, could they see the development of the
work which they began. . . .

Certainly the opportunities were there at such a time of pioneering

and development. Adam Paul's son, William, certainly made the most
of the chances surrounding him, accumulating and storing in his mind
his father's experience and knowledge, so that in 1848, at the early age
of twenty-five, he was in a position to publish one of the most important manuals on the rose ever written in this country: *The Rose
Garden*. But even before this he was a contributor to the *Gardener's
Chronicle* in its early days and had already published the pamphlet
"Observations on the Culture of Roses in Pots". In a review of the
second edition the *Gardener's Chronicle* remarked:

> Beginners, in this kind of cultivation, will find this a most useful
> pamphlet, and it may doubtless be read with advantage by persons
> even experienced in the art. The excellence of Mr Paul's roses, in
> pots, at our great metropolitan exhibitions, forms perhaps the best
> guarantee that could be offered of his ability to teach; and those who
> would wish to obtain similar results cannot do better than follow
> his instructions implicitly....

As a young man, therefore, William Paul was already an authority
on the culture of roses in pots, a relatively new idea at the time. Advo-
cating this method of growing for exhibition he wrote: "Roses in pots
during this season form highly interesting objects among the French;
and why should they not do the same here, since it is allowed that our
general cultivation of roses in the open ground is quite equal to theirs?"
Thus Reynolds Hole was in the forefront of fashion when he ordered
his first "*roses in pots*".

About this time, William Paul also came into contact with J. C.
Loudon. As Loudon was taken seriously ill in October 1843, dying two
months later on 14 December when he was struggling to finish his
Self-Instruction for Young Gardeners, it may, perhaps, be surmised that
William Paul, being at that time about twenty years of age, was one
of the "Young Gardeners" Loudon might have had in mind as he dictated far into the night to try to get the work finished before he became
too ill. (The work included instruction in arithmetic and book-
keeping, geometry, mensuration, practical trigonometry, mechanics,
hydrostatics and hydraulics, land-surveying, levelling, planning and
mapping, architectural drawing, and isometrical projection and per-
spective.) It is interesting to think that Loudon's teaching might have
been responsible for William Paul's later ideas on landscape gardening,
the planting of ornamental trees, etc.

The publication of *The Rose Garden* was a landmark in both the rose
world and William Paul's own career. Its well-deserved success was
soon established—it eventually went into ten editions—and anyone

reading through it might well be astonished at the vast store of personal experience which lies behind the knowledge expounded in its pages, especially taking into account the youth of the author. He had the Victorian capacity for conscientious application, coupled with all the integrity and energy of which he was capable. Like Loudon he must have worked through all hours. He also enjoyed the Victorian love of collecting; not only roses in his garden, but a vast number of gardening and botanical books in his library. Another Victorian trait— that of an upright character, with a streak almost amounting to severity —is illustrated in his reply when it was suggested that a suitable name for one of his new roses might be "Queen Mab, the queen of the fairies". He is reputed to have enquired: "Was she a good woman?" It must have been with pride and no kind of questioning that the Pauls propagated the lovely deep crimson rose, Reynolds Hole, in 1872.

However, this was still some years ahead, and we must remind ourselves that the battle of the roses had yet to be fought. William Paul himself predicts, in the *Horticultural Magazine* in 1848, that his pelargoniums have "a glorious career before them", and Shirley Hibberd, in 1859, mentions and recommends for planting at least fifty different varieties of fuchsia. So it is understandable that Hole records at this time: "But our warfare in those days was mere skirmishing. We were only a contingent of Flora's army—the rose was but an item of the general flower-show. We were never called to the front. . . ."

Had he but known at the time that this was only a temporary situation he might have comforted himself. But, in that case, he might not have put so much energy into his newly found "love", might not have brought the same persistence to bear. It was the growing zeal, fostered by his own realization of his ignorance, which sent him riding round the countryside to look at roses and to the library to find books and read about them. This was the period of building up resources by acquiring knowledge, making contacts, and planting in his own garden; all of which made the great achievement, that was to come within the next decade or so, possible.

For him the fever of rose-growing began first with a dozen trees, then a score and then a hundred. From one hundred he eventually reached one thousand and in time between four and five thousand. These were grown at Caunton on his father's land during the time that he was first curate and later vicar. He writes of this period:

My good old father, whose delight was in agriculture, calmly watched not only the transformation of his garden but the robbery of his farm with a quaint gravity and kindly satire, that, not doubting for a moment the lucrative wisdom of applying the best manure in unlimited quantities to the common hedgerow briar, he ventured nevertheless to express his hope that I would leave *a little* for the wheat.

Having surrounded himself with roses it occurred to him that this was a flower which should have a show to itself. There were already held carnation shows, dahlia shows, tulip shows and auricula shows. At Stoke Newington there was held a chrysanthemum show and there had even been known—a gooseberry show. What about the rose? And so there appeared, in the April 1857 number of *The Florist* magazine his suggestion that a Grand National Rose Show should be held, near some central station. Referring later to this enterprise he wrote: "And I must confess that, when I had made this proposal to the world, I rather purred internally with self-approbation. I felt confident that the world would be pleased."

But the world gave no sign, although he waited anxiously at home opening his mail in eager anticipation. Weeks went by and still there was no response whatever. Suspense emptied into disappointment— but not for long. Reynolds Hole was not the sort of man to be sunk in useless despair without making an effort to improve the situation. He wrote round to a few of the chief rosarians, asking them one simple question: "Will you help me in establishing a National Rose Show?"

The replies came back as soon as the mail could bring them, answering in the affirmative, offering willing help and giving their full support. The originator of this idea records that, in his delight, he rashly whistled while he was shaving and it was "a bloody business".

A meeting was arranged and held at Webbs Hotel, Piccadilly, where a good meal was first ordered and consumed and then the work began. Messrs Rivers, Turner and Paul were the backbone of his support. It was decided to hold a Grand National Rose Show about the beginning of July 1858, each person present subscribing five pounds towards a fund. A further meeting was arranged, details discussed, and the rose show was on its way.

Turning the results of the meeting over in his mind as he "went rushing down the Northern Line" on his homeward train journey, Hole confirmed his long-felt conviction on the value of friendship between lovers of flowers and gardens. This work had all been achieved in a comparatively short space of time between men, most of whom had only met together for the first time but who at once felt a bond of interest between them.

He reflected further on this important matter, the truth of which first came home to him through his experience, a very happy one, of

the "rose show" held in the upstairs room at the General Cathcart Inn:
"Were it my deplorable destiny," he wrote,

> to keep a toll-bar on some bleak, melancholy waste, and were I per-
> mitted to choose in alleviation a companion of whom I was to know
> only that he had one special enthusiasm, I should certainly select a
> florist. Authors would be too clever for me. Artists would have
> nothing to paint. Sportsmen I have always loved; but the brook
> which they will jump so often at dessert or in the smoke room does
> get such an amazing breadth—that stone wall such a fearful height—
> that rocketing pheasant so invisible—that salmon (in Norway) such
> a raging, gigantic beast—that, being fond of facts, my interest would
> flag. No; give me a thorough florist, fond of all flowers, in gardens,
> under glass, by the brook, in the field. We should never be weary of
> talking about our favourites and, you may depend upon it, we should
> grow *something*.

To illustrate the point he related the story taken from an after-dinner
speech of florists at Leicester by the editor of *The Gardener*. He had been
told by a Scottish clergyman that "in his visitations from house to
house he had never met with an uncongenial reception where he had
seen a plant in the window".

The great day of the first gigantic National Rose Show came.
St James's Hall had been engaged for the event, as well as the services
of the Coldstream band—"a mistake, because their admirable music
was too loud for indoor enjoyment". Large posters had been distributed all over London and subscriptions had come pouring in, enabling
a schedule of prizes to the value of £156.

Hole arrived at the hall at about 5.30 a.m. after a journey of some
120 miles. The carpenters were busy erecting stands as these could not
be put in position on the day before owing to a concert being held on
the previous evening. Then came the excitement of the staging of the
exhibits as vans and "four-wheelers" deposited their precious boxes
from "Cheshunt and Colchester, from Hertfordshire and Hereford,
from Exeter and Slough".

There were many anxious moments before the exhibition was due
to open. There was already an amount of £100 outstanding which
must be cleared before any profits could be made. An admission cost
of one shilling per head meant that a full hall was needed before the
organizers could feel easy in their minds. Hole writes that "a gentleman, who earnestly asked my pardon for having placed his foot on
mine, seemed perplexed to hear how much I liked it. . . ." One more
shilling, the head organizer must have been thinking to himself.

The undoubted success of the first national show was recorded in the *Gardeners' Chronicle* by Professor Lindley. "No words can describe the infinite variety of form, colour, and odour which belonged to the field of roses spread before the visitor." The mention of "odour" in this context is not, of course, surprising, but 120 years ago it meant more than it would today; and this point was made by John Leech in a subsequent issue of *Punch*: the sweet smell of the roses combating the stench invading London from the Thames. It is here described by Reynolds Hole at Leech's request:

In the days of the Great Stench of London, the Naiades ran from the banks of Thamesis, with their pocket-handkerchiefs to their noses, and made a complaint to the goddess Flora, how exceedingly unpleasant the dead dogs were, and that they couldn't abide 'em—indeed they couldn't. And Flora forthwith, out of her sweet charity, engaged apartments at the Hall of St James, and came up with 10,000 roses to deodorise the river, and to revive the town. . . .

4

A Little Tour in Ireland

1858–1859

REYNOLDS HOLE was introduced to John Leech on Easter Monday evening 1858. Leech had been having a day's hunting with the Belvoir and his host, Charles Adams, invited the Rev. Reynolds Hole over for dinner. In his writings he mentions the introduction with delight: "A few months before the Rose Show, I made the acquaintance, afterwards the dearest friendship of my life, John Leech, the artist . . . it was an epoch in my life, a green spot on the path of time, to look on his kindly, intellectual, handsome face."[1] Leech had been much amused by the attitude of other members of the hunt, some of whom had evidently expected to see great horsemanship and fearless riding from the famous hunting cartoonist, whereas he was neither a fearless nor an intrepid horseman. W. P. Frith wrote:

> Leech was a timid rider. He much preferred an open gate to a thick-set hedge, and the highroad to either. . . .[2] His constant charge to his friend (Mr Adams) to get him a horse suitable to a "timid, elderly gentleman", or to give the animal some preliminary gallops himself so as to take the *freshness* out of him . . .

Hole, who had been Vicar of Caunton since 1850, recalls that Leech had been known to say: "Give me an animal on which you can carry an umbrella in a hailstorm,"[3] which was not exactly indicative of a leader to hounds.

Leech was tall, "but slight in figure, with a broad forehead, large, blue-grey Irish eyes and a face full of expression".[4] He must have been about forty-one years of age when this meeting took place and Mr Hole thirty-nine. Leech was already of some consequence in society owing to his work with *Punch*, which was established in 1841, a few months before Leech's first contribution in 1842: "Though his first cut was late and sent the circulation down, his subsequent work soon repaired the damage . . . Extraordinarily prolific, in twenty-three years he did three thousand drawings, at least six hundred of them cartoons."[5] His Surtees illustrations had also begun to appear about this time; and his work with Albert Smith,* especially on *The Month*, had brought him into the public eye. As Frith writes that *The Month* essayed to give "a View of Passing Subjects and Manners, Home and Foreign, Social and General"[6] and contained "many amusing skits by Albert Smith and much of Leech's best work",[7] it is deserving of mention. It made its first appearance in July 1851, and as everyone knows, the great Crystal Palace Exhibition in Hyde Park had already been opened. (Frith had in February been to the site of the huge glass building with Dickens and the designer, Joseph Paxton.

Dickens was wrapped in furs and we shivered through the place which was only partially roofed and seemed altogether so far from completion as to cause great doubts in our minds of the possibility of its being ready for its contents by the first of May. I put the question to Paxton, and his reply was: "I *think* it will: but mind, I don't *say* it will.")[8]

In its first issue, *The Month* included a description of the reactions of a typical young lady visitor of the period known as the Belle of Hyde Park:

Yes; I like the Crystal Palace. Oh! I get so tired there—walking, and walking, and walking, you can't think how far! . . . I have never been out of the nave and the transept—nobody goes anywhere else. I did not know that there was anything to see upstairs, except large carpets. I am sure they would bore me dreadfully.

So much time did the exhibition take that she was nearly late for the next social round:

We had scarcely time to dress for the Grapnels' dinner party; and then we went to Mrs Crutchley's to meet the Lapland Ambassador . . . Old Mr Tawley was there, and would keep talking to me; he always bores me dreadfully. He is going to take mamma and me to see some pictures somewhere. I hate seeing pictures; they bore me dreadfully. After Lady [*sic*] Crutchley's we went to Mrs Croley's

* Albert Richard Smith, 1816–1860, author, lecturer, and in 1838 a member of the College of Surgeons. In 1841 he lived at 14 Percy Street, Tottenham Court Road, meaning to practise medicine, but became involved in literary contributions to the *Medical Times*, *Bentley's Miscellany* and *Punch*. Wrote many plays for London theatres. On 12 August 1851 he made an ascent of Mont Blanc. (It is on his writing paper headed "Mont Blanc" that he wrote a letter to "Pommy" of *Punch*.)

amateur concert, which was nearly over. She had only classical music. I don't know what classical music is; I only know it bores me dreadfully . . . .

John Leech's accompanying drawings to such a monologue may be imagined.

Another connection for Leech with the Crystal Palace was probably of greater interest to him. This was his introduction to the Duke of Devonshire, while staying with Millais at the Peacock, Baslow, close to Chatsworth. It was here, in 1854, that Millais's well-known portrait of Leech was painted. (Millais and Leech sometimes took fishing holidays together and in a letter to Millais dated June 1855, Leech records the catching of a large perch, "such a one as I have only seen stuffed in the fishing-tackle shops, and which I always believed to be manufactured by the carpenter or umbrella maker. He weighed three pounds, and *not* fisherman's weight.")[9]

Frith thinks the introduction was made by (Sir)★ Joseph Paxton and this resulted in a Leech drawing for the duke of the Crystal Palace. The duke was so pleased by this that he wrote asking for a sketch on a much smaller scale so that he could have a seal engraved of it.

In the postscript to a letter written to his hunting friend Charles Adams in April 1852, Leech wrote:

Look at the seal on this envelope. I told you, I think some time ago about my making a little sketch for the Duke of Devonshire, and how kind he was about it . . . I confess I am proud to send you an impression . . . The design of the seal is a spade turning up the Crystal Palace, in allusion to Paxton being a gardener. . . .[10]

Leech's connection with Surtees, the novelist, came about through an introduction by Thackeray. Having effectively illustrated his own *Vanity Fair* (1847-1848), Surtees invited him to try his hand for *Mr Sponge's Sporting Tour*. However, Thackeray turned this suggestion down but did put Surtees in touch with John Leech. Anthony Steel writes:

When *Mr Sponge* did eventually appear in monthly parts under the aegis of Bradbury and Evans, Leech duly provided the coloured illustrations and woodcuts which from this time on regularly adorn and enhance the value of the later works of Surtees: the alliance was in fact among the most successful of the kind in literary history. . . .[11]

★ Knighted for his services to the Great Exhibition.

The Surtees family lived at one time at Worksop Manor in the Dukeries, Nottinghamshire, and Reynolds Hole relates that "Surtees used to write after a day's hunting and a bottle of port; that what he wrote was excrutiatingly funny. . . ."[12] Unfortunately, much of the humour was watered down to a "mere skeleton"[13] of the original to fit in with the taste and decorum of that time and some of the best bits "cut out as unfit for publication".[14] But in spite of censorship the Surtees series and the Leech illustrations gave a remarkable documentary account of the life, habits and general social history of the mid-19th century. In dress there was the period of the "bloomers": for instance in *Handley Cross*, Mrs Mendlove's "lovely daughter Constantia may afternoonly be seen reclining elegantly . . . in the full-blown costume of a Bloomer" while the "less attractive Miss Grimes" in *Soapy Sponge* was described as "an ardent Bloomer". After this, there came the crinoline, in about 1860, here reproduced in the Leech drawing facing p. 64, showing an outsize lady in an outsize crinoline, Mrs Furbelow. It is a question of who should take her down to dinner—an achievement, from the look of things.

Then there was travel both before the railway and after, the barouche and the tandem, the dog-cart, the gig and the pony-phaeton. Lord Mudlark came to grief in Piccadilly driving his tandem and Mr Gallon's spring-cart in *Ask Mamma* was capable of twelve miles an hour. "Coaches are only for common people," said Lucy Sponge, and Mr Puffington, "the son of a great starch-maker at Stepney", cut a dash in the high mail phaeton.

Seaside resorts, entertaining, riding to hounds, girls' boarding schools, interior decoration—they are all clearly portrayed for us by Mr Surtees in his writing and by John Leech in his illustrations.

Leech also, of course, did many political cartoons, and an especially famous one came out in *Punch* No. 713, on 10 March 1855. The following note from Sir Ralph Abercromby was sent to Queen Victoria, written from The Hague, 2 March 1855, giving the news that "the Emperor Nicholas died this morning at 1 a.m. of Polmonic Apoplexy, after an attack of influenza". The Czar had contended that Russia still had two generals on whom she could rely during that terrible Crimean winter—Generals Janvier and Fevrier; and in his cartoon Leech shows "General Fevrier turned Traitor".

The Rev. Reynolds Hole wrote: "I had always longed to grasp the hand which diffused so much pure enjoyment and taught men how to be both merry and wise. . . ." Leech's immediate appeal for the Vicar of Caunton must have been reciprocated, as it was Leech who proposed that they should take a holiday in Ireland together during the following August. Hole accepted "with an eager gladness which was somewhat subdued when he (Leech) suggested, 'You shall write, and I will illustrate, an account of our little tour'."

In spite of his enthusiasm to go on the trip, Leech was apprehensive of the actual crossing being a severe sufferer of sea-sickness, that dreaded leveller of all men, above which no one can rise with any pretence at elegance, superiority of intellect or interest in the journey. In the depths of such misery one can only sincerely pray that the anguish will not be prolonged and that the ship will sink without delay. Leech had experienced such sensations on his crossing to Calais when going to visit Charles Dickens at a château in northern France. On that occasion he evidently presented such a dismal sight when he stepped off the boat that he was received "by the congregated spectators with a distinct round of applause" as being by far the most intensely and unutterably miserable object that had come ashore.

In a letter dated 5 August 1858 from Scarborough he is still anxious about the crossing—the Irish Sea being so many miles wider than the English Channel. He apologizes for not having given Hole his address:

Here I am, however, and propose starting on Monday morning for Newark—en route for Ireland. . . . I am already beginning to funk the sea passage, or rather voyage, four hours, oh dear! Suppose we make up our minds *not* to go until the channel is perfectly tranquil. We are out pleasuring you know. I know of nothing that combines the ridiculous with the truly miserable so much as a man, with no power in his legs, staring fixedly at a horrid steamboat basin. Ugh! I send you the diary which my friend has been good enough to make out for me. You may like to look over it. Of course I am willing to make any alterations of the plan that you may suggest. . . .

However, the Irish Sea respected the anxieties recorded in this letter and the journey took place without further delay. They must have been away for three weeks, for, on 30 August Leech is writing to his friend Charles Adams once more from the security of land, at Scarborough.

Frith reports that when John Leech had suggested to Reynolds Hole that he should write and "I will illustrate", Mr Hole's modesty took alarm, but with no reason, as was subsequently proved. For, the result of this trip was the publication, in 1859, of a volume entitled *A Little Tour in Ireland*; being a visit to Dublin, Limerick, Killarney, Cork, etc., by an "Oxonian". The "Oxonian" was, of course, Mr Hole; and the illustrations showed Leech in his happiest vein. For their own amusement on the trip, they gave each other pseudonyms—Philip for Reynolds Hole, Frank for Leech.

This book was not, as we are well aware, Hole's first expedition into the literary world, but it was his first collaboration in such distinguished company, and although one can understand his natural feeling of modesty, it is clear from his opening chapter that he need have had no reservations about his side of the work.

In *A Book of Ireland*[15] first published exactly a hundred years after the Hole-Leech production, Frank O'Connor chose for his prologue an anonymous 14th-century verse:

"The Irish Dancer"

> I am of Ireland,
> And of the holy land
> Of Ireland.
> Good Sir, Pray I thee,
> For of *saint charité*
> Come and dance with me
> In Ireland.

Being "of Ireland" and a sensitive writer, this verse sets the whole tone and feeling for Frank O'Connor's book. But Mr Hole had never been to Ireland before and could have little knowledge of what lay before him. He solved the problem by giving a personal approach to their visit, and chapter one is built around the romantic theme that *"I am always falling in love"*.*

He goes on with an innocent sincerity:

The moment I see a pretty face, I feel that sort of emotion which Sydney Smith used to say the late Bishop of London rejoiced to contemplate in his clergy, "a kind of drop-down-deadness". I cannot walk out, or drive out, or ride, or row out, but I am sure to have an attack. I have had as many, indeed, as two in one day ... with visitors, with ladies come in from the country to shop, I am perpetually and passionately in love. I don't like it, because there is not the most remote probability of my ever exchanging six syllables with these objects of my devoted affection, not to mention that they are equally beloved by some three or four hundred rivals; but I am powerless to oppose; I can't help it.

Here he describes the position in general; but it is one particular instance that he then relates and which, in all its misery of despair and frustration, is the deciding factor which sends him off to the Emerald

* His italics.

Isle. The occasion had been a picnic "enlivened by archery". Needless to say, the climax of the evening was at hand:

We were alone, and I resolved to propose. I seized her elbow with both hands, a ridiculous position, but I was very nervous and was about to ask the momentous question, when she said with such a tone of gentle pity as took away half the pain, "Philip, I am engaged . . . shall we go back for coffee?"

Fortunately for "Philip", he was able to pour forth his unhappy state to his friend "Frank" who happened to be staying with him. "Frank has Irish blood in his veins and his first impulse was to have 'A crack at——', but he ultimately took a less truculent view of the case and suggested brandy and water." Finally, as a long-term cure, they decided to go on a little tour in Ireland together.

And so the preparations began and became so engrossing and delightful that the incident of the archery evening became of less and less consequence than could ever have been believed. So much so, in fact, that on the day of their departure "Philip" makes a confession: "I fell violently in love at Crewe Station, whence my heart was borne away in the direction of Derby, by the loveliest girl. . . ." One might be forgiven for thinking that anyone who can fall in love on Crewe Station cannot be in serious need of moral support. From Crewe to Chester, from Conway to Bangor—"just allowing a glimpse of Telford's triumph"—to Holyhead, where the sea was calm and smiling and "Frank" began "in the joy of his heart, to sing songs of an ultramarine description, alluding to the land with severe disparagement . . .

Give to me the swelling breeze,
And white waves heaving high."

Happily these wishes were disregarded and they sailed smoothly across into Dublin Bay and were safely landed on Kingston quay, the journey to Dublin for passengers from London having taken twelve hours. Their first excitement on Irish soil was provided by the "outside car" on which they travelled "edgeways" from Dublin station to their hotel. Mr Hole describes this style of transit as "one of extreme insecurity, and though we laughed and made believe that we liked it, we were glad enough to hold on by the iron-work until we arrived at Morrisson's". The evening was well-spent in eating their supper accompanied by "large potations of *Guinness*" (under cover of an order to the waiter for a pot of tea) rounded off with a tumbler of Irish whiskey. Detailed instructions are given for serving this drink—warming the glass, dissolving the lump sugar, etc., ending up: "Frank suggests a soupçon of lemon; and this was the sole point upon which, throughout our tour, we were not quite unanimous!"

The next morning they explored Dublin by way of Merrion Square and St Stephen's Green, the University—including the Chapel of Trinity College which the Rev. Hole felt was similar to some of our English universities in being "more suggestive of sleep than of supplication", examination rooms and dining halls, where some of the walls were hung with portraits of great Irish writers. They saw the statue of King William III riding his charger on College Green and also those of Nelson and Moore, "the former being very effective and the latter (though suggestive in the distance of a gentleman hailing an omnibus) being impressive and pleasing on a nearer view".

The monument to the memory of the Iron Duke caused some comment, as it mentioned all his great battles but omitted "Waterloo". Mr Hole wrote that "there is something so delightfully Irish in this small oversight, that it seems quite natural and appropriate; and I should as little dream of being surprised or vexed by it, as if in an Irish edition of Milton I could find no 'Paradise Lost'."

Perhaps Phoenix Park impressed them the most, with its 1,700 acres of open grassland and some woodland, and the Constabulary Barracks where the men were drilling—"if a regiment could be formed from the Irish constables it would be the finest regiment in arms". Fifty of these constables had been sent off to Kilkenny that very morning to ensure that the peasants were stopped from smashing up some

reaping-machines recently introduced among them. The Irishman is not quick to appreciate agricultural improvements. It required an Act of Parliament to prevent him from attaching the plough to the *tails of his horses*; he was very slow to acknowledge that the plough itself was better when made of iron than of wood . . . and he denounced the winnowing-machine as a wicked attempt to oppose the decree of a good Providence, which sent the wind of heaven "to clane the whate and oats".

In the afternoon the travellers set off by rail for Killiney—a distance of nine miles—and as the journey was accomplished in three quarters of an hour the passing scenery was not "rendered invisible from extreme velocity". Here the grey stones contrasted with the heaths and heathers—"I never saw ericas in greenhouse or garden with such a fresh, vivid brightness" (and a footnote explains that this was so throughout Ireland).

They visited the "extraordinary structure" at the top of Killiney

Hill which seemed built to support a statue and while they were there "one of the loveliest girls I ever remember to have seen" went running up the steps and stood where the statue should have been. Mr Hole confesses that "something, beating violently under my left brace, told me that my heart had returned from Crewe. . . ." But he was still able to appreciate the view—"in silent admiration and took no note of time" so that they missed the train back to Dublin and on their return later "found our dinners and ourselves a little overdone at Morrisson's; . . ." Dickens, in a letter written from Morrisson's Hotel on Monday, 23 August 1858, to Miss Angela Burdett-Coutts describes his programme of readings: "The Carol here tonight the Chimes tomorrow—Little Dombey on Wednesday . . ." The two friends must only have missed him by about a fortnight.

Breakfast the next morning was rather stormy, for a "Scotch gentleman" read aloud his newspaper to his friend "in such loud tones" that Mr Hole and Mr Leech deemed retaliation essential. They tossed up as to who should recite the list of bankrupts in *The Times* and Mr Hole won, and thereby silenced the Scotsman. The two friends left Dublin by the "Midland Great Western Railway" at 10.30, arriving at Galway at 3.45. Going through County Meath they thought of Swift; and on their way to Athlone were reminded of Goldsmith, whose father's parsonage had been nearby at "Sweet Auburn" (Lissoy). At Ballinasloe, on the Galway border, they anticipated serious trouble with "some delirious driver", having heard legends of wild and reckless adventurers. "But", writes the Oxonian, "we travelled onwards, demurely and at peace; and, indeed, throughout our little tour, so far from being provoked or annoyed, we met with nothing but kindness and courtesy, and a good-humoured willingness to be pleased and to please."

They seemed to have the Railway Hotel, which contained "a power o' beds", almost to themselves, perhaps because the garden contained not only hydrangeas but cannon which pointed at the bedroom windows, and it "really required some little resolution next morning to shave ourselves with placidity 'at the cannon's mouth' ". They explored Galway and finally the Claddagh. This area with its meanly built huts of mud and stone and depending to some extent on the fishing industry for a livelihood, seemed to our friends to have a strange quality about it. Pigs are thought much of, as it is the pig *"that pays the rint"*. The Claddagh people appear to be of Arabian, Spanish as well as Irish descent and, however poor, to bear themselves with a certain dignity and grace.

It is in Galway that the friends—usually carefree and ready for a joke —came close to tears, for it was here that they heard about the Famine of 1845. There were many people still about who had vivid memories of the distress, starvation and often death which it had caused only fourteen years earlier. Amongst these was their "dear old waiter" at the Railway Hotel. The conversation began like this:

"Was the salmon caught this morning, waiter?"

"It was, sir. Faith, it's not two hours since that fish was walking round his estates wid his hands in his pockets, never draming what a pretty invitashun he'd have to jine you gintlemen at dinner." The salmon was followed by mutton from the Aran Islands, and the waiter continued:

> "That's right, good gintlemen, niver forget, when ye've had yer males, to thank the Lord as send them. May ye niver know what it is to crave for food, and may ye niver see what I have seen, here in the town o' Galway . . . poor craturs come crawling in from the country with their faces swollen and grane and yaller, along of the 'erbs they'd been ating. . . . I've gone out of a morning, gintlemen, and seen them lying dead in the square with the green grass in their mouths."

The failure of the potato crop was felt so acutely because it was almost the only form of sustenance known to the thousands of country people throughout Ireland. To depend entirely on potatoes was to "live upon the extreme verge of human subsistence", and when this source of food disappeared "there was nothing cheaper to which they could resort". (A later gardening friend of Mr Hole, Mr Shirley Hibberd—see chapter 8—carried out various experiments on the potato and the disease which caused the famine in Ireland.) Mr Hole also quotes Cobbett on the potato: "that root of poverty". In 1846 the potato disease was even worse and the terrible distress and starvation often meant that emigration either to America or England was the only answer. There is the story, told later on in the book, of a speaker at a public meeting (to deal with the distribution of food) saying that "rather than the people should starve, they might take his sheep from the hills; and how that, when want and hunger increased, they kept in remembrance his generous words and . . . turned ninety of his sheep into mutton".

And it was later, on their return journey to Galway from Joyce's country and Connemara, that the two fellow travellers watched "a most painful and touching scene" at the railway station—

> the departure of some emigrants, and their last separation, here on earth, from dear relations and friends . . . ever and anon, a mother or a sister would force a way into the carriages, flinging her arms

Mrs Furbelow by John Leech

Design by Leech of 'a spade turning up the Crystal Palace in allusion to Paxton being a gardener.' (Reported to have been used as a seal by the Duke of Devonshire.)

A famous political cartoon by John Leech, *Punch*, March 10, 1855: 'General Février turned traitor,'

Joseph Paxton, 1851

around her beloved, only to be separated . . . and parting from them
with looks of misery as disturbed the soul with pity . . . and I thought

recorded Mr Hole, "how bounden we are, with all our might, to avert
from them these overwhelming sorrows. . . ."

But to return to their journey through Connemara; this provided
opportunities for the finest of salmon fishing for John Leech, and at
Kylemore the catch was so stupendous as to inspire the scribe of the
expedition to break into verse:

> So long as Kylemore has such lakes and such fishing,
> As from Duncan's Hotel at this moment we see,
> And of salmon for dinner we bring such a dish in—
> *Connemara's* the planet for you, Frank, and me!

"After the banquet, 'Frank' caused us to be rowed in triumph over
the scene of his victory . . . surveying the waters with a grand com-
placency . . ." only vouchsafing the information afterwards that he had
"hooked and *lost* two much finer fish than that on which we dined".
Later on in the evening they met a landscape painter in the common-
room of the inn who confessed that he "could do nothing with Connemara", but as they all sipped their punch together he told them of the
derivation of the name "whiskey" from the Irish word *uiske* meaning
water, "the only water", quoth he, "that's good for a gentleman to
drink." (*Everyman's Encyclopaedia*[16] gives: "Whisky (Scotch and Canadian), Whiskey (Irish and Amer.) derived from the Gaelic *uisge beatha*,
the alchemist's *aqua vitae*, 'water of life'.")

As the evening went on the Oxonian asked the painter what he
"thought of Ireland's prospects?"

"Well", he said, after a long reflective pull at his little, black, *dudeen*,
"I am not so sanguin as some with regard to the prosperity of Ireland.
. . . Every history, or book of travels, written no matter when or by
whom, always has the same moral—Ireland is emerging from a
state of misery and degradation—followed by some fine, old,
crusted quotations with regard to our capabilities. The grand pana-
cea, Protestantism, has been administered to us . . . with so few
favourable results, that I begin to fear our malady is chronic and that
affliction must be regarded as our normal state."

(We may ask ourselves, in the 1970s, whether his words were just.)
It was a Saturday night and this discussion went on until late, with
"Frank" interrupting at intervals and calling them "two mythological

5

bloaters". However, the Irishman gave as good a summary of the question as any:

> Sure, we'll be the grandest nation upon earth the moment we get a taste of encouragement. Meanwhile I'll concede, that we're a trifle awkward to manage and, when we're not famished by dearth of food, nor depressed by a drought of whiskey, that we're mighty fond of a scrimmage.

After which they all ended up dancing to a fiddle in the kitchen.

After a happy although rather damp Sunday, spent in walking between the showers and arguing in friendly discussions about their respective religions, the two friends left Kylemore on Monday morning at breakfast-time with their Irish friend calling to them from his window "to give his love to the Bishop of London and to ask him what he fancied for the Chester Cup". This time they were travelling on an outside car which they enjoyed, being independent and able to stop where they pleased, having plenty of room and conversing freely together. They soon fell in with numbers of people on the way to Leenane to a fair to be held there. Some were coming across in boats from the other side of the water, many were walking, but most were riding. Leaving the fair behind them, after changing horses at the inn, they hurried on in order to meet the Clifden Car at the Cross Roads en route to Galway. Leaning over the bridge at Oughterarde they said their sad farewells to Connemara and the "glorious scenes where nature, with a calm, majestic dignity, which must impress and ought to improve, claims at once our reverence and love, awes us with her grandeur but charms us more with her smile".

Descending from these dizzy heights of poetic appreciation the friends admitted reluctantly that there had been one grave omission to their happiness in Connemara—"the want of ladies' society. English ladies can go, do go, and will go everywhere; but, generally speaking, they are unwilling, wisely unwilling, to encounter a wet day on an Irish car, or the carpetless, comfortless rooms of the Connemara Inns." Even some gentlemen may be deterred by the lack of small, comfortable amenities such as the marble bath filled with perfumed hot water or the delicate cuisine which can provide golden plovers, soups and sauces, Nesselrode pudding, et cetera. "Again", wrote Mr Hole,

> the fine gentleman may be disconcerted to find that windows very generally decline to be opened, or, being open, prefer to keep so, except in case of his looking out of them, when they are down upon his neck, like a guillotine. His looking-glass, too, just as it is brought

to convenient focus, may perhaps, dash madly round, as though urged by an anxiety which it could not repress, to assure him, in white chalk, that it really cost three and sixpence [17½p]. But . . . what are these trivial inconveniences which amuse, more than they annoy . . . and he who cannot enjoy Connemara fare, salmon, fresh from its lakes, eggs, newly laid, excellent bread and butter . . . who cannot sleep in a clean Connemara bed, after a day amongst its mountains and lakes . . . why he's not the man for Galway and had better keep away from it.

Leaving the station at Galway at 4 p.m.—where, as mentioned earlier they watched the sad scenes of emigrants leaving Ireland for new homes across the sea—the two friends arrived at Athlone, on their way to Limerick, a couple of hours later. It was pouring with rain, in traditional fashion, and the castle and barracks looked "their greyest and grimmest". But the thought of the Shannon river down which they were to take a steamer to reach Limerick, cheered them considerably. They discussed the fact that the Shannon, being fordable at Athlone, had sometimes altered the course of the town's history. And so, beguiled by the luxury of Mr Rourke's hotel with its "papered walls and carpeted floors and practicable windows and duplicate towels", they disregarded the rain and looked forward to seeing the beauties of the Shannon.

But those "beauties" of their river trip were not, after all, purely horticultural. For there on the steamer, in a deep purple gown wrapped round cosily in a green plaid shawl and on her dark hair one of the most bewitching bonnets ever created, tied with blue ribbons and bordered with roses, was THE BELLE OF THE SHANNON, and Mr Hole was "*again in love!*" There she was, the little enchantress, with her large eyes and a sweet, pink mouth and rosy cheeks, and she was carrying a long, narrow box from which emerged from time to time—of all things—a peacock's head, looking round unhappily. Failing to appreciate its proximity to such a divine female it only looked frightened and miserable.

Mr Hole was in a "state of most abject infatuation" and got no sympathy whatever from his travelling companion. "He'll forget her tomorrow morning", said "Frank" to his neighbour, in a pretended whisper which all could hear, "and it's better so, poor fellow, for the girl's ridiculously fond of me, and I've got no end of her hair in my pocket."

However that may be, Mr Hole wrote twelve verses—and sang them—in the smoke room that evening in Limerick. One of the verses went like this:

> Her very bonnet
> Desarves a Sonnet,
> And I'd write one on it,
>   If I'd the time.
> But something fairer,
> And dear, and rarer,
> In coorse, the wearer,
>   Shall have my rhyme.

which has a ring to it similar to a poem by the more established contemporary poet, H. A. Dobson, as the following shows:

> I intended an Ode,
> And it turn'd to a Sonnet
> It began à la mode,
> I intended an Ode;
> But Rose cross'd the road
> In her latest new bonnet;
> I intended an Ode;
> And it turn'd to a Sonnet.

Limerick and lace must be almost synonymous and the lace-girls besieged the two friends immediately they left their hotel to have a look round the town. To Mr Hole, whose home was close to Nottingham, the idea of beautiful lace would not have seemed so unique as to many other visitors. However, they took back "a miscellaneous assortment" which were declared to be "both pretty and cheap".

Leaving Limerick on the 11.30 a.m. mail train for Killarney, they reached their destination at about 4 p.m. The contrast between the wild mountains and lakes of Connemara and the tranquil scenes before them in Killarney seems to have been very great. Known widely as one of the world's outstanding beauty spots, it must be difficult to do it justice either in words or in paint. They hired a boat and set off at once for the island of Innisfallen. It was dusk and the moon was already rising on the one hand and the sun setting on the other. The boatmen were friendly —the tobacco pouch having circulated—and told them the legend of King O'Donoghue and his kingdom under the water, where banquets, courts and aquatic fêtes are held, reminding one of the history of Dunwich now under the sea where on a calm day, the church bells might be heard beneath the water. The beauty of the island impressed them both and they understood why St Finian chose it, more than 1,300 years ago, for his retreat.

After breakfast the next morning they set off in a hired motor to see the Gap of Dunloe★ and on the way had views across the River Laune of Macgillicuddy's Reeks, Ireland's greatest range of mountains. (For some reason which is not explained, "Frank" addressed Mr Hole as "Mr Macgillicuddy" during the whole of their time in Killarney.) The Gap of Dunloe is a wild pass through the mountains and here the cars are sent back and the journey undertaken either on foot or by pony. Dramatic it must have been and "Frank" was looking for an eagle which he insisted on seeing, as a large bird soared overhead. His delight was squashed when the guide murmured "raven" and Mr Hole "certainly thought 'Frank' would have hit him".

Having emerged into comparative daylight from the darkness of the Gap they had a view of the Black Valley ahead. Then they took to a boat again to traverse the river leading from the Upper and Middle to the Lower Lakes. One of the great beauties of Killarney is the wonderful variety of trees—birch, oak, arbutus, holly, yew, hazel and the mountain-ash—all in luxurious growth. Ferns, too, grew in abundance, and amongst the ruins of Mucross Abbey the next day, they found some fine fronds of the hart's-tongue fern, and many others which they were unable to name.

So much beauty—of nature, this time—had roused our scribe once more to the higher realms of poetry and he wrote something similar in length to a Shakespearian sonnet, leaving it in their joint writing-case. "Frank" was still out fishing, and Mr Hole took a walk to Killarney post office. On his return he found that every other line of his poetic achievement had been replaced in a lighter vein, and so read thus:

"Killarney"
When the pale morn streaks
Mr Macgillicuddy's cheeks
And the day-god shoots
Through the shutters, oped by Boots;
And from sweet Innisfallen,—
Jolly place to walk with gal in!
Which so lovely, and so lone is,—
Why, it ain't, it's full of conies.
Hark! a voice comes o'er the wave,
Now, old Buffer, up and shave!
As I watch the Heron's wing,—
More fool you, you'll cut your chin!
Sailing stately, slowly flapping,—
Better work away with Mappin!

★ See details of bill paid to Victoria Hotel, Killarney, facing p. 81.

Ah, sweet morning's face is fair,—
Not so your's, soap'd like that ere!
And she dons her summer garment,—
Get on yours, you lazy varmint!

"Frank" had obviously been otherwise engaged than fishing. But it
was impossible to be angry with him. "So we sat down to discuss in
affectionate unison, the delicious trout which he had caught (how could
I eat his fish and be sulky?) amplifying our ordinary allowance of sherry,
in honour of the Naiads . . . who look after the trout in particular."

They were now to go further south and the omnibus took them into
Killarney where they were to take the Glengarriff car. Having installed
themselves on "the Lake side" they sat there for some time before the
horses were brought. "But even Irish cars must fulfill their mission;
and we started at last," wrote Mr Hole. As they halted to pick up other
passengers some young girls and an older woman got on together,
selling various hand-made objects amongst the passengers suitable to
take home for gifts. One of the passengers, a flashy type of "Gent",
was approached by the older woman but he turned abruptly from her
saying "that he should buy from the young 'uns if he bought at all".
At this, our two kind-hearted friends—and it would be difficult, I
think, to find (in spite of any other failings they might have) two more
tender-hearted men, more touched by frailty, more anxious to help
the unfortunate—immediately invited her to show them what she had
to sell; "Frank" buying "her most elaborate bracelets" and Mr Hole
purchasing a box suitable for keeping gloves, "but subsequently used
by a small niece as a bed for her youngest doll, the sliding lid drawn
up to the sleeper's chin, forming a counterpane of unrivalled splendour . . ." They did what they could to comfort the elderly saleswoman
but she had obviously been deeply hurt by the unkind cut.

The scenery on this mountain drive was especially fine, "wild and
stern and desolate", and reaching the summit they passed through a
tunnel—a fine feat of engineering, leaving County Kerry behind them
and approaching County Cork.

After the steep rocks and forbidding mountains of Kerry it was
delightful to look upon the greenness of Glengarriff and the sunlit
waters of Bantry Bay. They stayed over a Sunday in Glengarriff and
climbed up the hill to the small cottage-cum-church for mattins. The
clergyman had other parishes to care for as well as this one and it
seemed strange to speak of "the beginning of this day" when they
were well into the afternoon. But the simple service was impressive
and they were glad to put their thanks for it into the offertory basin,
"though it was but a cheeseplate of the willow pattern".

It was at Glengarriff where a waiter from the stables had been introduced into the dining-room, hurriedly "garnished with an enormous
white neckerchief", and causing rather a stir by barging frequently
into his superior, "with such a clattering of plates, and dish-covers,
and knives, and jugs, and crockery in general" that they could hardly
hear themselves speak and "the noise made by a couple of waiters was
something to exceed belief". This incident caused Reynolds Hole to
make a general comment on the Irish waiter, much in his favour.

But the Irish waiter is, notwithstanding, a capital fellow, good-
tempered, prompt, colloquial, large-hearted. For example when
another diner mildly expressed his conviction that one waiter was
insufficient to satisfy the emergencies of seventeen persons, the individual referred to immediately exclaimed from the other end of
the apartment, but with all good humour and civility: "Shure, thin,
and every gintleman will be having his fair turn".

Such an optimistic outlook was much appreciated by our friends
preferring, as they did, "this scant attendance, with all its good humour
and elasticity, to the solemn dreariness of our English waiter". They
would rather have the waiter who will "favour you with a grin on
account" than the one who pretends not to hear and goes "rushing off
in a contrary direction".

The last stage of their journey now approached and they drove along
on the Cork car, going past the estuaries of Bantry Bay as they left
Glengarriff. The tide was out, showing—as an estuary frequently does
at low tide—the shape of the curving river banks more clearly and the
contrast of the river bed with the outcrops of sea lavender, sea pinks, or
coarse grass growing in tufted clumps. They saw a solitary heron, no
doubt surveying his surroundings with an eagle eye for any hope of
food, and curlews ran and flew and called amongst the seaweed.

They were offered a small excursion to an island about a mile away
from their route—Gougane-barra. This they accepted and visited the
"green island", "reaching it by an overland route" and the writer
adds: "a method of access which I do not remember to have noticed
out of Ireland". It was a place of pilgrimage (perhaps like Croagh
Patrick in Mayo), and with many "Stations" and lists of prayers to be
said there graven on the stones.

Returning to the car the journey was resumed, passing "small,
silvery streams from which the trout were leaping, 'Bekase', says our
driver, 'the wather's so full o' fish, that whiniver they want to turn
round they must jist jump out and do it in the air'." One of these
silver streams may have been a tributary—if not the river itself—of the

Lee which has its source at Gougane-barra and winds along on its way
to Cork. The city of Cork, standing as it does on an island, is so placed
because the Lee divides and flows around it, the scene backed by well-
wooded hills. Mr Hole quotes the old prophecy:

> Limerick was, Dublin is, and Cork shall be
> The finest city of the three.

They travelled the twelve miles from the city to the sea—to the landing place of Queen Victoria in 1849, called Queenstown in her honour
until 1922. At one time 100,000 emigrants embarked here annually for
America. (Mr Hole mentions that 7,520,000 dollars were sent from
America to help Irish emigrants during the years 1848 to 1854 inclusive.)
After their return to the excellent Imperial Hotel for lunch—fresh and
full-grown prawns with bread-and-butter accompanied by golden ale—
they set off by horse-driven car to Blarney, for the afternoon.

The old castle of Blarney has a fine position overlooking the River
Lee, but at this time there was little left except for a narrow staircase
leading up into the sole remaining tower. Ivy and wild myrtle were
growing up into the tower and close to the Blarney Stone. Mr Hole
noticed various people coming up the tower for the purpose of seeing
it and he writes: "Now it is my conviction, primarily suggested by my
own sensations, and subsequently confirmed by what I noticed in
others, as I lingered on that ancient tower, that the majority of those
who kiss the Blarney Stone, do wish and try to believe in it."

(A similar example in our own country might be the Giant of Cerne
Abbas.)

But this is being serious and with "Frank" at hand such a situation
must not remain for long. Afterwards, the old gardener was showing
our friends one of the Cromlechs, or burial grounds, in which they
both affected an all-absorbing interest. However, as they left the
gardens Mr Hole asked "Frank" what a Cromlech was. He replied
that, prior to inspection, his idea had always been that it was a species
of antediluvian buffalo!

Returning to Cork by a different route they had "a fine view . . .
of the beautiful city and its environs". Certainly it was a most well-
chosen ending before their return to Dublin by rail the following day.

They had a night in Morrisson's before sailing from Kingston Quay.
Mr Hole's last comment was a warmly appreciative one: "Looking
back upon that lovely bay, I thought of the poor Irishman's most
touching words, as he gazed for the last time on his native land, (Ah,
Dublin, sweet Jasus be with you!) and from my heart I breathed an
earnest prayer for the good weal of beautiful Ireland!"

Both the author and the illustrator had gone to a great deal of trouble
to ensure that everything was correct down to the smallest detail.
Leech, despite his fears of sea-sickness, "went a second time over the
Channel, and across Ireland to Galway that he might finish to his
satisfaction the wonderful picture of the Claddagh . . ."[17] Mr Hole had
evidently been trying to get certain facts and figures about farming in
Ireland, for, in a letter from Leech there is reference to a Census which
consists of twelve "volumes and weighs about a quarter of a ton". He
suggests, understandably, that perhaps Mr Hole can manage without
consulting such references.

After the publication of their joint effort in the following year they
eagerly awaited the reviews.

In a long letter written from Caunton and dated 20 September 1859,
Mr Hole writes:

My dear Leech, I am sure that I need not say that I am most sincerely
sorry to hear of your dear little boy's indisposition, and shall be quite
anxious to hear from you, when you can find a few minutes to give
me a bulletin. My address during this week will be at Springkell,
Ecclefechan, N.B., and an account of my little Tour in Scotland will
appear in the "Atheneum" with some very wooden cuts by H.D.

I have written to Milward by this post. I went over to Thurgaton
and had a shy at Aunt Sally* yesterday . . .

(In a letter a few days earlier Leech had asked Hole if he could possibly
go and take a look at the horse for him, and let him know the colour—
"not that I am very particular on that point as long as it is not pink or
green!")

. . . She is a gentlemanlike looking hack, *dark* chestnut. . . . She seems
very good-tempered, and I rode her close up to the gate of the rail
by Thurgaton as a train came up, but she took no notice. She is five
years old. I believe she would suit you exactly. . . .

The Little Tour is delightfully reviewed in The Gardeners'
Chronicle, published by B. and E. and number S.R.H. among its
contributors. But really it is a very pleasant bit of praise! . . . I
dreamed the other night that I wrote an article about you, in which
I proved you to be the greatest author, as well as artist of your time.
(Gardeners' Chronicle, by the way, terms you "our modern Ho-
garth"), and made it perfectly clear that you caused more cheerfulness in British hearts than all the philanthropists going.

Send me a line about your boy, and with our true sympathies, and

* A new horse.

our kind regards to Mrs Leech, believe me, dear Leech, yours very
sincerely, S. Reynolds Hole.

This was followed two days later, from Ecclefechan:

My dear Leech, I have read the review of our dear little Tour . . . in
"The Times" of yesterday, and have been drinking the Reviewer's
health ever since. . . . I don't know that I ever was so jolly in my life,
as when I first caught sight of the genial, graceful, glorious notice;
and I could *almost* have shaken hands with H— D—.
    How is your little boy? This is a lovely place, but the post leaves (of
course) in the middle of the day, and as we are going after grouse
and blackcock, I have no time for more.
    Besides I'm not sober, and don't mean to be for many months.
    Sir, the Press of this country is the Sun of the nineteenth century.
Let us bask in its rays and be glad!
    With kind regards, and love to the children—
    Yours ever and sincerely,
                                                    "The Oxonian"

Alluded to [in] *The Times* of September 26—whack! Here is the
review taking up two-thirds of a full column—

A pleasant little book has just got into the shop windows, and which
is as seasonable in its way as the handbooks for English travel. Its
effect is to give Ireland its turn of commendation to the tourist who
travels simply for his health and pleasure; that is to say, it is a model
run of some two or three weeks, recounted in so pleasant a vein by
an anonymous Oxonian, and so characteristically and gracefully
illustrated by Leech, that it must inevitably encourage others to
imitate their example. Its route via Dublin, includes Galway,
Connemara, Athlone, Limerick, Killarney, Glengarriff and Cork. It
is a mere loop, in fact, of an excursion into the sister island, but this
loop comprises, on the joint testimony of Leech and the author such
exhilarating scenes and influences, and such quaint characteristics of
race, that it refreshes any Irish reminiscences we retain and cheer-
fully stimulates our Irish predilections. Both author and artist saw
the persons and things they encountered in a humorous light, and
could have doubtless made a pleasant book from materials less
promising, but the enjoyments of Irish travel at the command of
other persons are made obvious here in an eminent degree. . . .
    We agree with the writer that the Englishman who desires a new
sensation should pay a visit to the Claddagh, Galway . . . "and to

my fancy", says the writer, "the most becoming dress in all the world is that of a peasant girl of Connemara." . . . there is little difference, on the testimony of the Oxonian and Leech, between Paddy in England and Paddy at home . . . the same in aspect, but in action how different! In England he will rise with the sun, reap under its burning heat until it sets and dance in the bara at midnight. In Ireland he always seems to be either going . . . —in brief, to be doing nothing.

. . . The Oxonian wisely warns tourists that they must still expect to rough it a little in the carpetless, comfortless rooms of the Connemara Inns. The tourist's addiction to his morning tub is still a pursuit of cleanliness under difficulties . . . these *désagrémens* are compensated to the humorist by Connemara scenery, and the appetite it encourages. . . . This our latest report from Ireland is, therefore, most encouraging and, as we said above, it is calculated to do Ireland the further benefit of sending Englishmen there in shoals in the course of this and the following seasons.[18]

Caunton Manor.
12 October 1859.

My dear Leech,
I have received a cheque from Bradbury & Evans for £105, with an allusion to future favours. I have thanked them sincerely, but my chief thanks and theirs (as I told them) are due, of course, to you. For they know, and I know, and you know, and all the world knows, that "A Little Tour in Ireland" would in all probability have made a Little Ditto to the Trunkmakers, had it not been illustrated by John Leech—God bless him.

I am the last man to say that there is nothing to recommend the text; but the first to maintain that the merits thereof (if any) would never have been recognised, had they not been chaperoned by you. And so, my friend, with the delightful document on "Smith, Payne, & Smith" before us, I see thro' the signature of "Bradbury & Evans" the name of John Leech, and to him I tender my most genuine gratitude.

The cheque is most acceptable, for my normal state, ever since I was weaned, has been to be in arrear, but far beyond the pecuniary pleasure is my real pride and delight in having "whipped in" to you during one of the pleasantest runs I ever saw in my life, and in having feebly assisted you in killing your fox, as you would do with the worst whip in England.

The Reviews, I suppose, are very satisfactory, because Evans says so. The citizen in "The Times" makes me thrill with delight, and I was immensely pleased with "The Spectator", "Examiner", "Globe", and "Illustrated"; the others read the book in no spirit of sympathy. All praise you, except H.D.—poor beast!

My dear Leech, I have so much to say that I shall not attempt anything of the kind. The chief thing on my mind is to ask you (and if you knew how really anxious I am on the point, you would not refuse, tho' you are such a granite-hearted old ruffian) to come here in November and do the Almanac. I can easily prove that it is your duty to do so.

I. You cannot get the little oxygen, which there is to be got in Nov', except in the country.

II. You want all the oxygen there is in the firmament to do justice to the Almanac.

III. We have horses and dogs and every adjunct of country life.

IV. You will be removed from the cares of housekeeping.

V. It is proved that Caunton is singularly adapted for the realisations of Art, all critics at home and abroad uniting in the assertion that the three drawings finished by you in one morning here were the best (with the trifling exception of 3 little sketches of my own) ever done in the same period of time.

No but really will you bring the mahogany box and come? Please do, for how else am I to tell you all I have to say and to hear all I desire to know? How else are you to get your gun, which I am thoroughly ashamed to have forgotten? How else are we to arrange about "A Little Tour in Holland", which I hope will be realised, and for which we can get some capital introductions? Echo answers, "Nohow", so fix your day. Bring Aunt Sally to "keep company" with my new horse, a beauty, and I will guarantee that you shall do twice the work you ever did in Town, far removed from smoke, and gas, late hours, &c.

Returning from Scotland I spent a few hours at the English Lakes. Windermere is a mere duckpool to the Lower Lake of Killarney.

Please give our united and very kind regards to Mrs Leech, I hope your children, those two "stars so blue and golden" [the allusion is to their pretty hats and hair] are blooming (Hang it! stars don't bloom) are shining brightly after their planetary visit to the sea.

I wonder whether you could persuade Lucas* to try change of air for a few days and come here with you. I should be so glad to see him. Believe me, my flinty friend, thine ever,

S. Reynolds Hole

* "A big 'shot'" [on The Times].

"A Green Spot on the Path of Time": A Portrait of John Leech

THERE IS LITTLE doubt that amongst the many friends that Rev. Reynolds Hole made during his long life it was John Leech who was the dearest of all. The *Little Tour* as a joint collaboration had gone so well that the friendship, begun a few months earlier, became cemented into an affectionate and sincere regard on both sides. A correspondence developed which shows their understanding of each other, their mutual love of humour, their kindliness and their industry.

"Friendship is a delicate plant and can only be grown very seldom for most of us. Acquaintances one can pick up any day, but a friend seems to me almost more of a rarity than a lover. . . ."[1]

What kind of person was John Leech—what had he been as a boy, as a young man, as the head of his family? Sent to Charterhouse at the age of seven, he remained there for about nine years and is described by a contemporary (the late Mr H. O. Nethercote of Northamptonshire) as "a nice-looking, genial lad, liked by everyone in the school for his good temper and winning manner". He was unable to take part in much of the sport at school such as cricket, racing, etc., owing to having broken his arm when falling off his pony as a small boy, but it is reported that he enjoyed his fencing lessons with Angelo more than his drawing lessons with Mr Burgess. After leaving school he entered the medical profession "under the auspices of Mr Stanley, surgeon of St Bartholomew's Hospital". Owing to certain financial embarrassments of Mr Leech senior, the young man went to reside with a Mr Whittle who was known to dispense extensively amongst his patients what was known as the *Pil. Hum* (abbreviation of Pill Humbug, or as he used to call them, the "Humbugeraneous Pills"), which was made of liquorice powder and yellow soap.

These rather questionable medical studies seem gradually to have slipped from the forefront of his interest and he exchanged the thermometer for the pencil. Art, in fact, took over. But while still at St Bartholomew's he had made many friends, amongst them Albert

Smith and Percival Leigh, both future comrades on the staff of *Punch* and authors in their own right. Little by little commissions came in and the real starting point was his skit on Rowland Hill's new penny postage stamp designed by Mulready.

Envelope ∧

His work for *Punch* has been mentioned briefly but as our concern is with Leech as a person, especially in his relationship with Reynolds Hole, it is from Hole's writings rather than from Frith's *Life* that most of the comments come.

It was about three months after their first meeting on that Easter Monday evening of 1858 that Leech invited Reynolds Hole to dine with him in Brunswick Square. (As an inducement to accept, Leech mentioned that Thackeray was to be present—an inducement hardly needed, in any case.) Hole records it as a "memorable night, 'a green spot on the path of time' at which I was introduced by the great artist to the great author". In a matter of minutes the ice was broken and Thackeray and Hole were standing back to back to see which was the taller. The other guests of the dinner party decided that there was little if any difference between them but Hole, overcome by modesty, made the well-known comparison: "Yes, the fiddle cases are of equal size, but in his there's a glorious violincello and in mine a dancing-master's kit."

It was only a few days later that Leech visited Caunton, "the first of many happy visits". He loved the country and country things and it was as he said, "a grand enjoyment to him simply to sit under a tree and rest". Hole took him over to see the enormous oaks of Sherwood Forest—Shire Wood as it was called then—where Leech took out his sketch book to do some drawings. But he was so overcome by the loveliness of the scene that he put it away. "Much too beautiful for work," he said. "I can do no work today."

Then came Leech's suggestion that they should do a little tour of Ireland together. It was Mr John Deane, one of Ireland's Royal Commissioners for many years including the time of the famine, who made out a route for them to take with only a limited time at their disposal. They wanted to be as leisurely as possible. "In fact, you cannot hurry in Ireland, there is something in the humid atmosphere and in the habits and demeanour of the people which ignores haste." They were both happy in this placid countryside

gliding along the rails, or riding in cars, or rowing in boats, listening to quaint carmen, oarsmen, and guides, talking and laughing in genial converse with each other, or silent in perfect sympathy, one of the surest signs, and one of the purest delights of a true friendship!

Mr Hole here remarks on the people who only feel they are being successful companions if they "go on gently buzzing in your ear" and so make one feel under an obligation also "to buzz".

Leech's ability to seize a situation, a comment, a profile was probably fifty per cent of his art and he often pointed out something quite small, hardly even a suggestion, to his friend, which he would register in his notebook as "just a few lines, and dots, and curves". Mr Hole relates with understandable pride that

> on rare, very rare occasions it was my privilege to tell or to show him something which took his fancy, and he would say, in a tone which told you at once that he really thought he was asking a favour, "May I make use of that?" Then would I draw myself up as a monarch upon his throne, and, extending my arms in royal clemency, would make reply, "You may!"

John Leech's thought and consideration for his fellows and companions, wherever he was or with whom, was outstanding, but "his anxiety for his friends in his own house was a very winsome sight to see". He met his wife, who was then Miss Eaton, while walking in London. "He followed her home, noted the number, looked out the name, obtained an introduction, married the lady." (A similar manner of meeting is supposed to have taken place with the Baden-Powells. Apart from the charming features, dark, wavy hair, and sweet expression of Miss Olave Soames, the late Sir Robert noticed especially how she walked, and liked it. Like Leech, he gained an introduction.) Mrs Leech was often used by him in his work for *Punch*, "one of those Anglican beauties whom he loved to draw". She was friendly and kind and understanding—"a devoted mother and wife".

Leech's son, John George Washington, was not only greatly loved by his father, but also returned the devotion. He loved to be with him, wanted to dress like him, and to draw at an easel like him. He was sometimes given a small easel where he painted engravings from the *Illustrated London News* with a gravity and seriousness worthy of his father. Perhaps he was precocious, too. Mr Hole recalls being in the house when the boy addressed a new nursemaid, "Nurse, Papa says that I am one of those children that can only be managed by kindness, and I'll trouble you to fetch some sponge-cakes and oranges!"

More than anything Leech had wanted to be a painter and when Hole rebuked him, reminding him of the great value of his talents, he said "that he would rather have painted a great picture than all he had ever done". He would not believe that "his pencil had done more good to his generation than all the brushes of the Royal Academy".

His value to his fellow artists was his craftsmanship, if they could but recognize and learn from it. This was a point brought out by Sickert writing of *The Artist As Craftsman*: "Millais had the benefit of Leech's friendship, but his example taught him nothing . . .";[2] which was not the case with Keene for "Let anyone look carefully at Keene's rendering of the rampant foliage of squares and gardens in London (always admitting Keene's debt to Leech), of sea, of snow, of rain . . ."[3] and, again, "A man who does not know Corot and Courbet can certainly not understand Pissaro, any more than a man can appreciate Keene fully who does not love Leech and Cruikshank, or Leech and Cruikshank without a knowledge of Gillray and Rowlandson."[4]

Frith, whose Derby Day is said to have accounted for more sixpences (in the days of sixpences) at the turnstile of the National Gallery than all the other paintings put together, had this to say on one aspect of Leech's influence:

> Speaking from my own experience, I have always found a difficulty in giving the effect of wind in a picture: the action of it on drapery, trees, skies, etc. is—from the almost momentary nature of the gusts— far from an easy task. No one who ever handled a brush or pencil has been so successful as Leech in conveying the action of wind on every object . . .[5] (see illus. facing p. 97.)

Frith also made the comment that Leech, "although a timid rider",[6] must have collected his immense knowledge of how to draw horses from his excursions into the hunting field, either frequently with his old friend Charles Adams or more recently with his new friend, Reynolds Hole. He goes on: "Landseer and all the animal-painters within my knowledge studied the horse from casts, often from the Elgin marbles, before they attempted drawing from the living animal."[7] Stubbs was so indefatigable in his research that, "It is told of him that . . . on one occasion he carried a dead horse on his back up a narrow staircase to his dissecting-room. . . ."[8] However, although unremitting in all his detailed work, "Leech, without any preparatory study whatever, drew the hunter, the cab-horse, the hackney, the rough pony, the cob—no matter which—in absolute perfection."[9]

Perhaps he may be compared with George Stubbs in that the backgrounds in his pictures were well up to the standard of the central theme. With Stubbs there may be a phaeton drawn by a superb pair of horses standing against a country scene with fine trees and a glimpse of waters and so with Leech, the background often showing finely drawn-in scenery behind the main drama. As Thackeray wrote, "homely drawings of moor and wood and sea-shore and London street . . ."[10] He took

THE BELLE OF THE SHANNON.

"With eyes like mayteors,
And parfect phaytures,
Which aisy bate yours,
Great Vanus, fair !"

Illustration from *A Little Tour in Ireland*—words by S. Reynolds Hole.

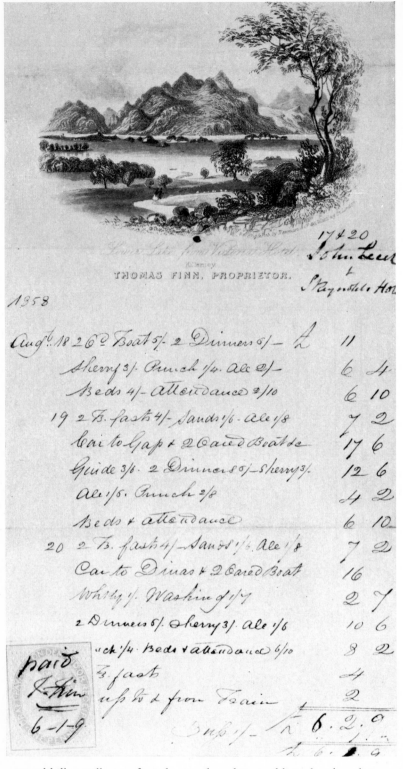

Hotel bill at Killarney for John Leech and Reynolds Hole when doing
their research for *A Little Tour in Ireland*.

his notebook everywhere he went, even to church, and the localities of many of his visits to the seaside are recognizable, whether he was at Folkestone or the Isle of Wight, Ramsgate or Scarborough, Lowestoft or Dover.

Mr and Mrs Leech often stayed with the Dickens family at the seaside and on one occasion there was a disturbing incident when they were all at the Isle of Wight. Occasionally there are, evidently, tremendous waves which roll up the shore at Bonchurch and one of these struck Leech on his brow and knocked him unconscious. He was, of course, taken back to bed and carefully nursed, with ice being applied to his head and bled in the arm. He was in serious danger of losing his life and Dickens suggested to Mrs Leech that he should try magnetism. He describes this in a letter to Charles Adams: "Accordingly, in the middle of the night I fell to, and after a very fatiguing bout of it, put him to sleep for an hour and thirty-five minutes. A change came on in his sleep, and he is decidedly better. I talked to the astounded Mrs Leech across him, when he was asleep as if he had been a truss of hay."

Dickens, who was also a close friend, wrote warmly of Leech's talents as well as his feeling for fulfilling a trust. "Some forms of our existing life will never have a better chronicler. His wit is good-natured and always the wit of a gentleman. He has a becoming sense of responsibility and restraint . . ."[11] It was this sense of responsibility which he had in common with Ruskin. As Eric Gill wrote: "He [Ruskin] is to be remembered as one of the few men of the nineteenth century who saw clearly that the roots of human action, and therefore, of human art, are moral roots."[12]

It was Leech's integrity of purpose both as an artist and as a chronicler of his time that often drove him to the pitch of exhaustion and despair over his work. Frith writes: "Leech's mental condition was certainly deeply tinged with the sadness so common to men who possess wit and humour to a high degree."[13]

Mr Hole reminds us of an incident when Mr Denison, later Lord Ossington, a neighbour living near Caunton and at that time Speaker of the House, met Leech on the train and remarked to him that he hoped he enjoyed doing his work as much as it was enjoyed by people who saw it. Leech replied: "I seem to myself to be a man who has undertaken to walk a thousand miles in a thousand hours." He always seemed to be trying to catch up and used to say that the world "itself waited for him and expressed its impatience in a smell of corduroy. That perfume, he was wont to affirm, never left his hall and it proceeded from the raiments of small boys who came continually to his house to convey thence to the wood engraver the boxwood 'blocks' on which he drew."

6

Remarking on these blocks and how they were done, Mr Hole
went on:

Sometimes his rapidity of execution was marvellous (I have known
him send off from my own house three finished drawings on the
wood, designed, traced and rectified, without much effort, as it
seemed, between breakfast and dinner), but there was never haste.
How I wish that the world could have seen those blocks! They were
committed, no doubt, to the most skilful gravers of the day, but the
exquisite fineness, clearness, the faultless grace and harmony of the
drawing could not be reproduced. If the position of an eyelash was
altered, or the curve of a lip was changed, there might be ample
remainder to convey the intention . . . but the perfection of the
original was gone.

Mr Hole recalls Leech's own reaction when he looked through the
latest number of *Punch*—his looking was usually accompanied with a
deep sigh. He knew exactly how the drawing should have been, and
only he. Others might only see charm, excellence and amusement but
for Leech there was nearly always some little line or curve missing
which meant all the difference between perfection and mediocrity. No
doubt it was a difficult operation to transfer a drawing from the wood
and Leech often acknowledged his debt to Mr Swain who, for about
twenty-five years, engraved nearly all his work. Mr Swain writes: "I
always found him kind, and willing to forgive any of my shortcomings
in not rendering his touches in all things." He went on to explain
how much easier it would have been if photographs of the drawings on wood had been known, in which case Leech could have
drawn on paper and had his drawings photographed on the wood, thus
preserving the finished drawings which would have been of great
value.

Constant frustrations of this kind may have contributed in no small
degree to the development of his nervous temperament. There are
many stories, for instance, of his hatred of excessive noise. This is
something with which, especially in this late 20th century, many of us
would be in sympathy and appreciate. But in Leech's case there are
occasions quoted which seem, perhaps, to be difficult to understand.
There is the case when he had been invited down to the country for
two or three days' hunting. He arrived during the evening and soon
settled down for the night only to be awakened the next morning by
the gardener, who was rolling the gravel underneath Leech's window.
This was a noise he particularly detested and so great was his reaction
to it that he jumped out of bed, put his things into his travelling bag

and had left the house to return to London before anyone realized that he had gone.*

Another noise, usually connected with a London square, which he disliked intensely was the barrel-organ. Having lived for many years in Russell Square, where barrel-organs appeared to flourish, he moved to No. 6 The Terrace, Kensington. Here he would show a visitor round and with especial pride draw attention to the double windows which he had "put in all over the house *to keep all noises out*". In those days the street hawkers "bellowed", the muffin-man no doubt clanged his bell, the lamp-lighter whistled, et cetera, but nowadays these background noises seem reasonably quiet compared to a motor-bicycle starting up, car doors being slammed, the incessant accompaniment of piped "music" or television sets going full blast.

A drawing which appeared in one of the early copies of *Punch* dealt with the matter of the barrel-organ. It had the title: "Wanted, by an aged lady of very nervous temperament, a Professor, who will undertake to mesmerize all the organs in her street. Salary, so much per organ."

(It appears that the barrel-organ was indeed a pest, so much so that an eminent artist of the day, finding that his work was continually interrupted by the strains of "Champagne Charlie", bought himself a pea-shooter in self-defence. This he aimed at the organ-grinder through one of the slats in a window-shutter. Having scored a direct hit, the notes of "Champagne Charlie" were interrupted temporarily and stopped altogether after a couple more successful shots from the seclusion of the shutter. Eventually a noise-abatement Bill was presented and passed by both Houses, the credit for which may partially have been due to the efforts of Leech in his cuts for *Punch*. See the Henry Silver Diaries, chapter 7.)

But above all Leech was a family man—"the best of husbands and fathers, and a most dutiful and affectionate son". And Dr Brown writes:

There is a genuine domesticity about his scenes that could come only from a man who was much at his own fireside, and in the nursery when baby was washed. . . . What he draws, he has seen; what he asks you to live in, and laugh at and with, he has laughed at and lived in. It is this wholesomeness and (to use the right word) this goodness that makes Leech more than a drawer of funny pictures,

* This incident is reminiscent of Gertrude Jekyll in her teens, who, wanting a little peace and quiet, laid the path to her garden hut with cinders as she knew her father hated the sound of their scrunching and would, in consequence, not approach the hut.

more even than a great artist. It makes him a teacher and an example of virtue in its widest sense . . .

The last word shall go to Mr Hole, to whom we return as they come back from Ireland:

After our Irish tour, the friendship between us was very brotherly and true, and a continuous intercourse, personal and epistolary, was continued up to his death. The city mouse and the country mouse paid each other many visits, but without any interruption of their mirth. It was a great intellectual treat to me to meet at his house Thackeray and Millais, Holman Hunt and Tenniel, Dasent, Wingrove Cooke, Knox, Mark Lemon and Shirley Brooks, and dear old Percival Leigh; and it was a refreshment to him to have a walk over the stubbles, or a gallop after the hounds, or a day of tranquil rest. The latter was to me the prime happiness of our communion—to sit and converse quietly with the friend I loved best on earth.

Next to this, to see him in his house, with his wife and children.

30 September 1859.

My dear Leech,

Tho' the article which you have sent me from the Unwelcome Pest is highly amusing to the public generally and to those who know you in particular, and ought only to be read with the serenest mirth, I must confess that my teeth snapped and my toes quivered, and I had not a single thought or feeling which a cool clergyman ought to have, when I reperused the dirty document in question. . . .

But I have no time to say my say, and I am glad of it, for the mountain air will restore my equanimity, and hereafter we shall have nothing but fun out of this excessively unclean production. The grub will attack the rose, my Leech: Would that I could take this—and treat him as I do the Caunton caterpillars.

You know how happy I am in hearing of your boy's convalescence. I do not return at present.

Well, well, I'm coming. Thine ever. S.R.H.

6

Punch and *The Cornhill*

March 1860

FOLLOWING THEIR RETURN from Ireland, Reynolds Hole found himself, through his friendship with John Leech, drawn more closely into the *Punch* circle. Mr Spielman, when writing *The History of Punch* many years later, refers to

the Very Rev. Reynolds Hole, Dean of Rochester, always a spoilt child of *Punch*s', and the intimate friend of Leech, was more of a *Punch* man than most contributors, as he was one of the very few outsiders who were ever entertained at the Wednesday Dinner. "Some six-and-thirty years ago", he informed me, "Mark Lemon wrote to me, 'Punch is proud of such a contributor' and I have his letter. I wrote a few short paragraphs about Oxford, and some longer articles in verse, entitled 'The Sportsman's Dream' and 'My Butler'. Leech told me, 'You are an Honorary member of our weekly meetings, and will be always welcome'."

His charming book "A Little Tour of Ireland" written "by an Oxonian" had the advantage of Leech's pencil, and by his friendship with that artist, as well as with Thackeray and others of the Staff, he was for a time identified in some measure with *Punch* itself, besides obtaining recognition as the beau-ideal of "the genial, jolly parson". That he did not become a regular contributor to the paper was due, it is believed, to a subsequent misunderstanding.[1]

There seems to be no record of the "misunderstanding" mentioned here, but even without it, the Vicar of Caunton would have had some difficulty in finding time to become a regular contributor to *Punch* as well as to continue with his work in the parish and also as President of the National Rose Show. The second of these was held in June 1859, and the third on 12 July 1860, owing to its much larger size, in the Crystal Palace at Sydenham. However, he did become more and more involved with some of these *Punch* friends, especially Leech and

Thackeray, and was privileged, as we have seen, to attend one of their Wednesday Dinners.

To understand the value of these dinners, the comradeship, the quickness of the fun and wit, presents a difficulty to anyone who was not there. However, to make things easier for us there are the Henry Silver Diaries (4 August 1858—23 March 1870) in which one finds recorded "with astonishing frankness" all that happened at these weekly dinners. Here are a few excerpts to give an impression of the friendliness and directness which prevailed:

August 4th, Wednesday, 1858, at 11 Bouverie Street, previously at the Star and Garter. "White soup and salmon—champagne out of tumblers—seltzer and cigars. No puddings allowed 'because we don't care for them' says S.B. in January, when E(vans) wonders we don't have them. E., like H.S., has a weakness that way . . . M.L. jolly and full of fun—takes a paternal interest in T. (Tenniel) now J.L. (John Leech) is in Scotland. 'My dear Tenniel, now don't eat too much salmon. Think of your big cut.' (illustration)".

December 9th, 1858. M.L. discourses parentally of his son Mark— fearing he may go wrong, etc. Confesses to having slept cum puella sempirivite sans kidding.* Amusing to hear the grave and sedate Professor holding forth on moral matters. S.B. openly bawdy—calls a spade a spade.

December 15th, 1858. Leech don't like Christmas generally and Xmas parties in particular.

December 22nd, 1858. J.L. on Sir Joseph Paxton—plain-spoken man, and drops an "H" occasionally—but clearly a clear head—and not a bit stuck-up. Sir J. "free of the table", B. says. Sits between us and champagnes with me. Says he has drunk enough champagne to *wine* the road from St Paul's to Hammersmith. . . . Then a discussion on the Franchise—Sir J. talking vehemently and T.T. knowingly. S.B. and P.L. the other chief speakers. Sir J. says Bright's plan would be most unfair—giving manufacturers much power and taking away from intelligent workmen (who in Coventry are a large class) all voice in the elections.

Jan. 12th, 1859. Mock turtle, red mullet, turbot, saddle of mutton and boiled fowl (Oh, I can't stand this, says J.L.!) kidneys, ptarmigan, brown flesh, deuced good. And all this after reading of The Homes of Our Poor in today's *Times*.

(The dinners were provided by Bradbury and Evans who thought nothing too good to put before their staff. Turtle soup, salmon cutlet,

* Would seem to mean "with a girl all night".

cold beef, pineapple fritters, cheese, strawberries and cream, cherries, pineapple punch, champagne, sherry and claret[2]—such was a typical menu.) "Man wants but little here below—but wants that little good," wrote Silver, when faced with such a menu.

Never did the evening pass without some amusement.

Mark, for one, could always provoke laughter. [Editor 1841–1870.] . . . At eight-thirty, the feasting over and everyone in an expansive mood, cigars were called for and the work of the evening begins. . . . Almost immediately he was jotting down notes for the Large Cut. Sometimes this business could be settled in a matter of minutes, but more often the deliberations continued well into the night.[3] *February 15th, 1860.* Present: B. (Bradbury). J.L. (Leech). T.T. (Tom Taylor). H.S. (Henry Silver). C.K. (Charles Keene). J.T. (John Tenniel). M.L. (Mark Lemon). S.B. (Shirley Brooks). Lucas (late). H.M. (Horace Mayhew—Pommy). W.M.T. (Thackeray). and Hole —Canon S. Reynolds Hole. "Reference for his Reverence. Shirley tells of sailor in bus and conductor, in a confidential whisper. Hole a big manly clean-shaven young parson of the Muscular Christianity order. Good at cricket and across country. Wrote 'The Little Tour of Ireland'. Ergo, has some fun in him—proves it too by his performance with a wet cork on a bottle. The Cork Robin, Mark calls it. A jolly evening."

Reynolds Hole's own impressions are given by Mr Spielman in some detail:

Guests at the Table.
Another visitor, as all the world now knows, was Dean [*sic*] Reynolds Hole, who has recorded in his "Memories" his impressions of that famous Dinner of February 15th, 1860. To me, also, he has given an idea of the effect wrought upon him by the frolic of the meal—an impression certainly not dimmed by time nor faded in his imagination. He says: "There was such a clash and glitter of sharp-edged swords, cutting humour, and pointed wit (to say nothing of the knives and forks), the sallies of the combatants were so incessant and intermixed, the field of battle so enveloped in *smoke*, that there was only a kaleidoscopic confusion of brilliant colours in the vision of the spectator, when the signal was given to 'cease firing'." Who would not attend a *Punch* dinner after that?[4]

Further entries in the diaries for the years 1860–1861, refer in some detail to Paxton; record the death of Albert Smith with whom Leech collaborated successfully ten years earlier; show a typical discussion—in this case on the work of Tennyson *v.* Thackeray.

May 9th, 1860. Sir Joseph Paxton enjoyed the frequent privilege of dining with the *Punch* folk. . . . Then cigars were lighted—cigarettes were things despised then: even fast young ladies carried a cigar case.* Bradbury proposes P.'s health and P. in reply says it was 34 years this day that he first went to Chatsworth . . . reached it by a rival coach at 4.0 a.m. . . . recollects helping to put horses to—instead of going to bed walked round grounds and so set men to work at 6.0— being young this gave him authority which he wanted—says he lived a life in that 3 minutes' speech of Bradbury's . . . Evans asks if it wasn't that morning he first saw Lady P., and he says "yes" and without a good wife a man can't well succeed.

May 16th, 1860. Albert Smith died. [Some references give his death a week later, 23 May.]

October 23rd, 1861. E. heard Jenny (Lind) last night, in Elijah, her first reappearance—liked her better than ever—voice, if less powerful, has even more expression. Such dramatic warmth—prefers her to Malibrau.

November 13th, 1861. J.L. hates crinolines, on ladies as well as servants. S.B. don't—in moderation. When the Prince of Wales marries a pretty ankled girl, away will go the crinoline.

November 20th, 1861. Didn't Tennyson hate Elizabeth Browning, asks S.B. Isn't it natural for rival writers to be enemies? W.M.T. dissents—calls Tennyson the greatest man of the age—"has thrown the quoit the furthest". S.B. says *Vanity Fair* ranks higher than anything of Tennyson's and asks, "Would you change your reputation for his?" "Yes." "I don't believe you . . ." P.L. thinks Tennyson is to Wordsworth what Mendelssohn is to Beethoven; graceful but not sublime. . . . All three praise Scott, S.B. and P.L. the most—stirs the blood—"but" says, Thackeray, "I don't want my blood stirred". "Like a trumpet call," says S.B. . . . Thackeray thanks God that the world is wide, and that tastes are various, and whatever mental food be offered there are sure to be customers. "Tennyson on a level with Milton and Shakespeare." "No, Mr. Thackeray, I can't agree to that. . . ."

It may be noticed that Thackeray was amongst the regular members present when Reynolds Hole was the Guest at the Table. This must

---

* This was the time, after all, when Lord Lytton was "regularly puffing his way through seven cigars between going to bed and getting up in the morning". (Philip Howard, *The Times*, 5 May 1973.)

have meant a good deal to him as, next to Leech, it was Thackeray to whom he had come closer in friendship than any of the others in the *Punch* Circle. Hole writes that they had "many a pleasant reunion. Whenever we met, he invited me to his house, and always, before the guests went home, he whispered in my ear, 'Stay for the fragrant weed'."[5] (It was Thackeray who, two years later, proposed him for the Garrick Club where they frequently dined together.) "He said so many good things, being the best talker I have ever listened to, when it pleased him to talk, that they trod down and suffocated each other."[6]

But there was one conversation which stood out in Hole's mind. It related to the publication of Buckle's *History of Civilization* where the power of the "human mind and the progress of scientific discovery"[7] could set out to eliminate all unhappiness and sorrow. "Thackeray spoke, as Newton spoke about gathering pebbles on the shore, and affirmed that one of the best results of knowledge was to convince a man of his ignorance. He seemed to preach from the text, though he did not quote it, that the wisdom of this world is foolishness with God."[8]

Thackeray's humility about his own work was endearing. He related one particular occasion when, travelling abroad and entering a hotel after a tiring day of sight-seeing, he lay down in the sitting-room on a settee. By his side there was a small table and on it a book. He turned the pages to find that it was a copy of *Vanity Fair*. "I had not read it since I corrected the proofs and I read a chapter. Do you know, it seemed to me very amusing!"[9]

At the time of the *Punch* dinner just mentioned Thackeray was editor of *The Cornhill* and he invited Hole to write something for it. The entry consisted of three verses "which he commended so highly and rewarded so munificently"[10] that the author took heart and quoted them some years later in a sermon. Much to his pride, as they were leaving the cathedral together, the Dean of St Paul's remarked: "Were not those lines from Hood?"[11]

"Mabel"

I

In the sunlight:—

Little Mab, the Keeper's daughter, singing by the brooklet's side,
With her playmates singing carols of the gracious Eastertide;
And the violet and the primrose make sweet incense for the quire,
In the springlight, when the rosebuds hide the thorns upon the briar.

II
In the lamplight:—
With a proud defiant beauty, Mab, the fallen, flaunts along,
Speaking sin's words, wildly laughing, she who sang that Paschal
    song,
And a mother lies a-dying in the cottage far away,
And a father cries to heaven, "THOU hast said, 'I will repay'."

III
In the moonlight:—
By the gravestone in the churchyard, Mabel, where her mother
    sleeps,
Like the tearful saint of Magdala, an Easter vigil keeps:—
There, trailing cruel thorns, storm-drenched, plaining with piteous
    bleat,
The lost lamb (so her mother prayed) and the Good Shepherd meet.

Other contributors to *The Cornhill* during 1860 included Ruskin,
with *Unto This Last*, Thackeray *The Four Georges*, and Trollope
Framley Parsonage. Poetry was represented by Tennyson, Emily Brontë
(who wrote "The Outcast Mother" which sounds rather the same
theme as "Mabel"), Thomas Hood and R. Monckton Milnes.

One of Thackeray's characteristics which appealed most to his
friends and especially to Reynolds Hole was his pride in his elder
daughter's books. "I assure you", he said (but we tacitly declined to be
sure), "that Anny can write ten times more cleverly than I."[12] She had
indeed received a "rich inheritance" of her father's brains—"excep-
tional. . . ."[13] Perhaps we might not be wrong in suggesting that this
"rich inheritance" may have been developed on account of his deep
affection for his "dear little girls".

The eldest of Thackeray's two daughters was born on 9 June 1837 at
his parents' home, 18 Albion Street, Hyde Park. Thackeray had been
working as the Paris correspondent for a London newspaper which had
suddenly been closed down, necessitating the Thackerays' speedy
return to England. They moved to a home of their own in the spring
of next year: 13 Great Coram Street, Bloomsbury. It was quiet and full
of character and conveniently close to the British Museum where
Thackeray liked to do research for his journalism. It was to this house
that, even as a small child under three years old, Anny could remember
Tennyson coming. "One does not remember enough in after life the
extraordinary variety of experiences which are comprised within the
first two or three years of one's existence—these dawning hours when
the whole world is illuminated and enchanting. . . ."[14]

But the peace and magic of these memories were rudely interrupted four years later, when Anny's mother became mentally ill and the home was broken up. Then began the first of many visits to grandparents in Paris for Anny and her younger sister, Minnie (born in 1840). Anny began to show signs of an independent character: "She fights every inch of her way—if it's only to wash her face or put on her stockings she will not do it without an argument",[15] her father reported in a letter to his sister-in-law.

In *Chapters From Some Memoirs*, Anny wrote years later her memories of this Parisian home, too.

We lived now in a sunny flat on a fourth floor, with windows east and west and a wide horizon from each, and the sound of the cries from the street below, and the confusing roll of the wheels when the windows were open in summer. In wintertime we dined at five by lamp-light at the round table in my grandfather's study. After dinner we used to go into the pretty blue drawing-room, where the peat fire would be burning brightly in the open grate, and the evening paper would come in with the tea. I can see it all still, hear it, smell the peat, and taste the old herbaceous tea and the French bread and butter.[16]

It was while staying with her grandmother that Anny was taken by a friend of the family to visit Chopin. She describes the visit in detail which, for quite a young child, shows remarkable talent for observation. Chopin opened the door to them himself. He was "slight, delicate-looking"[17] with "long hair, bright eyes and a thin, hooked nose".[18] They followed him "into a narrow little room with no furniture in it whatever but an upright piano against the wall and a few straw chairs standing on the wooden shiny floor".[19] She was struck by his courtesy and the fact that when asked if he had slept well or eaten any food he merely "shrugged his shoulders and pointed to the piano. He had been composing something—I remember that he spoke in an abrupt, light sort of way—would Miss X like to hear it?"[20] And so Anny heard him play—she heard the room "filled with continuous sound".[21] Golden memories for a small girl.

In 1846 the children returned to England, "to the quiet and sleepy village of Kensington" and once more to a home of their own with their dearest papa. Writing to his mother excitedly at the thought of having his two little daughters with him again, Thackeray described the house in Onslow Square: "There's a good study for me downstairs and a dining room and a drawing room, and a little court or garden

and a little greenhouse: and Kensington gardens at the gate, and omni-
buses every two minutes. What can mortal want more?"[22]
Anny's description was more detailed.

I liked the top schoolroom the best of all the rooms in the dear old
house, the sky was in it and the evening bells used to ring into it
across the garden, and seemed to come in dancing and clanging with
the sunset; and the floor sloped so that if you put down a ball it
would roll in a leisurely way right across the room of its own
accord.[23]

They were there for seven years and amongst their visitors was
Leigh Hunt—they "wondered at his romantic, foreign looks, and his
gaiety and bright eager way".[24] On another occasion Trelawny stood
by the fireplace, "a dark impressive-looking man, not tall, but broad
and brown and weather-beaten, gazing with a sort of scowl at his own
reflection in the glass".[25] And then there was Charlotte Brontë,

a tiny, delicate, little person whose small hand nevertheless grasped
a mighty lever which set all the literary world of that day vibrating.
. . . The moment is so breathless that dinner comes as a relief to the
solemnity of the occasion, and we all smile as my father stoops to
offer his arm; for genius though she may be, Miss Brontë can barely
reach his elbow. . . . I can see her bending over the table, not eating,
but listening to what he said as he carved the dish before him.[26]

7

Engagement and Marriage

1861

WRITING OF ONE of Leech's creations—the Briggs family—Thackeray describes how the drawings show them in the pleasure of their domestic life:

How cosy all the Briggs party seem in their drawing room, Briggs reading a treatise on dog-breaking by a lamp, mamma and grannie with their respective needlework, the children clustering round a big book of prints—a great book of prints such as this before us, at this season, must make thousands of children happy by as many firesides! The inner life of all these people is represented. Leech draws them as naturally as Teniers depicts Dutch boors or Morland pigs and stables. It is your house and mine; we are looking at everybody's family circle.[1]

It may be remembered that the Vicar of Caunton, remarking on his affection for Leech and of "the prime happiness of our communion"[2] being to sit together in the quiet countryside, ended by adding that next to this happiness was "to see him in his house with his wife and children".[3]

This was the comment of a bachelor of forty who, according to his own confession, had a weakness for "falling in love".[4] What was more natural than that his thoughts should turn towards furnishing his own fireside with all the cosiness of a much-loved wife, where he might peacefully read by the light of a lamp, meanwhile watching his children turning the pages of a family album. At this stage in his life Reynolds Hole did not return home to an empty fireside—his father was there to be interested in his doings—but somehow this was different from the delights provided by a "family circle".

Somewhere in his writings on Leech's work, Frith especially comments on his excellence in depicting scenes of croquet and archery. The introduction of gunpowder had meant the end of archery as a method of fighting; but it died slowly and its revival in this country as a social sport for health and exercise broke out again during the 18th and 19th centuries.

In 1861 the Grand National Archery Society was founded and is today the main legislative and administrative body, holding championship meetings in which members of local or regional clubs may compete. Many bows were made of yew but as this wood became more difficult to obtain this has been replaced by some wood, combined with steel or sometimes plastic.

Reynolds Hole began life, as he describes it, "in alphabetical order". And archery came under the heading of "A was an Archer, who shot at a frog". "Having just read Maria Edgeworth's story of 'Waste not, want not'," he recalls in his *Memories* written some years later how they went down

> to the brook for the stiff, straight reed, which we shortened into arrow form, and the blacksmith converted long nails into pointed piles, and the shoemaker fixed these firmly with waxed thread, and I sallied forth, as it seemed to me, a combination of Apollo, and Robin Hood and William Tell. . . . How delightful it was when first I shot an arrow into the air, and it fell to earth I knew not where . . .

This was what archery meant to a young boy growing up in Caunton village, but now he was a man and a skilled archer. The sport took on a more social aspect and he writes invitingly from Caunton in 1848, four years after his ordination, to his great friend of Oxford days, J. W. Maxwell Lyte: "I yearn to grasp your true hand again and have pyramids of things to talk about. Could you not come to our Archery Meeting on the 8th, tomorrow week? *Do*, Peter! I would give anything to see your long pliant old back whirling once more round the ballroom at Southwell." And later on in the same letter he presses him again: "Now do come over to the Archery."

An archery meeting had become quite a social event since the days, when as boys they had scrambled along the banks of the brook to find the "stiff, straight reed" which they "shortened into arrow form". Now someone else did the scrambling up and down banks of streams, and the young men and ladies may be pictured in graceful postures, walking across green lawns lit by bright sunlight or chequered with the deep shadows of tall trees.

And then, it seems, after suitable refreshment where no doubt they were served with delicious cold salmon and a sparkling wine or a cool claret cup, they took to the dance floor. It is not surprising, therefore, to read that the dress worn by the future Mrs Hole—known as her "archery dress"—should consist of flounces of butter muslin edged with lace over a fitted underslip of taffeta, simple materials made up into an enchanting style and worn by a beautiful girl just out of her teens.

It was said of the Genoese at Crécy that their bows had been "made useless by a recent shower, which had whetted their strings",[5] and it seems reasonable to conclude that, as with tennis, archery is a sport primarily undertaken in good weather. This being so, it would be reasonable to assume that the couple met during the late summer or early autumn of 1860. For we know that Mr Hole fell finally and for always "in love" at an archery meeting, and the following letter to his sister, Sara, in which he announces his engagement to be married is dated the first week of February 1861. Also, the third Rose Show being held in July 1860, and organized by Reynolds Hole, would have kept him fully occupied until that date.

The letter to Sara is addressed to "Kaipoi", Christchurch, New Zealand, and it was posted in Newark on 8 February, travelled via Marseilles and arrived in Lyttelton, New Zealand on 28 April.

Caunton Manor. 8 Feb., 1861.

My very dear Sara, I am engaged to be married! After prowling about the hen roost for "many roving years", I have made selection of a beautiful pullet, and intend to carry her off. Wish the old fox success, and a career of happiness! More earnestly, my [illegible] I have been for some time oppressed with drear anticipation of that loneliness, which, long distant as I hope and pray, would overshadow Caunton when the good Lord of the Manor should have it "as full of grace and years" and had resolved to seek a congenial helpmate, one "born alike my tears and joys to share". And I have found, and have wooed, and have won, such a sweet, bright, gentle lady, that I am really astonished at the impudence of my own conjurations, and entirely *spifflicated* (Keble) by *her* condescension in endorsing them. I can only wonder, and be thankful, and ask to be made more worthy of this crowning happiness of my very happy life. Sometimes I think that our dear Mother and Sister, who loved me with such a deep undeserved love, have asked and obtained this blessing for me.

The lady is Miss Francklin, of Gonalston, in this county, a *lady* in the fullest meaning of the word—a lady by birth and education, a lady in mind and mien. She is rather young, 20 yrs (I have spoken to her seriously concerning this delinquency, and note improvement), tall, "a daughter of the gods, divinely fair, and most divinely tall" for she is 5 feet 8 inches in height, fair with much roseate glow, her hair the colour of yours. You will form a good idea of your sister from the photograph★ which I inclose, remembering that this style of portraiture always adds some dreariness to a face, and never improves the expression thereof. Her brother, the heir of Gonalston etc. (the estate is said to be worth between 3 & 4000 a year) is at Harrow, and there is another brother and a sister. Mr Francklin only left his daughters 2000 pounds each, but an Aunt, with a discretion and elegance of mind which command my liveliest sympathy, has since bequeathed to each of them 7000 in addition. Grosvenor Hodgkinson has been to London concerning settlements and reports satisfactory progress. As Miss Francklin (her name is *Carry* in private and by that name you must think of her) is a ward in Chancery, the permission of Court is necessary to the consummation of courtship: but I hope we may be married in May.—What other news have I? Your Uncle William is dead, but you need not put your family into mourning for more than a year, nor ask your Cousin Anne to live with you. All well at Beckingham: Gina and Edith both handsome dear girls and Ashhurst a jolly young giant, full of affection and fun ... at Southwell Harriet Williams has married Mr Rolfe, a London Artist, of whom we hear favourably. In the village there are few changes. Oh, my sister, when, when shall we wander by the brookside again? My heart in its great joy yearns and craves for you. George Riddill has lost his second wife (Anders assisting) and is in anxious quest of No. 3. Nothing of import in Literature. Hope you saw my lines on Mabel in the Cornhill. They have been both painted and set to music. Next Christmas if Matrimony allows I mean to bring out a Book for Gardeners—now publishing in the Florist and called "The Six of Spades". Always believe me my very dear sister your very fondly affectionate brother, S. Reynolds Hole.

Perhaps the letter needs one or two explanations.

Sara was his "very dear sister" who had married the Rev. John Raven in 1847, and later they sailed for New Zealand as early members of the Canterbury Settlement. The family returned to England in 1868. Reynolds mentions the birth of her first child, Sarah Maria, in a letter written to J. Maxwell Lyte dated 31 May 1848, and that as she arrived while he was visiting the house, he saw the baby shortly after she was born. (The illustration facing p. 116 shows the cradle the Ravens took with them to New Zealand.)

Towards the end of the first paragraph of the letter he writes that he sometimes thinks "that our dear Mother and Sister, who loved me with such a deep undeserved love, have asked and obtained this blessing for

★ See facing p. 113.

Portrait of John Leech—from the water colour by Millais in the National
Portrait Gallery.

Scene at Sandbath by John Leech. "I have always found a difficulty in giving the effect of wind in a picture: the action of it on drapery, trees, skies, etc. is—from the almost momentary nature of the gusts—far from an easy task. No one who ever handled a brush or pencil has been so successful as Leech, in conveying the action of wind on every

me". His mother had died in 1852, and his sister Mary Elizabeth, who married John Hilton, died in May 1859.

After giving the lady's name and adorning it with most of the requisite adjectives of a newly affianced bachelor, he goes on to mention the fact of a "settlement", not large, "but an Aunt, with a discretion and elegance of mind which command my liveliest sympathy, has since bequeathed to each of them [the sisters] about £7,000 in addition".

Might he be criticized for paying too much attention to the question of a settlement? If such a question arises in the reader's thoughts, may I mention in this connection the attitude of the day to such matters? For instance, in *Emma* when Mr Elton returned to Highbury after becoming engaged to Miss Hawkins it was discovered that in addition to all the usual advantages of perfect beauty and merit [she] was in possession of an independent fortune, of so many thousands as would always be called ten— ". . . The story told well: he had not thrown himself away—he had gained a woman of £10,000 or thereabouts and he had gained her with rapidity; . . ." In a letter to Mrs Buxton, dated January 1816, Maria Edgeworth writes, "The authoress of *Pride and Prejudice* has been so good as to send me a new novel just published, *Emma*."[6] And in Mrs Hole's diary for the year 1844, Mr Hole's mother mentions reading Miss Edgeworth. *Emma* was only about forty years earlier than his own engagement, and in mentioning the settlement he was merely following the fashion of the times.

The reference to Uncle William's death and the fact that she need not have her cousin Anne to live with her is an example of his gift for putting matters into a nutshell: no waste of words here. In much the same way, he writes in the letter later on: "George Riddill has lost his second wife (Anders assisting) and is in anxious quest of No. 3." It may be remembered, from his mother's diary, that Anders is the local doctor, of whose advice he obviously thought little.

Following the engagement to Caroline, Hole's general idea was to cut down on outside activities and, writing about the fourth National Rose Show, he mentions his gratitude in being able to hand over much of the work to other recruits, as the show

> interfered at times unduly with my other engagements. Moreover, to tell you all the truth, in the happy springtide of 1861 I had a correspondence which occupied all my time, upon a subject which occupied all my thought—a subject more precious, more lovely even than Roses— I was going to be married in May.[7]

Caroline, born in 1840, was a Ward in Chancery, being orphaned whilst still a minor. Her mother had died in 1849 leaving her, when only a still child, to take over the care of a young family as well as of her father. Following his death in 1858 she and the other children had been cared for by her grandparents, Mr and Mrs Edgell. It was they who offered to arrange the wedding, as is shown by the following two letters from the prospective bridegroom. (Samuel Hole was by now an old man and it would have made serious difficulties to have held the marriage proceedings at Caunton.)

Lowdham Grange 3 May 1861.

My dear Mrs Edgell, Pray allow me to express my sincere appreciation of all your kindness to me, but especially of your goodness in undertaking so very generously, and, I fear, to your own great inconvenience, the reception of the marriage-party. We both of us, I can assure you, feel most grateful to you for suggesting and arranging a plan, which seems at once the most proper and the most pleasant; and we shall never, I hope, forget your kindness. My gratitude will be best proved, I know, in my endeavour to make her happy, for whom you have shewn so much affectionate love, and in this, with God's blessing, I do not fear to succeed.

We shall not, I think, interfere *very* much with your comfort, but it must be, at best, a great anxiety and self-sacrifice, and the least that we, for whom all this is endured, can do, is to assure you, as we now most heartily assure you, that we are unfeignedly thankful to you.

I must confess that I looked forward with much anxiety as to the arrangements for our marriage, as there seemed much real difficulty in the case, but now, thanks to you, all is fixed, and that for the best in every way.

With our united love, and hope that Mr Edgell is finally well, believe me, my dear Mrs Edgell, Yours very sincerely and *gratefully*, S. Reynolds Hole.

Caunton Manor, Newark, 9 May 1861.

My dear Madam, I am desired by my Father to express to yourself and Mr Edgell his very sincere thanks for the kind and courteous invitation contained in your letter to me; and I am to assure you that, while he is prevented by the distance and his advanced age from attending the marriage, he equally appreciates the politeness shewn to him, and heartily reciprocates the kindly feelings which prompted it.—With regard to our Wedding Tour, we have given up all idea of visiting Italy, and shall not attempt any extensive route. You may depend upon it, my dear Madam, that I shall keep her, whom I love so dearly, from all avoidable fatigue and excitement, knowing as I do that she is by no means so strong as she seems, and inclined to undertake more than is prudent.

Would you allow me to send you up next week some of our superabundant supply of spring chickens and other country produce? As I am leaving home, it would really be a prevention of waste, and they might be suitable for the luncheon on the 23rd, which, with a very rare abnegation of *self*, you so kindly propose to give us.

My father begs to offer his best compliments to Mr Edgell and yourself, and I remain, my dear Madam, yours very gratefully, S. Reynolds Hole.

In his *Memories* Reynolds writes with appreciation of another's support:

Leech took as much lively interest in my engagement and marriage as though he had been my brother; insisted on accompanying me when I went on the somewhat anxious mission of discussing settlements with the young lady's guardian, to the door of his house . . . and having requested, and received long notice of the wedding-day, "Because", he said, "his coat, waistcoat, trousers, and especially his scarf, must be gradually and carefully developed," he appeared in due course, a combination of good looks, good temper, and good clothes, as my best man.

The couple were married on 23 May 1861. In a honeymoon letter to Mrs Edgell dated 17 June and written at Thun, Caroline related travels which included Paris, Macon, and Geneva where "Reynolds gave me such a lovely watch, in a double case, and outside a wreath of roses and forgetmenots on both sides"; from when they travelled to Chamonix which she found too much "confined by the mountains. We left there on *mules*, with our baggage tied on behind us . . . the scenery we passed through was certainly most splendid, it was worth bearing some inconvenience for." They visited the Castle of Chillon which Lord Byron made famous and saw the clock at Bern on their way through to Thun. She loved the quiet and peace of Thun, watching the steamers go up and down the lake, sometimes carrying people, sometimes a horse and a few cows, and liked the "homelike" feeling about the whole place.

Her next letter to "dear Granny", dated 1 July, was the first which Caroline wrote from her new home at Caunton Manor. It describes their arrival at Newark in the afternoon "on Thursday, about half past three, all safe". The carriage was waiting to conduct them to Caunton where the whole village had turned out to welcome them. They passed under triumphal arches and garlands of flowers to the house, where a long table was laid in the garden for everyone to have tea, followed by dancing until about 10 o'clock. "I have a good deal to do to put all my things away especially as I find the house full everywhere with Reynolds' books and papers and rubbish. No end of old clothes of all sorts ... enough to clothe the parish."

"To His Wife"
And shall I see her face again?
And shall I hear her speak?
I'm downright giddy with the thought,
Good troth, I'm like to greet.

The parish perspired with joy.

                                    5.29 tomorrow.[8]

Letters from John Leech, cheerful letters which came with some frequency, now always ended with a note to include Mrs Hole. "Give my kindest regards please to Mrs Hole and to your Father ... " "Please give our very best regards to Mrs Hole and to your Father ..." "Mrs Leech is out and will write to Mrs Hole ..." "With my most kinderestestestest regards to everybody ..." In a letter with the envelope franked 15 February 1862, and stamped Garrick Club there comes something different—another literary plum: "You have just been elected at the 'G' unanimously". And in a following letter, dated 19 February 1862, this short statement is amplified: "I am very happy that you are pleased with your election at The 'G'. It would have gratified you I think to have heard the good word, or rather good words, that Thackeray said for you ..."

John Leech goes on, in his letter, to enumerate some of the blessings of becoming a member of the Garrick Club. He is looking forward to showing Mrs Hole over the club on a visiting day, the reading and lecture rooms, and hopes that it will mean they can all pay a visit to the opera together—in fact, he longs to introduce Mrs Hole to this "box of delights".

But one of the first of many letters of love and affection from Mr Hole to his wife does not come from the Garrick Club—it is from a rose show in Birmingham:

Queens Hotel,
Birmingham,
July 1 1862.

Own Darling, how I wish you were here! The loveliest Show of Roses I ever saw, and ours, altho' competing with the best in England, carrying off the *first honours*. They have won the *two best prizes*, namely the first for 48 varieties and the first for 24 varieties (not to mention the second for 18, and the third for 12) and are acknowledged both by nurserymen and amateurs to be unsurpassed by either of them. The immense Town Hall of Birmingham is completely filled with roses, from 14 different counties, —and seen from the galleries above is one of the most charming spectacles I ever looked on. In addition to the flowers, there is a most interesting collection of garden implements and ornaments and of most beautiful articles for the dessert table & I have selected my two best prizes from the latter (to the amount of 7£ and 5£) and I think you will allow that you never saw more graceful things of their kind.

I have never had such a complete victory, since I have fought in these Wars of the Roses; and again and again I keep longing for you, to see and share it with me. You would hardly believe how well the roses have travelled, and I was really surprised when I lifted the lid this morning—many of the flowers having expanded and all looking as freshly as in the garden.

I shall travel to Derby and sleep there tonight and meet you at Thurgarton tomorrow, you tweetiest tweet! The train arrives there at 11.22 . . . . Ever believe me, my own dear love,

> Your fondly affectionate husband
> S. Reynolds Hole

I have very nearly secured a first-rate appointment for Harry, namely that of Thirty-second swill carrier to the prize pigs at the next Birmingham Show—

Their son, and only child, was born in October of this year and in the next letter his delighted father sends a special message to "that tweet". Writing to Mrs Edgell, Caroline's grandmother, in a letter dated 16 October, he tells the glad news: "I have the happiness to inform you with a thankful heart that my dear wife is the mother of a fine little boy, and that doctor and nurse unite in assuring me that both she and her baby are as well as could be hoped. Her troubles began at 1.30 this morning. The doctor arrived at 3.30 and her son at 6. . . ."

The Deserted Village,
Tuesday.

Deliciousest Ownums,

Limp as a balloon without any gas in it, and residing in a mansion, which, ever since you left it, has been about as merry as a mausoleum, I do not feel at all equal to any cheerful correspondence, can't crow, like an old cock with the gapes, and must sit like Constance (not Burnell, but the girl in the song) "sad, silent, and alone", until the happy morrow brings me to my Love. Nevertheless, having promised to write, I will endeavour to awake from my stupor ("rouse me, Sarah"), and say what there is to be said.

The Boddhams, mère et fille, with two Misses Castle called yesterday, but I did not see them. I enjoyed (if a man without his wife can be said to enjoy anything) the evening at Beesthorpe as I had much pleasant talk with pleasant Mrs F. Lumley, partly with reference to mesmerism, about which she told me the most interesting *facts* I ever heard from an authentic source. I need hardly say that Mrs Becker filled her mouth so full of Dessert that her conversation was unintelligible, reminding one of that very unscrupulous angler, who, when his friend enquired what he had in his mouth, responded that it was "*wururms* for baits". . . .

. . . Our bedroom looked awefully dismal, and almost reminded me of poor John Manners's description of "the *dungeonest* place as iver he see". I made the best of it by saluting the pillow, but I can't say that I got much *flavour* out of it. . . .

. . . Give that Tweet a few *thousand* extra ones for me. I shall expect to see him much grown.

Poor Mrs Doncaster was buried to-day, brought in one of those hideous hearses, which are so unsightly and unChristian——

. . . believe me, my own darling darling Wife, your most fondly and faithfully loving

S. Reynolds Hole

It had better be explained here that Caroline did not enjoy good health and she often spent short periods away from Caunton recuperating.

Caunton Manor,
    alias
The Deserted Village.
Dec. 9 1862.

"Tweet of the tweetiest", it seems already a fortnight since I saw baby, and three weeks since I saw you; and so many events of immense importance have occurred since your departure, that I hardly know how to begin their history.

The first incident which happened was a sorrowful one (humanly speaking), namely the death of the remaining twin—those two lovely babes, which I Baptized so recently.

At luncheon, Ashhurst and Arthur arrived in a high state of perspiration, having walked from Beckingham★ in 2 hours & 20 minutes. . . . Had a cigar at night (which you will be glad to hear made me very restless). . . .

We have a dinner-party this evening, James and Willie, but the house looks awefully dismal without *the Dear Thing*, and no *music* charms the listening ear.

. . . Benedict's mouth was quite hard to-day, and he showed an inclination to pull, so says I to Johnson on my return home, "did the horse pull at you much this morning, when you took him to Covert?" "Oh yes, Sir, says he, very much indeed." Now the horse does not usually pull an owner, and has an excellent mouth, so that I must let Joe ride him for the future.

I wish you could have seen a figure, which appeared in Richard's bed last night. I made the face by smoking the bottom of a certain utensil with a candle, and then delineating the features with my finger thus

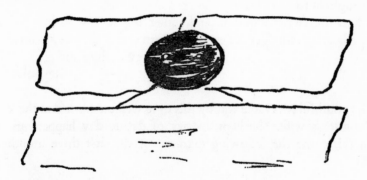

The effect was very refreshing——

I hope, own darling, to come & see you by Rail on Thursday, and to find your *beauty self* stronger & better.

Give my very sincere regards to Mrs Storer, the Doctor, & the young ladies, & believe me as ever, nay more than ever, your most fondly loving Husband,

S. Reynolds Hole

★ As this was about five miles from Newark on the Sleaford road, it meant they had walked probably ten miles in the time.

ROYAL HORTICULTURAL SOCIETY
MEMORANDUM.   5 o'clock p.m.
                                July 1. 1863.
From Revd Reynolds Hole   To His Wife Caroline.

Dearest Darling, This is the only bit of available paper I can find in
the superintendent's office, and I have about five minutes in which
to fill it.

The southern roses, fully in bloom, have beaten mine, as I thought
they would, but I am *quite as good* in quality tho' not in quantity.

The Queen of Prussia and the two Princesses, Helena and Louise,
came, while we were judging the roses, *and I was presented to them!*
So if I am rather high, when I return, you will know the reason.
Perhaps it would be better if you were to call me "Sir" for a few
days at all events.

I have seen darling Bud looking much better, also yr. Aunt came
& Barbara.

Hay fever entirely gone, since I took the camphor this morning,
and this under a morning sun!

I shall . . . return by the train what leaves *between five and six tomorrow* afternoon. Please look it out in Bradshaw, and send the
Brougham to meet us.

Kiss the tweet a million and rather less to my Father and the
Marlborough Slodger believe me always and in my very heart
                                Your loving husband
                                            Reynolds

The youthful Mrs Hole was by this time well established as the Vicar
of Caunton's wife. She kept a diary of day-to-day happenings and
from this come the following extracts for the first three months of
1868:

Saturday 11 January.
Very snowy all day and quite thick on the ground. . . . Mr Hole
[her father-in-law, in his ninetieth year] much worse and at times
unconscious. . . . Mr Ward came twice and said the dear old man
was going. . . .
Sunday 12 January.
The Father quite unconscious and seems in much pain. . . . Reynolds
and I sat up till ¼ before 3 when the dear good old man passed away
so peacefully and so quietly in his sleep. . . .
Monday 13 January.

Lovely morning, Jenny and I went in the brougham down to
Newark to get mourning. . . .

Tuesday 14 January.

. . . at two o'clock got a note to say that Sara Raven (returned from
New Zealand) was coming and she arrived an hour after. . . .

Saturday 25 January.

After lunch Reynolds and I started for a ride, he on "Blackie" and I
on "Jacobite". Very cold we went round by the common. . . .

Monday 27 January.

Reynolds started at $\frac{1}{4}$ past 8 for London to see Mr H. Bristowe. He
got back at 7.30 to dinner having done his business and lunched in
Portland Place.

Thursday 30 January.

Fine morning. The hounds met at Hockerton. Mr M. Reynolds and
I drove to the meet where our horses met us. Mr M. rode "Jacobite". . . .

Tuesday 18 February.

Reynolds went to town early. Lilly, Fred and I went to Newark
with him. I to see the dentist but did not.

Tuesday 3 March.

Reynolds took me to Newark to Mr Hepburn to have a tooth out
and he gave me great pain and broke it in. . . .

Thursday 26 March.

Beautiful fine day after the rain. Mr D. . . . lent me a brown cob to
ride and I went with Reynolds to meet the hounds at Winkburn.
Hugh rode his little pony without being led . . . and enjoyed it very
much. Killed a fox in Park Springs after a good deal of running and
another in the open after six hours and 10 minutes.

Friday 27 March.

Fred and Lilly came over to lunch and Mr Thorley. Fred rode
Mr Dufty's cob and bought it.

The only reference to any local person apart from the family is on
9 January when the butler, Wilks, was found to have taken prussic
acid. ". . . had often said he would make an end of himself . . . Reynolds sent for and came in less than an hour. . . ."

From the diary extracts it will be gathered that riding was a great
love, and it transpires that "buying lovely horses" for Caroline was
one of the extravagances in which Reynolds Hole indulged. As her son
wrote years later: "Sydney, Lord Manvers, used to say that she was the
most beautiful woman on a horse that he had ever seen";[9] so it is not
surprising that Leech sometimes asked her to sit for him. Spielman
wrote that

Leech would never employ artists' models—partly because his *chic* drawing, like Sir John Tenniel's, came natural to his genius, and his memory was extraordinarily retentive, and partly because when he began to draw for *Punch*, and for a long while after it, it was unheard-of for black-and-white men on comic papers to do anything so seriously academic . . . On one or two occasions he would ask Mrs Hole, the wife of the Dean of Rochester, to sit for him in her riding habit—but this was the nearest approach he ever made to the "model".[10]

Caroline was a lover of country things, social life, for itself alone, meant little to her. She was known, in fact, to have put the kitchen staff into a turmoil on more than one occasion when guests arrived, apparently uninvited. Food had to be prepared hurriedly while the mistress of the house came in perhaps from riding or a walk, having forgotten completely about any such engagements. However, her youth and charm meant that such lapses were soon overlooked and forgiven, and numerous visitors came happily to Caunton Manor, some of them for a meal, others to stay.

In one of his many letters John Leech writes: "Seriously, my dear Hole, I am cordially obliged both to Mrs Hole and yourself for your great kindness in offering us a fortnight at Caunton. . . ." This particular letter was addressed from 8 Esplanade, Lowestoft and a later one from the same address is full of apology for lateness in answer to an invitation to Caunton: "I go down upon my bended knees and beg your wife's pardon. . . ."

There are frequent references in the Leech letters which illustrate the growing intimacy between the households:

I have sent the saddle by Gt Northern Rail this afternoon, and that your father may ride upon it many a time and often is my earnest wish. . . . You have spoiled us for London . . . I feel all the better for my delightful rest at Caunton. . . . The hamper from Macgillicuddy arrived safely. . . .

There are of course congratulations on a certain "event" at Caunton: "Both my wife and I are indeed delighted to hear of such an addition to the happiness of your house and home . . ." and Leech ends another letter with: ". . . my very kindest regards to Mrs Hole and to your Father and a kiss to the Baby which I know is a commission you will HATE. Yours always," and, again: "My very best regards to Mrs Hole and to your Father, not forgetting the Rosebud. . . ."

8

Sadness in the *Punch* Circle

1863–1864

MANY MEMBERS OF the *Punch* circle used to congregate in the Garrick Club; and a newly elected member writes: "I found Millais one of the foremost amongst the distinguished men frequenting the old Club House in King Street. Night after night twelve or fifteen men gathered in the smoking-room of the Club—Thackeray, Dickens, Anthony Trollope, John Leech ... Shirley Brooks ..."[1] When Reynolds Hole was elected to the Garrick in February 1862, he must have been heavily involved in domestic matters. However, he is writing to Caroline from the Club in September 1863:

> I dined here last night with Leech, Millais and Percival Leigh, and tonight repeat the performance, Thackeray being substituted for Leigh. Leech and I called on the great man this morning, and Miss Thackeray, the authoress of "Elizabeth is," very anxious to make your acquaintance.

The two friends had paid many visits together to the Thackeray household in the past few years, most of them to 36 Onslow Square, South Kensington, from where Miss Thackeray had written to Mr Hole on 4 January 1862:

> 36 Onslow Square, S.W.
>
> My dear Mr Hole,
> Now that it is eaten up I must write and tell you how good the game was and how much obliged we are. All this year we have been so unlucky for though all our friends have been kind we have hardly been able to eat any of the game they have sent us. But your pheasants were everything that pheasants ought to be—Everybody is grateful but I am most grateful because I was ill at home on New Year's day and dined off one of them.

Papa is very busy upstairs so that I must be his secretary and write
to you for him and wish you and Mrs Hole a Happy New Year
from us all. I hope we may make her acquaintance in it and I'm
yours,

very truly, Anne Thackeray

Anny had already been her father's secretary for some time as it was
during their first few months at Onslow Square that he wrote the last
part of *The Newcomes*, the lectures on *The Four Georges*, *The Virginians*
and part of *Philip*. She records:

I remember writing the last chapters of "The Newcomes" to my
father's dictation. I wrote on as he dictated more and more slowly,
until he stopped altogether, in the account of Colonel Newcome's
last illness when he said he must now take the pen into his own hand,
and he sent me away.[2]

Anny had been writing herself since she was a young girl. In a letter
to George M. Smith, the famous publisher of Messrs Smith and Elder,
she explained the situation:

I had written several novels and a tragedy by the age of fifteen, but
then my father forbade me to waste my time any more scribbling,
and desired me to read *other* people's books.

I never wrote any more except one short fairy tale, until one day
my father said he had got a very nice subject for me, and that he
thought I might now begin to write again. That was "Little Scholars"
which he christened for me and of which he corrected the stops and
the spelling, and which you published to my still pride and rapture.[3]

In his own *Reminiscences* George Smith wrote about this essay:

Thackeray sent it to me and a letter containing the following
passage: "And in the meantime comes a contribution called *Little
Scholars*, which I send you, and which moistened my paternal
spectacles. It is the article I talked of sending to *Blackwood*; but why
should *Cornhill* lose such a sweet paper because it was my dear girl
who wrote it? Papas, however, are bad judges—you decide whether
we shall have it or not!"[4]

There was yet another move of house, this time to Palace Green and
the first writing Thackeray did here was to finish *Philip*. Anny was
just twenty-five and of invaluable assistance to her father; she was

again working with him. "*Philip* was finished on Thursday (3 July 1862)", she writes, "and on Friday we made holiday. That Friday was a red-letter day for us all, and how well I can remember it! The sun shone, the shadows lay soft upon the lanes and commons as we drove out with our ponies from London towards the open country. . . ."[5]

There were not to be many more such holidays together.

An outing mentioned in Thackeray's diary as taking place in April 1863, was a week's visit to the Monkton Milnes★ at Fryston Hall. This was significant for the presence of another guest, Algernon Charles Swinburne. Edmund Gosse describes Anny's reactions:

She was in the garden on the afternoon of his arrival, and she saw him advance up the sloping lawn swinging his hat in his hand, and letting the sunshine flood the bush of his red-gold hair. He looked like Apollo or a fairy prince. . . . On Sunday evening he was asked to read some of his poems. His choice was injudicious; he is believed to have recited *The Leper*; it is certain that he read *Les Noyades*! At this the Archbishop of York made so shocked a face that Thackeray smiled and whispered to Lord Houghton . . . *Les Noyades* was then proceeding on its amazing course, and the Archbishop was looking more and more horrified when suddenly the butler—"like an avenging angel"—threw open the door and announced, "Prayers, my Lord!" Swinburne and Anny remained friends till the poet's death.[6]

Anny mentions a more typical outing with her father which took place later in the same year. As they were driving along in the dusk by the Serpentine they passed

Carlyle walking across the park, and my father, seeing him, leant forward and waved his hands. "A great benevolent shower of salutations" Carlyle called it, when he spoke in after days of this last meeting. How often have I seen Carlyle in Kensington Gardens walking on and on. . . . As children we did not have much of Carlyle's company; if he came in and sat down in the arm-chair which was his, on the opposite side of the sofa, we immediately went away; but the sense of his presence overhead in the study distinctly added to our enjoyment so long as he remained upstairs.[7]

Virginia Woolf, reviewing Anny's published *Correspondence* years later remarks specifically on her ability to see things "precisely as they

★ Monkton Milnes became Lord Houghton in August 1863.

were. Old Carlyle was a god on one side of his face but a 'cross-grained, ungrateful, self-absorbed old nut cracker' on the other".[8]

Anny's first novel *The Story of Elizabeth* was published in 1863. Rhoda Broughton wrote of her amazement when she read this book "written as I was told by a girl hardly older than myself".[9] She describes Anny's "exquisite literary gift".[10] As Mr Hole remarked, she had indeed "received a rich inheritance".

Meanwhile the *Punch* lunches went on, usually attended by Thackeray, although his general health was beginning to give cause for some anxiety.

July 1st, 1863.
H.M. applauds bright speech last night on the Roebuck and Napoleon interview . . .
J.L. tells of Millais at swell's playing alphabet game and saying, "I want a P".

June 24, 1863.
Leech salmon with Millais; happy fellow! . . . Is he? Talk of the Murdered Milliner, and Mr Isaacson's beautiful letter in *The Times* today . . . Thackeray says his daughters always order their dresses a month beforehand—and E. contends that the Mantalinis can't help the press of business. Bosh! M.L. and P.L. stick out for the common-sense view—that the Mantalinis overwork their slaves, and wear them up because there's always a fresh supply of flesh and blood material. Journeymen tailors work at 6d. [2½p] an hour and won't work more than 12 hours a day—milliners keep their girls in the house and work them at 6/- [30p] a week, and so get all the work they can out of them. . . .[11]

On their last visit to Thackeray's house, shortly before his death, Leech and Hole owed it to Anny that they were able to see him. They were being turned away by a servant when Anny opened the door and called out to them. "Of course, papa will see you."[12] And so they were taken up to his study. He must have been looking tired and ill because Hole recalled the suggestion made by Leech that Thackeray should have a holiday "and take the girls to the seaside".[13] Two days before his death he sent for Anny to give her some notes and directions about his work as he was too ill to manage himself. He died suddenly in the early morning of Christmas Eve 1863.

December 30th, 1863.
No Dinner. Funeral of William Makepeace Thackeray: who d. on Christmas Eve—not long after we left the *Punch* table last week. S.

tells me of his sudden death, after breakfast on Saturday—they would not spoil my Xmas Day by letting me hear of it. I never felt a loss so much, except of course those of my relations. And yet I was not privileged to rank myself as more than a casual acquaintance. But his kindliness extended to the smallest of his visitors, and he never snubbed one or ignored one's presence. What the loss must be to his old chum and schoolfellow Leech, who can pretend to estimate? And what the loss must be to his daughters who owed everything to him, in position and in fortune, and were ever petted and much thought of, one shrinks from considering—The loss is a national one . . .[14]

The loss was indeed a "national one", and was felt not the least in Edinburgh. Dr John Brown, well known as an essayist for *Rab and his Friends, Marjorie Fleming*, and *Horae Subsecivae*, and as a doctor of medicine first met Thackeray in December 1851, when the latter went to Edinburgh to lecture. A close friendship sprang up between the two men involving a great amount of correspondence, in which they often spoke of matters close to their hearts. For instance, in a letter written from Brighton on 31 December 1854, Thackeray gives a typical comment on a *Blackwood* article showing his own brand of philosophy:

Blackwood sent me his magazine with an article which pleased me very much, and which I think uncommonly friendly and timely. I don't believe Bulwer is the first of that triumvirate the reviewer talks of: I think Dickens is . . . but, Sir and Madam, what after all does it matter who is first or third in such a tuppenny race? Kindness matters, and love and goodwill, and doing your duty if you can and leaving a little store for young Jocks and Helens [the Brown children] and Annies and Minnies.[15]

In 1856 Thackeray was again lecturing in Edinburgh and in a letter to a friend, Dr Brown writes: "I knew Thackeray would go to your heart. . . . We have just come home from the third George. We liked it better than the first time. What power and gentleness and restraint! I wonder at and love him more and more. Tonight he took the whole house by the heart, and held them; . . ."[16] And in a postscript Dr Brown compares the genius of Thackeray to the "Fidelio of Beethoven, or The Magic Flute or Jupiter of Mozart".[17] Dr Brown especially mentions *The Newcomes*—"what a quantity of good matter in that book and what a thoroughly good style".[18]

Writing of Thackeray the artist in his essay on "Thackeray's Death" in *Horae Subsecivae* he says:

It should never be forgotten that his specific gift was creative satire—not caricature, nor even sarcasm, nor sentiment, nor romance, nor even character as such—but the delicate satiric treatment of human nature in its most superficial aspects, as well as in its inner depths, by a great-hearted and tender and genuine sympathy, unsparing, truthful, inevitable, but with love . . .[19]

Such, especially, are the characteristics of Colonel Newcome in his relationship with his son Clive: the colonel's return from abroad to be near him growing up into manhood, in the hope of sharing things with him, his pride in him, and the slow realization that a relationship is possible although a different one from that which he had imagined. The Newcome family are drawn finely and distinctly, sometimes a complete impression being conjured up in a few words: "Barnes Newcome never missed going to church, or dressing for dinner".

And of Thackeray himself, apart from his writing, Dr Brown wrote: "No one, we believe, will ever know the amount of true kindness and help, given often at a time when kindness cost much, to nameless, unheard-of suffering, a man of spotless honour, of the strongest possible home affections and the most scrupulous truthfulness."[20]

Henry Silver in his diaries wrote, "What the loss must be to his old chum and schoolfellow Leech, who can pretend to estimate? . . ."

Leech's letter, dated 18 February 1864, from 6 The Terrace, Kensington, says that he had been meaning to write but "had not the heart. If I tried, I could not express in words what the loss of my dear friend is to me . . ."

It was shortly after Thackeray's death that Leech told Millais of his presentiment "that he also should die suddenly and soon. His nervous system became more and more unstrung; in London, the street music produced an intolerable irritation; . . . yet he went working on."[21] And it was not long before, in numerous letters to Hole, Leech began referring to the deterioration in his health: ". . . I am not the thing at all [written from Brighton] . . . you have no idea how I am driven with my work . . . I am still so pressed with my work that I hardly know which way to turn. . . . How much I should like to run down some Saturday I cannot say, but just at present it is out of the question . . . I was so unwell at Brighton that I have not been able to make any social arrangements . . . I will not bother you with too much about how I have been and am pressed and worried . . . I shall try and come to you for a day's rest. . . ."

There is mention of Mr Hole sending his friend an extract from an

Anny and Minny from a water-colour sketch by W. M. Thackeray.

Caroline Francklin, 1860.

Caroline's archery dress worn by her great-great grand-daughter.

article by Dr Brown: "It is certainly most complimentary and I value it highly because it comes from a good quarter—Dr Brown's is praise worth having." He ends one letter emphasising the rush of his work, with the well-known reference to "a boy, who diffuses an odour of damp corderoys over the house and who is waiting . . . and be blowed to him, for funny drawings, so excuse more. . . ."* which serves to emphasize the rush he was in to get his work done. Another letter (envelope franked 20 February 1864) is short and to the point and more cheerful: "All right—G. at 6.30—I will order Turtle and Venison with Champagne and Burgundy, which is not a bit or drop too good for two such extraordinary fellows as we are. Yours always, J.L."

Perhaps this last letter shows a temporary improvement in Leech's health. He was still producing regular work for *Punch* and attending the *Punch* dinners and an especially interesting one dealing with the question of the Penny Post, was recorded in his diary by Henry Silver:

March 9th, 1864.
Talking of Rowland Hill, Shirley says in the next century perhaps there'll be no letters written—all correspondence done by telegraph —Leech pictures a swell saying, "Aw, I never write a letter—such a bore writing—I send a little gram!"—Also pictures Man sending a message to his sweetheart, "Dearest, I love and adore you, etc., etc." and pretty telegraph clerkess saying, "There's a word or two too much, Sir—perhaps you'd better strike out the 'adore'. . . ."

Sir Rowland Hill's retirement, the Subject, says Mark . . . Shirley insists that Hill has done more to civilize England than half a dozen Shakespeares. No poor person ever wrote to another till the penny post came. Suggests Hill falling asleep and dreaming of the good effects of his work. "Pity he's not dead", says Charles Keene—"I mean for the artist's sake"—Leech suggests Hill smoking and the pictures of his work seen in the fumes—"How am I to draw Posterity," says Tenniel—Charles says, "But if Hill hadn't invented it, somebody else would—" "Then we'd better have a Monument to Somebody Else," says Burnand. . . .
March 16th, 1864.
Mark begs for earlier copy—and Evans says the circulation now renders it necessary that the number should go to press Saty. night— then we must try and reduce the circulation says Leech . . . Shirley thinks there should be open voting in Club—has seen how ballot is abused. Leech thinks personal objections shd. not weigh in voting but bores should be blackballed merely for their boorishness. Leech

* See chapter 5, p. 81.
8

talks of Herbert who has just finished his House of Lords fresco. Affected Roman Catholic—went to Paris for a week and now speaks broken English.

March 30th, 1864.

Garibaldi the other cut—his visit to England is to get support and money, in case the war goes on in Denmark. G. will attack Austria and all Lombardy will be up. . . . J.L. rather sneers at G. and M.L. thinks him the greatest man of the age—so unselfish and brave hearted. But weak in head, says Shirley: who suggests Punch rowing him ashore—or receiving him on landing . . . P.L. suggests G. glad to breathe the English air—the air of freedom—"Yes", says Leech, "make him landing in a good English fog."

April 7th, 1864.

J.L. lets out his hate of pet dogs—all dogs should be shot except sporting dogs . . .

April 11th, 1864.

Arrival of Garibaldi. "Leech of course hates the whole thing. . . ."

April 20th, 1864.

Garibaldi to the City. Eulogy on Garibaldi. . . . Subscription begun for G.

May 4th, 1864.

J.L. hates boys to go birdnesting.

On the 17th of that same month, a sad letter from 6 The Terrace, Kensington, reached the Holes. They had asked Leech to stay with them, but, full of foreboding, he replied that he had visited another doctor whose advice he must follow. He had to go to "Hambourg", the sooner the better, where he was to stay for about a month and take the baths. He was not allowed to do any work while undergoing the treatment.

He cannot have gone at once as he was present at the *Punch* dinner, recorded by Henry Silver, of 15 June: "J.L. wrote to Gladstone about street music, G. having spoken against Bass's Bill. The Band in the Park's a very different thing to a street organ, methinks, Mr G. J.L. off to Hambourg with Elinor tomorrow and we all shake him by the hand and wish him better."

Mark Lemon had given full support to the Bill introduced some months earlier in the House of Commons by Michael Bass, partially on account of the effect of street noises on Leech. "I am so greatly interested in the success of your measure", he assured Bass, "that I am desirous of strengthening your hands by putting you in possession of some facts within my knowledge."[22]

In his notes to Dr Brown's essay on John Leech the Vicar of Caunton wrote of his final illness and the effect of Thackeray's death:

Then the shadow of a coming danger fell upon the hearts which loved him best. "Can't you take him back with you into the country?" Thackeray had asked almost angrily . . . but I strove and pleaded in vain.

Then the great man, who had been to him as a brother, the schoolmate of his childhood, [they were both at Charterhouse] the chief friend of his manhood, Thackeray, died.[23]

Once again referring to John Leech Henry Silver records:

Then we revert to poor Leech—his *voluntas* was stronger than his *arbitrium* says P.L.—he could deny no one—not excepting himself and laments those dear old days when Leech first married and what a pleasant little unaffected wife he had and how delightful were the little homely banquets of mutton and gin and water to which she welcomed his friends.

P.L. tells of the old father calling on him this morning and bow-wowing about the article in the *Times* which implied that family money matters had injured Leech's health. . . . Old Leech was keeper of the London Coffee House—and M.L. says he knows that Leech accepted bills for the old man and his daughters for £3,000 or so; which swept away the sum he received for his first 100 paintings. While J.L. was at Hambourg the father called to borrow £50 of old Joyce and then of M.L. and hearing this made J.L. very indignant and angry, and M.L., seeing how agitated he was said: "Your duty is to work for your wife and children and not to let your mind be harassed and if buttoning up your pockets leads to a quarrel with your father, I still should advise you to button them up.

Reynolds Hole continues: "At last the brave heart broke. 'Please God, Annie, I'll make a fortune for us yet', he said to his wife on the morning of the 29th of October, 1864, and, a few hours afterwards, that same voice whispered into the same loving ear, 'I'm going'."[24]

News of the death did not reach the little village of Caunton for two days.

I did not know of my friend's death until the 31st, when, with a grief which will never leave me, I read it in the *Times*. Very, very sadly I thought next morning, as I went to my daily service, that we should no more take sweet counsel together, and go up to the house of God in company. And then the great solace came, came in these glorious words, which I read to my little flock, in the first lesson of All Saints' Day: "But the souls of the righteous are in the hand of God, and there shall no torment touch them. In the sight of the unwise, they seemed to die; and their departure is taken for misery, and their going from us to be utter destruction: *but they are in Peace.*"[25]

At the funeral there were scenes of real affection for a man who had been so greatly beloved. Du Maurier is quoted by John Millais:

I was invited by Messrs Bradbury and Evans, the publishers of *Punch*, to the funeral, which took place at Kensal Green. It was the most touching sight imaginable. The grave was near Thackeray's, who had died the year before. There were crowds of people, Charles Dickens among them. Canon Hole, a great friend of Leech's, and who has written most affectionately about him, read the service; and when the coffin was lowered into the grave . . . we all forgot our manhood, and cried like women! I can recall no funeral in my time where simple grief and affection have been so openly and spontaneously displayed by so many strangers as well as friends—not even in France, where people are more demonstrative than here . . . he was only forty-six.[26]

On 12 November 1864 Shirley Brooks wrote the public eulogy in the magazine that Leech had served so truly. He begins: "The simplest words are best where all words are vain . . ."[27] and ends with a paragraph, every line of which is charged with deep and sincere feeling:

While society, whose every phase he has illustrated with a truth, a grace, and a tenderness heretofore unknown to satiric art, gladly and proudly takes charge of his fame, they, whose pride in the genius of a great associate was equalled by their affection for an attached friend, would leave on record that they have known no kindlier, more refined, or more generous nature than that of him who has been thus early called to his rest.[28]

Not only amongst his associates on the staff of *Punch*, but in many other spheres of life, John Leech seems to have attracted a most sincere affection, an immediate appeal, and to some of these men he became one of their closest friends. In a letter to Mr Evans, dated much later, Millais writes: "I loved John Leech (and another who is also gone) better than any other friends I have known."[29]

Mr and Mrs Reynolds Hole after their wedding, May 1861.

The cradle taken to New Zealand by Sara, Reynolds' sister. She had married the Rev. John Raven in 1847 and they emigrated as early members of the Canterbury Settlement in 1852.

CAUNTON MANOR.

JANUARY 21st, 1864.

THE

TRAGEDY

(WRITTEN FOR THE OCCASION)

OF

GOUGE

THE GAROTTER:

OR, THE

MANIAC MAID.

Randolphus, Duke of Hoveringham	MR. LONGMAN.
Bruce Mac Gregor, Duke of Gretna Green	MR. MARLBOROUGH.
GOUGE, THE GAROTTER	THE AUTHOR.
Chokem, Deputy Assistant Garotter	MR. H. FRANCKLIN.
Hawkshaw, Detective Officer	MR. FLAMSTEAD.
Duchess of Hoveringham	MR. ALVERY.
Lady Battersea Field	MR. PEEL GARNETT.
THE MANIAC MAID	MR. MOORE HALL.

TO CONCLUDE WITH

WHITE-BAIT AT GREENWICH.

Buzzard	MR. WHETHAM BODDAM.
Glimmer	MR. REYNOLDS HOLE.
John Small	MR. FREDERICK BURNABY.
Miss Lucretia Buzzard	MRS. COOK.
Sally	MRS. REYNOLDS HOLE.

TO COMMENCE AT EIGHT O'CLOCK P.M.

CHARLES JOHN RIDGE, PRINTER, MARKET PLACE, NEWARK.

Playbill, Caunton Manor, 1864.

Trelawny (who, it may be recalled, was a visitor to the Thackeray household) "said that Shelley and Leech were the two men he had loved best. . . ."[30] And of Thackeray: "It is said that when he was asked to name the most intimate and dearest friend of his life, he replied, 'John Leech'."[31]

Mr H. O. Nethercote of Moulton Grange, Northamptonshire, who was at school with him, and with whom Leech stayed towards the end of his life, wrote: ". . . I lost sight of him for many years; but through the medium of our common friend Reynolds, now Canon Hole, we came together again. . . . I am inclined to think that the man he liked best in the world was R. Hole, and then Thackeray and Millais; but of course I cannot say with any certainty."[32]

In a letter to Reynolds Hole dated 9 December 1864, Shirley Brooks wrote:

My dear Reynolds Hole,

Thank you much, very much, for your welcome letter. It is among the most valuable to me of all the proofs I have received that in the memoir of our dear friend "gone before", I wrote what the hearts of his friends approved. The paper in the Cornhill M. was written by E. S. Dallas, of the Times, who also wrote the first announcement of the death. But a real biography remains to be composed, and I am rejoiced that you think of doing it. You knew him as well as did any of us, and perhaps better than most, and the correspondence is invaluable. I wish you would think of doing it, not in any partial form, but as "*the* Life of J.L." and would call in any who can furnish you with additional materials, to do so we should all feel that the work could not be in such good hands. Any aid I could give in seeing publishers, or otherwise, you know you have only to desire and have.

As regards his property, I am as yet but ill-informed, but I have reason to believe that Mrs Leech will not be so well situated as one hoped and believed. Friends are applying to Lord Palmerston for a pension for her, and I think would not do what *he*, as you know, would have so much detested, were it not needful. Another matter, strictly of course entre nous, has been revealed. It was believed that Charles Eaton* would do a great deal for her, and I think she hoped that he would live with her, and thus that the house might be retained. He *may* do something, but it seems that he has been privately married for about two years—I suppose "ineligibly", as he has kept it secret. I cannot hear whether there are children, but in any case

Mrs Leech's brother.

this fact is against Mrs Leech. Millais anticipates the obtaining a great sum for the drawings. I hope he does not exaggerate their market value—but even if he does not, I conclude that the Agnews have a heavy claim, which I make no doubt those shrewd Swedenborgians will duly set up. On the whole, my impression is that the family will have little more than a competence, but I speak without book, as yet. When I hear more, I will let you know.

The town mouse, and I may add mousess, are much obliged for the game, which, or part of which, is to be nibbled on Sunday by some specimens of the Illus Literarius, and the sender will be remembered when they "dip their whiskers and their tails into the malmsey", or whatever substituteth it.

Believe me, my dear Hole, ever faithfully yours, Shirley Brooks

There was also a letter from Dr Brown (edged with black as his wife had died on 6 January 1864) dated 22 March 1865.

My dear Sir—you have given me a great pleasure. Such ex[illegible] from you, are I assure you very precious to me. I know how intimate you were with that great and good man. I know that you read over his body the divinely beautiful and comforting service of your Church, and that you were one of his 3 or 4 most cherished friends, therefore it is to me a great comfort and joy to know that what I so imperfectly said of your friend, has pleased you. I am delighted at what you tell me [illegible] you preparing a memorial of him. I hope I may live to see it . . . I know you were the Oxonian who wrote The Little Tour—I also thank you for telling me in his own words about what I said of him in the *Horae*. I often looked forward to seeing him at my cousin's house—John Scott of Calnaghii—a . . . [illegible] . . .

but he too has gone now to the majority. I send you a copy of the paper containing a cut that was omitted in the review. I think it completes the moral significance of Leech's work.

I regret exceedingly a pressure of professional work made me so hurried in the writing of the paper—it should have been much better than it is. I hope if you are ever in Edinburgh you will come and take up your bed with me.

Yours ever truly and gratefully—J. Brown

The *Punch* circle was sadly depleted and the meetings at the Garrick Club must have lost some of their sparkle. For, although there were arguments and even some personal animosities, the general feeling at these gatherings was of friendliness and good humour, of loyalty and cheerfulness. Now two of their number were missing, and during 1865 Paxton, who was an unofficial "member", also died.

In July of that year, Henry Silver's diary mentions the Staplehurst train disaster, as recorded to him by Mr Read: "By the way, I met Sam Read on Monday; he was in the river 'covered with mud and blood' in the Staplehurst accident—escaped unhurt, man killed by his side— nerves unshaken. No time to think—3 bumps and a smash. Dickens' carriage kept on the line. Sam got £20 for his ducking."

It is recorded elsewhere that part of Dickens's carriage was on the line and the other part up in the air, that he had to scramble out and jump down and that, having done so, he remembered a script he had left in the train and so climbed back again to recover it. Although not suffering actual injury he was shaken by the accident to the extent that when he died five years later it was said that he had never completely recovered from the shock.

Meanwhile there was practical help to be found for the Leech family and Mr Hole writes to his wife from 7 St James's Place, on Tuesday 25 April 1865, that he spent the previous evening "with the father, mother and five sisters of my dear friend" and in a note added at the end of the letter he tells of the sale of Leech's work, amongst which was a famous hunting sketch in which Mrs Hole was one of the figures. "5.30 p.m.—The Sale has gone off most successfully. The pencil sketch of Joe Johnson and my Carrie sold for *Twelve Guineas*."

In another letter from the same address (undated) which must have been written about this time he begins:

I immensely enjoyed my sweet darling's note this morning and kissed the "affectionate wife", as also the letter from my son, which I think shows great talent . . . Hurra for home tomorrow . . . I have all my shopping to do and more literary enquiries and investigations, so don't blame a hasty note. I saw poor Mrs Leech last evening. She does look so sweetly sorrowful in her widow's dress that it is heart-breaking to see her and her fatherless children. I had a long conver-sation with her, and was very pleased to hear from *his* wife that Millais and I were the dearest friends he had. She inquired about you, my father, and Tweets—I dined last night with the Cooks. Salmon at 5/9 a lb. (so Billy said). Turkeys as big as Benedict,* ice in every form . . .

As a memorial Reynolds Hole later dedicated a window of St Luke in the chancel of St Andrew's church, Caunton, with the inscription: "To

* His favourite horse.

God and in memory of a beloved friend John Leech this window is offered by Samuel Reynolds Hole, Priest."

The deaths of Leech and Thackeray left, in both cases, a sorrowing family as well as friends and public. In the case of Leech his widow and children survived him but a few years. The Thackeray daughters, whilst desolate, fared rather better.

9

Thackeray's Daughters

HENRY SILVER HAD written of Thackeray's death: "... what the loss must be to his daughters who owed everything to him, in position and in fortune, and were ever petted and much thought of, one shrinks from considering ..."[1]

Anny was twenty-seven and Minny twenty-four when the sorrowful event took place, and Anny writes of it from their new home at 16 Onslow Gardens, in October 1864:

> I know Papa was tired and that he did not want to live except for us and yet my heart sickens and aches and I feel that he might have been with us now. ... It makes one so humble and so ashamed to hear of his tender goodness and to remember his unceasing love and partiality—and it is like a torture now to remember how little we understood it. Though indeed we did care very very much. ... Sometimes Minny looks very like Papa and sometimes she says things so like him that it is a wonder. She can remember things he said and he liked and his words and she has all his tenderness. I mean it is like his. ... Minny is going out for a drive with Mrs Carlyle this afternoon—we met old Thomas the other day on his horse and he suddenly began to cry. I shall always love him in the future, for I used to fancy he did not care about Papa. ... I try and write a little but I've nothing to say ...[2]

Through their father the girls had a large circle of friends and invitations came in from all around in an effort to help them to overcome their grief. They had been invited that summer to stay at Freshwater in the Isle of Wight, with the Ritchies at Henbury, and at Wykehurst, Bolney in Sussex. There must also have come an invitation from Caunton Manor which evoked the following reply:

> Dear Mr Hole,
> Your kind letter is *so* kind and comforts me so much. What years ago it is since we first met.

I should like to come for a Sunday very greatly or any other day,
and so make Mrs Hole's acquaintance and see 4,000 roses and any
day that Lady Barker likes and that is convenient to you will suit
me . . .

Did my Father ever pay you a visit—I think I remember your
asking him. It is always a happiness to us to hear people speak of
him—and when I read your letter it seemed to me almost as if we
were all at home in the old home again.

Yours sincerely,

Anne Thackeray

There is, unfortunately, no record of Miss Thackeray following up
her suggested visit to Caunton to meet Mrs Hole and to "see 4,000
roses", but her writing, although providing a solid background for
building her new life after her father's death, did not prevent her keeping up with old friends or making new ones.

Although she must have begun work almost at once on her new
novel *The Village On The Cliff*, which she finished in time for serializa-
tion in *The Cornhill* during 1866–7, her journal also records a visit to
the Anthony Trollopes at Waltham Cross, where she must have been a
welcome visitor as Trollope writes of her with affection:

I have loved [her] almost as though she belonged to me. . . . Miss
Thackeray's characters are sweet, charming, and quite true to human
nature. In her writings she is always endeavouring to prove that
good produces good, and evil evil. There is not a line of which she
need be ashamed—not a sentiment of which she should not be
proud.[3]

She went to the National Gallery with Millais, walked with Tennyson along the cliffs at Freshwater where she "almost expected to see
poor Boadicea . . . with her passionate eyes", and went to the House of
Commons to hear Gladstone on the "redistribution of seats".

On 9 June 1866 close friends came to her birthday picnic, among
them Leslie Stephen, the current editor of *The Cornhill*, and in October
he asked Minny to marry him. "I was finishing *The Village on the Cliff*
[for which Frederick Walker did the illustrations] when she came up to
my study to tell me." A year later they were married. After a honeymoon when Anny had "such happy letters from my bride and bridegroom who are scrambling about, Minny on and Leslie walking beside
the mule, which has to have steps cut for it as if it were a member of
the Alpine Club . . ." they returned to Onslow Gardens where they all
"shared the same home . . ." (In view of the reference to the Alpine

Club it ought, perhaps to be mentioned that Leslie Stephen went climbing in Switzerland every summer and was President of the Alpine Club for three years.)

While editor of *The Cornhill*—Thackeray had resigned in 1862—Leslie Stephen on one occasion invited two young contributors to dine: Robert Louis Stevenson and Sir Edmund Gosse. Evidently their shyness was only equalled by the silent Stephens, who hardly opened their mouths, and it was left to Anny Thackeray to fill up "the hiatus with soft and unbroken monologue".[4] But more usually she left them to their own devices, following her own life, although sometimes spending holidays abroad with them, in Paris, Rome, Switzerland, or visiting friends.

Robert Browning was staying in Normandy when Anny was there with the Ritchies and she gives her description of a lyrical picnic: "The feast was spread out of doors on the terrace with a view of the sea between the lilac bushes. . . ."[5] Of his wife:

I think Mrs Browning the greatest woman I ever knew in my life. She is very small, not more than four feet eight inches I should think. She is brown, with dark eyes and dead brown hair, and she has white teeth and a low harsh voice, her eyes are bright and full of life, she has a manner full of charm and kindness. She rarely laughs but is always cheerful and smiling. . . . Her husband is not unlike her. A dark, short man, slightly but nervously built, with a frank, open face, long hair streaked with grey and a large mouth which he opens widely when he speaks, white teeth, a dark beard and a loud voice with a slight lisp, and the best and kindest heart in the world.[6]

These were almost golden days again—certainly they were for the Stephens. For Anny fresh sights, new friendships and the happy settled atmosphere of their home background all contributed towards a peace of mind she was glad to recapture. In 1870, a daughter, Laura, had been born to Minny and Leslie, and in 1875 Minny was again pregnant. But in October she became ill. Following the birth of Laura she had recovered from the ill effects and become almost well again: this time things were different. She died suddenly on 27 November. It was the end of peace, happiness, and a home where Minny had built up an atmosphere of loving thought combined with a delightful sense of fun and humour. A light had gone from their lives.

Leslie Stephen's sister, Caroline, wrote of Minnie: "She had a singular and indescribable social charm—a humorous, wayward and changeful grace, which captivated not only for the moment but for life, because its freshness was so unmistakably the outcome of transparent sincerity. She was, beyond anyone I have known, quaintly picturesque, tender and true . . . Altogether the eight years of their married life were a spring-time of beauty and gladness for both."[7] As for her sister: "In a way it was the death of Anny too. Little by little a new life was to come to her, full of interest and purpose, but she herself was never quite the same again."[8]

Anny, like many people who, having lost someone they deeply love, found that work, whilst not lessening the pain, did help to make it more tolerable. She turned to her writing. She would say: "Without my work I should be lost."[9] Like much of the best writing, hers seems effortless. She frequently conjured up a bright, vivid picture of a setting or a personality in comparatively few words. This applies especially in her references to Ruskin whose ideas are constantly quoted by Reynolds Hole. (In a letter to James Blackney he advises him "stick to Ruskin", and in his advice to young gardeners he quotes Ruskin: "A child is always asking questions and wanting to know more. Well, that is the first character of a good and wise man at his work. To know that he knows very little; to perceive that there are many above him wiser than he; . . ." And he concludes "The young gardener should learn these words by heart . . .")[10]

Anny, Leslie and the little girl Laura, went to the English Lake District during the year after Minny's death and in a paragraph Anny sums up the Ruskin household at Coniston in a letter to her publisher as a

> lovely little aesthetic encampment here. They are all in fits of delight over *scraps*, not the lake and the mountains, but a gooseberry or a feather off a chicken's head or something of that sort. But I do like them so and he is a kind gentle dear old fellow and sometimes he talks quite beautifully. There is Mr Severn who floats off bare-headed in a small sailing yacht . . . Ruskin has beautiful old bibles, and missals and above all such nice strawberries at his house. He says if you can draw a strawberry you can draw anything . . .

She was now writing frequently to her cousin, Richmond Ritchie: From Coniston, "Mrs Severn sat in her place behind a silver urn . . .";[11] of the terrace at Clevedon Court, "with a fountain dropping into a marble basin, and beyond a sight of all the summer in the valley . . ."; from Blois in the Touraine: "I can't think how to tell you what a lovely old place it is, sunny-streaked up and down . . ."; from Cornwall: "The elements are our one excitement. You walk through a great blowing wind into a mist, across a moor with brown, cropping cows . . ."; and from Interlaken: "how I wish one could send all that one sees to you . . . I should like to send you a pine tree and a bunch of

Part of a letter from Anne Thackeray to the Vicar of Caunton, in January, 1862.

Letter from Reynolds Hole to Caroline's grandmother telling of their child's birth.

Minny. "She had a singular and indescribable social charm—a humorous, wayward and changeful grace, which captivated not only for the moment but for life, because its freshness was so unmistakeably the outcome of transparent sincerity. She was, beyond anyone I have known, quaintly picturesque, tender and true. . . . Altogether the eight years of their married life were a spring-time of beauty and gladness for both." (Leslie Stephen's sister, Caroline.)

Leslie Stephen (*left*) with friends and family including —sitting, from the left—Vanessa, Virginia and Adrian.

wild strawberries, a valley of sloping nodding flowers with thousands of glittering spiders' webbs, the high up snows and far below lakes . . ." (Here she seems to anticipate the deep satisfaction one could store up for the future if a precious moment could be caught and captured and put into a beautiful case to be opened in need.)

Richmond Ritchie was seventeen years younger than Anny. Notwithstanding, they were married in August 1877. To Charlotte Ritchie she wrote: "People do not seem as shocked as I expected . . ."[12] Millais stormed, but from George Eliot came an "earnest desire that you may have the best sort of happiness".[13]* The following year Leslie Stephen married again. His second wife was Julia Duckworth, the daughter of Maria Jackson (née Pattle), and of this marriage there were four children—Thoby and Adrian, Vanessa and Virginia.

During her travels, both with and without her husband, Anny had made many friends; in much the same way that Reynolds Hole would when he later began to travel. The circles in which they both moved were very similar and consequently the friends they made either through travel or interests were common to both, or at least indirectly connected. It might perhaps be interesting to see how these friendships did connect up. In Paris Anny had known Madame Mohl, and it was at a party at her house one evening that she met Madame Bodichon (née Barbara Leigh Smith), a founder of Girton and an artist of some standing. Describing her Paris stay Anny wrote that she was enjoying "a mad but delightful extravagance".[14] Madame Bodichon was a close friend of Gertrude Jekyll; the latter sometimes visiting her in Algiers or staying with Madame Bodichon at Scalands, her house designed by William Morris. Madame Bodichon was also, like Anny, a friend of George Eliot, and is the prototype for *Romola*.

The Ritchies both loved music and Leonard Borwick, the pianist, used to play at their musical evenings. He also played duets with Hercules Brabazon, the water colour painter, at the Sedlescombe parties—"Eight hands on two pianos would be going for hours, the floor of the room would be littered with the scores of operas . . ."[15] and Brabazon would suddenly rush into the garden "to catch a sunset".[16] Miss Jekyll and Madame Bodichon were both members of this musical group of friends.

Although Miss Jekyll's connection with Reynolds Hole and his wife was gardening she numbered amongst her closest friends many artists, and one of these was Frederick Walker who illustrated Anny's books, *The Story Of Elizabeth* and *The Village On The Cliff*. Of the latter book Anny mentions her difficulties in getting it into shape: "When I was writing *The Village On The Cliff*, I was very nervous about it, and quite

* It was understood that George Eliot was later influenced by Anny's example when she decided to marry J. W. Cross.

at an end of my ideas and resources, when one day came the first proofs of the lovely drawings by Frederick Walker. They were so completely everything that I had ever hoped or imagined, that the sight of them gave me a fresh start . . ." Unfortunately he became ill and this happy— and for Anny, inspiring—partnership had to end.

On account of his delicate health Walker was spending the winter of 1873–1874 in Algiers when both Miss Jekyll and Madame Bodichon were there, and it was Miss Jekyll who helped him on his return journey to England in the spring, "almost like a poor stray kitten under her arm."[17] He had felt ill and far from home and remarked "that if only he were once again in a hansom cab in London, he should be quite happy".[18] Miss Jekyll saw him safely back and bade him farewell: "There, Mr Walker", she said, "this is Charing Cross and there is a hansom cab."[19] He died the following year aged only thirty-five. The illustrations for Anny's book, *Old Kensington*, which was published in 1873, were done by George Leslie, another friend of Miss Jekyll who lived near her at Wargrave.

Logan Pearsall Smith was a neighbour and friend of the Ritchies in Chelsea and a frequent visitor to Miss Jekyll in Munstead Wood who delighted in battles of words with him. She had always been interested in the use of words and caught him out nicely on one occasion over the word *"epergne"*. After his election with Robert Bridges, to the Committee of the Society for Pure English he always sent her copies of his pamphlets written for the Society, for her comments.

But amongst so many it is Ruskin's name which stands out as being of common interest. (It was, after all, Anny's father who had given an airing to *Unto This Last* in *The Cornhill*, controversial as these ideas were at that time, in which Ruskin pleaded for state factories as well as private enterprise, more education for the young and provision for the unemployed and old.) Anny and her husband visited him at Coniston and corresponded—Anny smoothed out problems in one of his many unhappy love affairs. Reynolds Hole quoted Ruskin frequently in his writing. He once "called on Mr George Allen at Sunnyside, Orpington, with some enquiry about Ruskin's work: *The Seven Lamps of Architecture*", which had lately been re-published. As he left the hall, he struck smartly with his head a hanging lamp. The last thing that, as a rule, comes off a man's tongue in a case like this is a witty remark; but Hole instantly remarked with good humour, "If I am not careful there will only be Six Lamps left." Miss Jekyll knew Ruskin through Arthur Severn and Brabazon, and had been brought up from schoolroom days to read his essays. But perhaps Ruskin's ideas meant most to William Robinson, who, with Miss Jekyll pioneered the "natural movement" in gardening. He is known to have admired *Proserpina*, published in 1875, and it was here that Ruskin gave his explanation for interpreting Latin and Greek flower names for the benefit of his "young English readers". To him, as well as to Robinson, the unnecessary use of Latin names was a lifelong irritant. "A good English name should have precedence of all others for general use . . ."[20] Robinson wrote with special reference to trees.

On 18 May 1868 Reynolds Hole received from William Robinson an inscribed copy of his book, *Gleanings from French Gardens*.[21] Sent by separate post was this letter:

28 Scarsdale Villas, Kensington, W.

Sir, I trust you will accept a copy of my little book on French gardening sent yesterday simply as a small testimony of the great pleasure I have derived from your writings—and for long before I ever thought (?) of becoming a writer on gardening matters or any others, I am, Sir, very respectfully yours, (signed) Wm. Robinson.

This was a year before *A Book About Roses* was published—in fact, Mr Hole was probably busy correcting the proofs of his work when Robinson's book arrived. As Robinson states specifically that the copy is given because of "the great pleasure" derived from reading works by Mr Hole, it seems that this must apply to *A Little Tour in Ireland* and to gardening articles published in papers or magazines. But *A Book About Roses* would establish Hole's reputation once and for always as both an authority on the rose and as a skilled writer, combining knowledge with a kindly wit and common sense.

A Book about Roses

A Book About Roses opens with a frank account of the invitation which Reynolds Hole received, as a young man, to judge at an April rose show; an account, which, it may be remembered, he at first thought to be a hoax—after all, roses at Easter! Between this opening account and the specialized chapters at the end, there is a store of valuable information, including the historical report of the founding of the first National Rose Show. The book is written with a lightness of touch that is endearing; there are no pompous statements or displays of knowledge which might immediately depress the novice. Instead one is reminded that the author had no roses in his garden when invited to judge that first provincial show, and, on returning home, feeling humble and, almost, hypocritical, he at once wrote off "for an assortment of *roses in pots*".

The theme of the book, although practical and direct in its approach, is a well-known one, more often associated with people than with plants. The theme is love. Again and again he emphasizes the point that love is needed in growing a rose.

> As with smitten bachelor or steadfast mate the lady of his love is lovely ever, so to the true rose-grower must the rose-tree be always a thing of beauty. To others when its flowers have faded it may be worthless as a hedgerow thorn! To him, in every phase, it is precious.

Again he says: "I will tell what may be done in a very small garden by a very poor man who *really* loves the rose." And perhaps the most often quoted: "He who would have beautiful roses in his garden must have beautiful roses in his heart."

Reynolds Hole condemns the rose-grower who takes no trouble and who blames everyone but himself when the trees are covered not with roses but with grubs:

> The earth is set and sodden; no spade nor hoe has been there. As for manure . . . we know that they have never seen it, and yet they are

expected to bloom profusely; . . . The owners will complain: "Is it not sad that we cannot grow roses? We have spared no trouble, no expenses, and we do *so* dote on them."

Even Hole's habitual good temper wilted before such arguments and he replied with vigour:

You have taken no trouble which deserves the name; and as to expense, permit me to observe that your fifty rose-trees did not cost you a fifth of the sum which you paid for your sealskin jacket. You don't deserve beautiful roses and you won't have any until you love them more.

To illustrate his idea of taking trouble "which deserves the name" Hole relates the story of a friend who won a first prize at a Newark rose show. A competing gardener remarked to him: "I believe, sir, that you have got the only soil in all Lincolnshire which could grow such blooms." "And I brought it there", was the reply, "*in a wheel barrow.*"

The romance of that first April rose show is described in chapter two and is followed by others on conditions, manures, selection, aspect, et cetera, as well as by tributes to the early rose-growers.

Of these early rose-growers it is Mr Paul's name which stands out today in some of the most widely grown of all roses. Paul's Scarlet climbing rose is seen in many gardens and is probably one of the best in colour among red roses and most reliable in its manner of growing. Paul's Lemon Pillar is profuse in flowering and of superb colouring— white with a touch of ivory or palest lemon. It is vigorous in growth (will attain a height of ten or twelve feet) and has a long flowering season. Paul's Himalayan Musk, blush to rose in colour and with a rich scent, will achieve a height of forty feet and is grown to some effect through a yew at Hidcote. He also gives various examples of the right conditions in which to grow roses and these instructions are illustrated by lively anecdotes which indicate a genial sense of humour as well as much practical knowledge in the author. Writing of the first efforts of an amateur rose-grower he says:

As a rule, the amateur rosarian has made about as much progress as George III with his fiddle. After two years of study the King asked his tutor, Viotti, what he thought of his pupil. "Sire," replied the professor, "there are three classes of violinists; those who cannot play at all, those who play badly, and those who play well. Your Majesty is now commencing to enter upon the second of these classes."

9

In a spirited account he describes his first "battle of roses" with a neighbouring parson who had "long maintained an absolute monarchy at all our country flower-shows"; the Vicar of Caunton decided it was time to *"have a go at him"*.[1] Having noticed that the Reverend Jones had always exhibited his entrants in ginger-beer bottles Mr Hole consulted Mr Lane of Berkhamstead who suggested zinc tubes as being superior. This was surely a step forward. The next thing was to produce better roses to put into the zinc tubes. Amongst others of his collection he remarked on "a Baronne Prevost"[2] on which he rather flattered himself and thought "would make Jones gasp".[3] Preparing their flowers for exhibition on the morning of the show in one of the ante-rooms provided for this purpose, the two combatants emerged at the same moment, bearing identical boxes—Jones with zinc tubes instead of the usual ginger-beer bottles, and a Baronne Prevost rose beating the Caunton exhibit by "half an inch in diameter".[4] The climax came three hours later when the Rev. Jones came up to his vanquished rival and remarked: "They've disqualified you for extra foliage, or I really believe that you would have come in *third*."[5]

However, there were occasions when Mr Hole was successful, which sometimes proved embarrassing when he had helped to organize the show. Like Mrs Nickleby, when her eccentric lover would carve her name on his pew, the process of presentation at these times could be "gratifying, but embarrassing", even "suggesting to a suspicious mind the trustee described by Mr Wilkie Collins in whose accounts occurred the frequent entry, 'self-presented testimonial, £10' ".

Mr Hole, with all his knowledge, is refreshing about botanical classifications, et cetera.

As to any scientific arrangement, ethnological, genealogical or physiological classification, I am helplessly, hopelessly incapable. I have as poor brains for these studies as Cassio for strong drinks. "I am no botanist" as the young chap pleaded to the farmer who reproved him for riding over a field of wheat.

This type of approach is encouraging in these days when botanical qualifications rank high in the gardening world, especially to people who may love their plants and shrubs and tend their gardens with affection but who cannot remember, or pronounce if they did, many of the Latin names by which familiar flowers are sometimes known.

In the matter of practical advice the book stands on firm ground. One chapter deals, for instance, with the best position in the garden to select for rose beds. It is just as bad for roses to have too much wind—

draughts or gusts—as it is for them to be suffocated by other trees or large shrubs. He writes:

Some, having heard that a free circulation of air and abundance of sunshine are essential elements of success, select a spot which would be excellent for a windmill, observatory, beacon or Martello Tower. ... Others, who had been told that the rose loves shelter, peace, etc., have found "such a dear snug little spot", not only surrounded by dense evergreen shrubs, but overshadowed by giant trees. A rose under trees ... can no more flourish than a deer can get a good "head" who never leaves the forest for the moor.

Then come direct instructions:

... expose to the morning's sunshine, protect from cutting wind. Give the best place in your garden to the flower which deserves it most. In the smallest plot you may make, if you do not find, such a site as I have described. You *will* make it if you are in earnest. I have seen old boards, old staves, old sacking, torn old tarpaulins—yes, once an old black serge petticoat—set up by the poor to protect the rose.

He always expresses most fervent admiration for those gardeners who may not be blessed with the most propitious growing conditions, but who are yet undismayed by whatever difficulties befall them. In connection with ideal situations for rose-growing which might include clean country air, a sunny aspect, some shelter, et cetera, he quotes the case of his friend Mr Shirley Hibberd:

... if he could grow good roses within four miles of the General Post Office (London)—and I have seen the proofs of his skill and perseverance at one of the great London rose-shows, to my high surprise and delectation—it is quite certain that he would have been *nulli secundus* with the full advantage of situation and soil.

Soil is the heading of another chapter and the same principles apply here as were mentioned in connection with the position of the rosebeds. Not everyone has perfect soil for rose-growing. Some people have, for instance, to contend with heavy clay where the first step to be taken must be some form of drainage—roses do not care to stand with their feet in a pool of water throughout the winter any more than most other plants. Drainage of soil must be followed by lightening with every possible means, even if it involves using old feather cushions, worn-out mats or carpets, spent hops, soaked cardboard broken up into small pieces, tea leaves, et cetera. Others have to deal with too sandy a soil, where the roots may have difficulty in finding an anchorage. But there is always some means of balancing up these extremes and much of the ordinary garden soil does not fit into either category.

To complement the case of Mr Hibberd growing first-class roses under difficult town conditions, Mr Hole quotes that of a railway worker who applied for and obtained a tenement adjoining the line to which was "attached the meanest apology for a garden which I ever saw in my life . . . it seemed to me a gravel-bed and nothing more". He knew this man and knew also that he was fond of flowers, and so offered him his condolences on such a gravel patch. However, he had reckoned without the man's persistence or his ingenuity. On seeing this same "garden" about one year later, full of flowers, fruit bushes, vegetables and fruit trees all "in vigorous health", he expressed his amazement. "Why, Will, what have you done to the gravel-bed?" "Lor' bless yer," Will replied grinning, "I hadn't been here a fortnight afore I *swopped it for a pond*." This determined gardener had removed from his own patch of land a stratum to the depth of three feet and carted it to the edge of an old pond, which had become filled with silt and leaves over the years. It was this mixture that he had brought home a distance of about 200 yards in wheelbarrow loads. He had worked hard for his garden and he was soon insisting on "stirring up them cottagers at next show with roses . . ."

On the subject of manure Mr Hole collects together the opinions of about ten of the leading rosarians of that time. The answer, although there may be a few variations, is always the same—farmyard or stable manure. Mr Keynes of Salisbury recommends as his recipe "a good wheelbarrowful of compost, two thirds good turfy loam and one third well-decomposed animal manure", and adds the following reminder: "It is difficult to give the rose too good a soil."

There is little variation on the time-table for applying manure. It should be given liberally to rose-trees in November when the ground is dry, leaving it "as a protection as well as a fertilizer through the winter months" and dug in during March. This application should be supplemented in late May or early June by a strong liquid stimulant. If our neighbours expostulate over the extravagance of such a procedure, Mr Hole suggests that we remind them of Victor Hugo in *Les Miserables*: "the beautiful is as useful as the useful, perhaps more so."

Describing his own efforts of applying the later dose of a liquid stimulant he writes:

I wait for the indications of rain, that the fertilizing matter may be

Rose: Gloire de Dijon. This and the two plates following
are reproduced from the *Amateur Gardener's Rose Book* by Dr Julius Hoffman, 1905.

Rose: Maréchal Niel

at once washed down to the roots. . . . During the extraordinary drought of the summer in 1868 I watched day after day . . . and at last, feeling sure of my shower, wheeled barrow after barrow . . . and distributed it . . . Soon the big rain came dancing to the earth and when it had passed, and I smoked my evening weed among the rose-trees, I fancied that already the tonic had told.

(It was this year that Mr Hole won fourteen first prizes out of sixteen collections shown, including that which was then considered the champion prize of all, the first awarded to amateurs at the Grand National Show of the Royal Horticultural Society.)

A convenient summing up of important points to remember about roses in connection especially with these three chapters on position, soil and manure comes as follows:

Let them be planted in the best place and in the best soil available, avoiding drip and roots. Let them be manured in the winter and mulched in the spring. In the summer months let them be well watered below and well syringed above, two or three times a week. Let grubs and aphides be removed, and sulphur, or soot, or soap-and-water be applied as soon as mildew shows itself.

Now we come to the lists of recommended roses and from these it is only possible to select a few. Mr Hole had one or two especial favourites, as most rose-lovers have, and one of these grew on the chancel-wall of his church. He writes: "I have just measured a lateral on one of my trees, and of the last year's growth, and found it to be 19 ft. in length, and the bole of another tree at the base to be nearly 10 inches in circumference. . . ."

The one on the chancel-wall "has often had two hundred flowers upon it in full and simultaneous bloom".

The name of this favourite climbing rose is Gloire de Dijon.

One of the favourite roses of a man who grew not just a few hundreds but thousands can surely claim special attention for anyone who grows any at all. There are available, nowadays, even longer and longer lists of roses, some of them recommended for scent but most, it seems, for colour, shape, length of flowering season and ability to stand up to pests. Let us see what the Gloire de Dijon has to say for itself:

"It is what cricketers call an 'all-rounder', good in every point for wall, arcade, pillar, standard, dwarf, en masse, or as a single tree." This is his own personal recommendation, confirmed by the fact that he grew it, at one time or another, in most of these situations, and that, as already mentioned, he had a climbing variety against the

chancel-wall of his church upon which he often counted 200 blooms.
All this speaks well for the sturdiness and profuse flowering of the
Gloire de Dijon; but what are the characteristics of the actual
rose?

First, its colouring is unique. I think I am right in suggesting that
there is no other rose—even today and allowing for the introduction of
so many new varieties and tones and shades—which so resembles the
soft velvet of a ripe apricot. The catalogues, obviously in understandable difficulty, vary in their descriptions, from buff, yellow and fawn
to orange and salmon. Then comes its flowering season which begins
early and lasts until late. Best of all is its perfume—subtle and not
always noticed by the rose-lists on this account. Miss Eleanour Sinclair
Rohde in *The Scented Garden* asks: "Why does one so seldom see now
the splendid old Gloire de Dijon, introduced in 1853, for this rose is at
home under any conditions, one of the earliest to bloom and the last to
give out, and has in abundant measure the true tea perfume."[6]

Miss Sackville-West described Gloire de Dijon with affection as
"that fragrant crumpled straw-coloured old stager, equally charming
as a climber or a bush".[7] And to revert to Mr Hole's personal selection
once more, he concludes by saying that if, for some terrible crime, he
were sentenced to owning but a single rose-tree, he would "desire to be
supplied, on leaving the dock, with a strong plant of Gloire de Dijon".

Other special favourites were Cloth-of-Gold and Maréchal Niel,
both of these Noisettes and neither completely hardy, so only recommended with reservations. Others, well known and loved today, include Aimee Vibert, a double white; Boule de Neige, a small and very
double white; and Madame Alfred Carrière, a most prolific ivory
white, beloved by Miss Jekyll and seemingly just as happy on a north-
facing wall as anywhere more propitious. This is a rose which flowers
first in June and goes on through the summer until the end of October.
These Noisettes are descended from the White Musk Rose, or Rosa
Moschata, the most splendid of parents.

Reynolds Hole also testifies to the charm and beauty of the Banksian
rose, introduced to Europe from China in 1796 and into this country
first in 1807. The double yellow climbs famously against a south-facing
wall, achieving tremendous heights once it is established. He recalls a
French writer telling of a tree at Toulon "which covered a wall 75 feet
in breadth and 15 to 18 feet in height and which had fifty thousand
flowers in simultaneous bloom". (Even allowing for a little French
exuberance here, the number must have been outstanding.) However,
there are examples today of great height being achieved in this country
and at Birr Castle, the Irish home of the Earl and Countess of Rosse, it
is recorded as climbing at least thirty feet.

Writing in *Old Fashioned Flowers* Sacheverell Sitwell extols especially the profusion of the Banksian rose: "I remember it growing on my grandmother's house in Surrey in such profuse richness of cluster that it is associated for evermore in my mind with the strawberries and cream of June afternoons."[8]

Having noted Mr Hole's admonitions with reference to the Banksian rose—that it needed a "southern wall" and that "It cannot be warranted perfectly hardy but *with careful mulching* there is scarcely one frost in a lifetime which will kill it"—I felt nervous about my own garden exposed to south-west Kentish gales and planted two for safety, both in sheltered positions. They have reached a height of about fifteen feet in five years and one survived a serious buffeting during a winter gale. It was not staked sufficiently high enough up the wall of the house and blew down, lying bent almost double across the path. It was a tragic sight but after being cut back, as little as possible, and fixed once again in position—this time more firmly—it is now flourishing.

His mention of the yellow rose found by Robert Fortune—who took with him, on his trip to China in the early 1840s, some of the new Wardian cases to bring back his plants—is interesting owing to the fact that it was of relatively recent discovery at that time, having been found in a garden at Ningpo. Whilst Fortune's yellow is today one of the older roses, at the time of Hole's book it was almost a new introduction. Robert Fortune had been the superintendent of the hothouse department of the Horticultural Society's garden at Chiswick before his adventurous three years in China and on his return was appointed Curator of the Chelsea Physic Garden. The rose he described as having "yellow flowers; . . . the colour was not a common yellow but had something of buff in it".[9] Mr Hole, commenting on its relatively recent introduction, said that it had not yet received "in England the attention which it deserves, as one of the most attractive and abundant of roses".*

Looking through someone else's list of varieties of a favourite flower it is natural, perhaps, to notice how many of one's own selection are included. So far I have not discriminated to the exclusion of ones which I like to grow in my own garden, but as it is impossible to go through Mr Hole's selection in detail and entirety, I shall end with making a personal selection. The rose is Blairii No. 2.

I first saw Blairii No. 2 climbing far and wide over the front of a cream-coloured house in County Waterford. It had been given to the owner by Mrs Fleischman whose garden in the Cotswolds was world-famous for old roses. The delicacy of colouring in this flower is like a painting by Rachel Ruysch. Mr Hole writes: "No. 2, with its large

* This lack of appreciation must have been righted later as Mr Edward Bunyard describes it as "the sensation of its day".[10]

globular flowers, the petals deepening from a most delicate flesh-colour without to a deep rosy blush within, is a gem of purest ray serene." Perhaps the word "globular" gives an impression of bunchiness, perhaps not. It is not a bunchy rose—it is neat and compact, with a gentle scent and an almost velvet texture to its petals. One confession must be made—it is subject to mildew, but perhaps forewarned is forearmed, and good mulching together with plenty of spraying at the first sign may do something to avert the trouble.

Miss Jekyll describes it as a "beautiful old rose".[11] Writing in 1902 she says: "For full fifty years this fine thing has been with us, and in its own way there is as yet nothing better."[12] The perplexing title of Blairii No. 2 is explained by Reynolds Hole (who heard it transformed to "Bleary Eye" on more than one occasion), because two seedlings of the rose were raised by Mr Blair of Stamford Hill, London. No. 1 proved to be unworthy of further cultivation; No. 2 was the one we know.

A Book About Roses has three chapters which deal entirely with exhibition roses, which to show and how to show them. But for the amateur there is a most valuable appendix entitled "Memoranda for the Months"; here are some notes from it.

October: I begin with this month because both he who desires to form, and he who desires to maintain, or extend, a rose-garden, must now make his arrangements for planting in November. . . . The ground intended for rose-trees or stocks must be thoroughly drained and trenched to receive them.

November: is the best month for transplanting. Ah, how it cheers the Rosarian's heart amid those dreary days, to welcome the package from the nurseries, long and heavy, so cleanly swathed in the new Russian mat, so closely sewn with the thick white cord! . . . Let him plant his rose-trees as soon as may be after their arrival; but if they reach him, unhappily, during frost or heavy rains, let him "lay them in" as it is termed, covering their roots well with soil and their heads with matting, and so wait the good time coming. When planted they must not be set too deeply in the soil—about 4 or 5 ins. will suffice—but must be secured to stakes, firmly fixed in the ground beside them. Established rose-trees should, if the ground be dry and the weather fine, have a good dressing of farmyard manure. And in *December:* you should take advantage of the first hard frost to wheel in a similar supply for the new-comers. In both cases the manure must remain upon the ground to protect and to strengthen too, and need not be dug in until March.

January: . . . We must make up our minds to some losses among the old and young . . . but, with our ground well drained, and our rose-trees well secured and mulched, we need not fear for the hale and strong. . . .

March: is the month for our final planting of all save Noisettes and Teas. . . . Different varieties will, of course, require different treatment. . . . Some roses of very vigorous growth, such as Blairii No. 2 . . . will not flower at all if they are closely pruned. . . . See to your stakes when the stormy winds do blow, and towards the end of the month dig in the manure left about the newly planted rose-trees and briers.

April: Prune tea-scented, noisette, and Bourbon roses, observing the previous rule—that is, cutting very abstemiously, when the growth is vigorous, as with . . . Gloire de Dijon. . . .

May: . . . Of all the months, this to the Rosarian brings most anxiety. Nothing so adverse to his roses as late vernal frosts, cold starving nights in May. . . . The trees, which were growing luxuriantly, suddenly cease to make further progress. . . . Wisely did our forefathers fix their Rogation Days at this most perilous time. . . . A surface application of manure, as previously recommended, should now be laid on the surface of the soil.

June: . . . If May has been genial, June will be glorious. . . . If situation, soil, and supervision be such as I have suggested nothing but weather of unusual severity will bring aphis or harm to the rose. Once a Rosarian asked me, "what I did for green-fly?" I told him truthfully that they never troubled me; and I suppose I spoke too conceitedly; for soon afterwards they attacked me in force for the first time since I understood the art of rose-growing. But in that year, the bitterness of May was extraordinary, as the farmer, the fruitist, and the florist know to their cost; and it was evident, in the dull look of the leaf, that the trees were frost-bitten, and that the usual consequences must come.

July: . . . Should mildew make its appearance, remove the leaves most affected, and cover the rest with flower of sulphur when the tree is wet from shower or syringe, giving them another good washing next day. Mr Rivers recommends soot as a remedy, and kindly sent me a letter some years ago, the result of a successful experiment. Have you mildew? he asks—*try soot.* . . . That yellow-bellied abomination, the grub which produces the saw-fly, in this month attacks the rose, sucking the sap from under the leaf, and changing the colour of the part on which he has fed from bright green to dirty brown. The process of "scrunching" is disagreeable, but it *must* be done. . . . During the continuous droughts which frequently occur in July, it is desirable, of course, to water every evening. . . . Everywhere, I would advise that the surface of the beds be loosened from time to time with the hoe . . . but there is nothing like a mulching of farmyard manure. Fading roses should be removed from the tree. . . .

August: . . . if the weather is hot and ground parched, it will be desirable to give the beds a good drenching with water "when the evening sun is low".

September: brings us little to do, except to remove suckers and weeds, and to enjoy our second harvest of roses. . . . When at the end of this month the chill evenings come, and curtains are drawn and bright fires glow, who is so happy as the rose-grower, with the new catalogue before him?

Afterwards comes a list of exhibition roses.

But no record of his favourite flower would be complete without mentioning his club, The Six of Spades, articles on the activities of which appeared in *The Garden,* 1872. These were finally incorporated into *A Book About the Garden.* The club is described as meeting on wintry evenings to discuss a variety of subjects relevant to gardening:

We touch promiscuously upon boilers, flues, and stoves; heating, shading and ventilating; washing, sulphurating and fumigating; disbudding, stopping and pruning; tying, training and packing; manures, solid and fluid; soils, sand and peat; . . . traps for earwigs, birds and mice, et cetera.[13]

The meetings were reputedly held in the garden-house:

a warm and cosy chamber, I can tell you, or what would happen to those seed-bags hanging around or to those roots and tubers piled, dry and dormant in the background? . . . There is a potting-bench beneath the closely shuttered window, with a trowel protruding from well-matured and mellow soil. . . . Hard by, two bulky bags of sand from Reigate lean lazily against each other. . . . Beyond is a pyramid of boxes with many a railway label on their green exteriors, to tell of anxious miles they have travelled with auriculas, pansies, carnations, verbenas, roses. . . . Before our blazing fire, which roars a hearty bass to the mirthful tenor of the kettle is a table for our pipe and glass. . . . A wrathful canary, roused from its slumbers, twitters expostulations from its case and wishes "The Six of Spades" at Jericho.[14]

Sometimes special meetings were noted—round Christmas, when each member was asked to give a talk on a favourite subject, tell a story or sing a song. The Vicar of Caunton's talk was given on his favourite flower and entitled "Rose Bonheur". He described going for walks as a small child when he noticed the beauty of the wild rose in the country lanes. But then came a stretch of about fifteen years when his thoughts were centred on food-producing plants to the exclusion of anything else. As a schoolboy he enjoyed luscious gooseberries, pears, peaches, apples, but in defence he quoted Sam Weller when caught kissing the pretty housemaid: "It's natur, ain't it?"[15]

In spite of Sam Weller he gave the impression that he felt time had been wasted when, as a boy, he had received no encouragement in the study of flowers or the use of a spade, and in the introduction to these articles on his club he mentions the importance to be placed on rousing this early interest. He tried to do this for the children of his parish by taking them for walks in the woods and fields on summer evenings, and recalls at least one excellent result from these walks:

Twenty years after I had some hours to wait for a train at a great Yorkshire station and recognized in one of the porters a schoolboy who had often joined our floral promenades. He invited me to visit his home and when we reached a long row of houses, exactly alike in size and structure, he stopped and asked, "Now, Sir, can you tell me which of these houses is mine?" "Yes, Joe, that is your home with the little flower-beds in front and the climbing plant on the wall." And I remember the smile on his face as he said, "I have never forgotten those Sunday walks."[16]

Purpose
1869–1879

THE STORY OF Joe which ended the last chapter clearly illustrates the sense of purpose which lay behind so much of Reynolds Hole's work. George Herbert, in his *Country Parson*,[1] has a chapter on "The Parson's Completeness" in which he considers a knowledge of plants to be necessary in a parson, that he would be incomplete without it; and the Rev. John Laurence in *The Clergyman's Recreation*[2] emphasizes the help that a parsonage garden can be in his ordinary parish work. "I am not in the least ashamed to say that most of the time I can spare from the necessary care and business of a large parish and from my other studies, is spent in my garden—having myself reaped so much fruit both in a figurative and literal sense."

Many years later, looking back over his life, Reynolds Hole wrote:

> I have lived to see good results from a custom which I observed, some fifty years ago, of taking the boys of my Sunday-School for walks by the brook (Caunton Beck) and in the fields to gather wild flowers in the summer . . . I took with me the small volumes by Ann Pratt, with coloured illustrations and from these we learned the names and habits, with other information, of the specimens which we collected. In the interval between that time and this, I have been much gratified to meet with those who associate the love of flowers, which has never left them, with our Sunday evening walks. In cities and towns, far from the meadow and the wood, they have cherished in small gardens, window-sills and flower-pots, the old affection.[3]

When speaking at a City banquet he mentioned the story of Joe as an example of the penetration of gardening interests into an industrial area in the shape of window-boxes or small flower-beds, climbing plants or tubs. After his speech the toast-master, a dignified liveried gentleman whose powerful voice was used to commanding attention, quietly put a small card down in front of him. On it were the words:

Rose: La France

ROSE. REYNOLDS HOLE

JOHN BRAND & C? LITH. LONDON. E.C.

Rose: Reynolds Hole reproduced from *A Book About Roses* by Dean Reynolds Hole, 6th ed., 1877.

"As a boy I captured first prize for wild flowers in my native county, Devon".

But there were two aspects to this incident of Joe's garden. One is obvious—his continued love of plants and flowers, and the difference it made to his life. The other was the interest in him taken by Mr Hole. Whether it is the same Joe would be difficult to ascertain, but there is a long correspondence between a young shepherd boy named Joe Birley and the Vicar of Caunton, which they both continued into old age, and which resulted in a life-long friendship. Joe subsequently left tending the sheep to take up duties at the manor and it was shortly after that the Caunton beck flooded, rushing down through the water meadows to the Trent. One of the horses was swept away by the flood water until the desperate animal became caught up in some wooden poles stretched across the banks. It had already been in the swirling water for two hours when Joe came to its rescue, risking his own life, and freed it from entanglement. His bravery was appreciated by the whole household and a small ceremony held where he was thanked by them, and blue ribbon, with a gold coin enclosed in it, was pinned to his coat.

Joe eventually left Caunton to go out into the wide world and this was when the letters began. On the vicar's side they are full of concern and interest, of humour and of affection. He has pet names for Joe which include "Jilly Flower", "Cololy Cololy Cololy!!!" and "Keck-leckity Joe!!!!" and "Topper". Joe remembers the vicar's birthday, and Hole writes back:

I am heartily pleased to be remembered on my birthday, and thank you sincerely for your kind wishes. . . . I have just returned from a 10 days' Mission in East London. The amount of sin and misery is appalling. Such scenes as make the heart bleed. Large families crowded in a small room. Three children in a bed, two of them sick, one *dead*. The little corpse taken out at night, and put on the floor to make room for the parents! A husband brought home drowned— the wife takes off his boots and pawns them for drink! It was a great day at Northampton! . . . As to my *refusal* of the *Bishoprics* it reminds me of a certain Miss Baxter, who thought that a gentleman proposed marriage, when he had no such intention, and . . . her brothers used to tease her by saying:

"Poor Miss Baxter, poor Miss Baxter!
Refused a man, wot never ax'd her."

During these years many such missions as the one referred to in this letter took place, in Nottingham, Derby, Manchester, Preston and

London. He often wrote home to Carrie, even though he might be, and usually was, tired and exhausted at the end of a heavy day's work, to keep her in touch with what was happening, how things were going. Perhaps it should be realized, that it was because he had an understanding wife, interested in his work, welcoming him back, loving him, that he was able to take on so much travelling, prepare so many addresses, deliver them with such sincerity and never shrink from the day-to-day slogging which all this mission work involved. As they were so happy together she must have missed him very much when he went off on these journeys. It would have been easier for him to stay at home, to ride to hounds, to care for his parish and his roses, with his wife at his side; but his love of his fellow man, especially of those driven hard by overwork and frequently facing disgraceful living conditions, was uppermost in his mind and heart.

The welcome and sympathy which Caroline Hole gave to her husband's friends sometimes meant that they came to depend on her help even more than on his. The following letter from William Robinson makes it clear that she was looking out for a house-keeper for him and might even, if he required her to do so, be ready to introduce him to a possible wife:

Bray,
Dublin.   Nov. 4th, 1874.

Dear Mrs Hole,

I shall be glad to see the person you kindly write about as soon as I return. In *this* case I shall dispense with a certificate of youth and beauty! In another (which I need not particularise) by no means! We are never satisfied alas! I now begin to long for somebody to superintend the domestic department if I may put it in that prosaic way. I think I must appeal to my friends! Quite right to stop the needless ending of the walk. I am buying chickens here every day and regret they are not those enemies of the alpine flora at Caunton. Chickens, bacon and Potatoes are the grand resources here!

Pray make my apologies to Mr Hole for making such deep forays into his purse for the improvements and garden changes. However, I am hopeful that, two or three seasons hence, the harvest of beauty will be richer than you anticipate! I get such a nobly comprehensive and vigorous appetite (in your northern air) that I seriously advise your becoming a member of the C.S. Supply association or some other body which supplies large quantities of simple food at wholesale prices before I go down for "that week"! Kindly save the alpine

flowers from those dreadful hoofs and believe me always faithfully
yours,

William Robinson

In much the same way, just over a year later, she received a letter
from Edward Lyttelton* of cricketing fame. On the third page he
writes:

Will you please thank Mr Hole for his last letter. I have placed it
among those few which I have thought worth keeping and I haven't
had above a dozen such in my life. . . . P.S. The malformation in my
eyebrow turned out as you said, mostly a chill. It lasted about a
week and was a great nuisance though very interesting. Now all is
well.

Sometimes Reynolds' letters to Caroline are sent from Caunton.
She might be away having a change of air. As has been mentioned, her
health was not robust; but he was always in close touch.

Own darling, I need hardly say that the Newark train had left Doncaster about two minutes when ours arrived, and I had a couple of
hours to wait, so I went to see the Parish Church, one of the grandest
Petrifying Wells I ever entered, (after some walking round in the
snow, and telling everyone I met how disgraceful it was to shut up
God's House of Prayer, before the key arrived) no *sign* of Priest or
Services or Life. Rather like a Swell House, *when the family* are
abroad.

So I said my prayers and went back to the Station and sent the
Vicar "A Stranger's ideas of his Church" on a postcard, and had my
luncheon.

Well, I have been to look at myself in your glass since I came home
and find there's a good deal left . . . but I never worked so hard in my
life as in these eight days:

11 sermons
6 instructions spoken in the central aisle
4 addresses, 2 to women, 2 to children
4 catechisms in school
24 services in Church, visiting parishioners, sick people, and all

* *Edward Lyttelton* (1855–1942), a nephew of W. E. Gladstone and one of the youngest
of Lord Lyttelton's eight sons. With the addition of a couple of uncles the family could
produce a cricket eleven and it is reported that owing to practice in their home, much of
the furniture suffered severe knocks and dents. Years later, after having been ordained,
and as headmaster of Eton (1905–17), he admitted that he seldom walked up the aisle of a
church or cathedral without judging the distance as a spin bowler would judge a pitch.

without a note to help me. I do not say it with any conceit, because I feel ashamed to know how much more I might have done. Last night the church was crowded (*a great number of dissenters leaving their "chapels"*) and a jolly old farmer, who drove me to the station tells me that the Mission has been successful beyond all their expectation . . .

An undated letter from Caunton:

My own dearest and best, I reached home yesterday for dinner and was very thankful to find comparative rest for a brain which has been going at top speed for the last 10 days. It's not quite half a home, with the better half away, but after lodgings (my landlady's name was *Dinah Kendall*, and a kinder hostess I could not have found), everything seemed to look and to taste delightfully.

Today I have been much occupied—letters, school, invalids, (Annie Morris gradually weaker, Brown very bad from inflammation of the lungs and Tom Chappell, the widow's son, very ill with some internal disorder, Mrs C. says, which Mathison does not seem quite to understand) and a speech to prepare for Nottingham tomorrow. Tomlinson has called and sends his love, and I am to tell you he has been a prisoner, like yourself, with gout and rheumatism. He says Tom Parkinson told him that Mr Milward was decidedly better. . . .

Tomlinson seemed to be much refreshed by Mrs Smith's confinement which lasted from Monday to Thursday, Job and Elliott (and a few horses) pulling at the baby all the time! Her shrieks were distinctly heard at Upton. . . .

Parochial matters were still uppermost in his thoughts, even when so much of his time was being dedicated to his Church in Home Missions. This mission work was not going unnoticed and in a letter dated 15 November 1875, the Bishop of Lincoln invites the Vicar of Caunton to become a canon of Lincoln Cathedral. He mentions that "financially it is not only of no value but . . . that certain fees amounting to about eight pounds are required to be paid . . . on installation"; and goes on: "But it may have some attraction in your eyes as connecting you as canon with one of the grandest Cathedrals in Christendom and with a spiritual ancestry of good and great men who have been a blessing and a glory to the English Church for eight centuries."

A close relationship grew up between Bishop Christopher Wordsworth (nephew of the poet) and his new canon, built on mutual respect and affection, which was to continue for ten years, until the

PRESIDENTS OF THE
ROYAL NATIONAL ROSE SOCIETY

1877–1904 The Very Rev. DEAN HOLE, V.M.H.

1905–06 CHARLES E. SHEA	1943–44 HERBERT OPPENHEIMER
1907–08 E. B. LINDSELL	1945–46 A. NORMAN ROGERS
1909–10 Rev. F. PAGE-ROBERTS	1947–48 A. E. GRIFFITH
1911–12 Rev. J. H. PEMBERTON	1949–50 E. J. BALDWIN, O.B.E.
1913–14 CHARLES E. SHEA	1951–52 D. L. FLEXMAN
1915–16 EDWARD MAWLEY, V.M.H.	1953–54 WILLIAM E. MOORE
1917–18 Sir EDWARD HOLLAND	1955–56 OLIVER MEE, O.B.E.
1919–20 H. R. DARLINGTON, V.M.H.	1957–58 A. NORMAN
1921–22 Sir EDWARD HOLLAND	1959–60 F. FAIRBROTHER, M.SC., F.R.I.C.
1923–24 SYDNEY F. JACKSON	1961–62 E. ROYALTON KISCH, M.C.
1925–26 C. C. WILLIAMSON	1963–64 Maj.-Gen. R. F. B. NAYLOR, C.B.,
1927–28 H. R. DARLINGTON, V.M.H.	C.B.E., D.S.O., M.C.
1929–30 ARTHUR JOHNSON	1965–66 F. A. GIBSON
1931–32 HERBERT OPPENHEIMER	1967–68 Maj.-Gen. R. F. B. NAYLOR, C.B.,
1933–34 Dr. A. H. WILLIAMS	C.B.E., D.S.O., M.C.
1935–36 Major A. D. G. SHELLEY, R.E.	1969–70 JOHN CLARKE
1937–38 HERBERT OPPENHEIMER	1971–72 FRANK M. BOWEN, C.ENG.
1939–40 JOHN N. HART, C.B.E.	1973 R. C. BALFOUR, M.B.E.
1941–42 CHARLES H. RIGG	

THE QUEEN MARY COMMEMORATION
MEDAL AWARDS

1957 ALEX DICKSON & SONS	1957 OLIVER MEE, O.B.E.
1957 SAMUEL McGREDY & SON	1957 A. NORMAN
1957 E. B. Le GRICE	1964 BERTRAM PARK, O.B.E., V.M.H.
1957 HERBERT ROBINSON, M.B.E.	1971 C. GREGORY & SON

THE DEAN HOLE MEDAL AWARDS

1909 Rev. J. H. PEMBERTON	1950 JOHN RAMSBOTTOM, O.B.E.,
1910 EDWARD MAWLEY, V.M.H.	Dr.SC., M.A.
1912 GEORGE DICKSON, V.M.H.	1950 F. S. HARVEY-CANT, M.B.E.
1914 CHARLES E. SHEA	1950 E. J. BALDWIN, O.B.E.
1917 E. B. LINDSELL	1952 D. L. FLEXMAN
1918 Sir EDWARD HOLLAND	1952 BERTRAM PARK, O.B.E., V.M.H.,
1919 Rev. F. PAGE-ROBERTS	Mérite Agri.
1919 GEORGE PAUL	1952 Dr. A. S. THOMAS, O.B.E., V.M.A.
1920 H. R. DARLINGTON, V.M.H.	1954 W. E. HARKNESS
1921 S. McGREDY	1956 OLIVER MEE, O.B.E.
1923 Miss E. WILLMOTT, F.L.S.	1958 A. NORMAN
1924 SYDNEY F. JACKSON	1959 W. J. W. SANDAY
1925 COURTNEY PAGE	1960 F. FAIRBROTHER, M.SC., F.R.I.C.
1926 C. C. WILLIAMSON	1962 H. G. CLACY
1930 Dr. J. CAMPBELL HALL	1962 E. ROYALTON KISCH, M.C.
1930 WILLIAM E. NICKERSON	1964 G. D. BURCH
1931 ARTHUR JOHNSON	1964 Maj.-Gen. R. F. B. NAYLOR, C.B.,
1933 HERBERT OPPENHEIMER	C.B.E., D.S.O., M.C.
1935 Dr. A. H. WILLIAMS	1965 H. EDLAND
1935 WALTER EASLEA	1965 E. BAINES
1936 ALISTER CLARK	1966 EDGAR M. ALLEN, C.M.G.
1937 Major A. D. G. SHELLEY, R.E.	1966 F. A. GIBSON
1940 JOHN N. HART, C.B.E.	1967 ALEX DICKSON
1942 CHARLES H. RIGG	1967 W. KORDES
1942 Dr. HORACE J. McFARLAND	1969 J. W. MATTOCK
1945 Dr. H. V. TAYLOR, C.B.E.	1970 JOHN CLARKE
1947 A. NORMAN ROGERS	1971 L. A. ANSTISS
1948 Dr. G. E. DEACON	1971 D. BUTCHER
1949 W. E. MOORE	1972 FRANK M. BOWEN, C.ENG.
1949 A. E. GRIFFITH	

8

A page from the 1973 *Rose Annual* showing the Presidents of the Royal National Rose Society, the Queen Mary Commemoration Medal Awards and the Dean Hole Medal Awards from the date of the founding of the Society, 1877, in the first instance, and from 1909 in the third.

Bishop Christopher Wordsworth of Lincoln invites the Vicar of Caunton to become a Canon of Lincoln Cathedral, in November, 1875. "It may have some attraction in your eyes as connecting you as Canon with one of the grandest Cathedrals in Christendom . . ." (*Photo Edwin Smith*)

Bishop's death. (Bishop Wordsworth's manual, *Theophilus Anglicanus*, was said to have had more influence on students and candidates for Holy Orders than any other book in its day.) In a message to Reynolds Hole, shortly before his death, he said: "Tell him who is so fond of flowers, that no bed in the Garden of the soul is so beautiful as the bed of sickness and of death, on which the penitent seems to be in the presence of the Gardener. . . . Tell him that these thoughts may give him a subject for a sermon."[4]

Canon Hole never forgot his words and some years later he preached his sermon on this theme, trying to show how "every man may make the desert smile".[5] This was in the "archdeaconry" of Westminster, (perhaps at the invitation of Dean Farrar who became a canon there in 1876) where Bishop Wordsworth had ministered as canon from 1844.

But there would always be time for roses and, when in December 1876, the Rev. H. Honywood D'Ombrain (vicar of the beautiful 13th-century parish church of St Mary, Westwell—sometimes known as the cathedral of the Kentish marshes) called a meeting at the Horticultural Club which he had started, Canon Hole took the chair. The purpose of the meeting, which was held in Adelphi Terrace, was to form a National Rose Society. Canon Hole was elected its first President, D'Ombrain its first Hon. Secretary—joined two years later as joint Hon. Secretary by Mr Edward Mawley. "For the next forty years these three men dominated the affairs of the Society."[6]

D'Ombrain took an especial interest in looking for the best new varieties of rose in France and there is the story of a visit paid to Verdier's nursery near Paris to see new varieties which were being sent out. When these had all been shown to him there still lay at the bottom of the box "a yellow ball".[7] On asking what it was, Verdier replied that it was "only a yellow rose".[9] D'Ombrain realized that it was much more than "only" a yellow rose and said at once that it was worth all the others that he had seen. He was right, as it turned out to be Maréchal Niel which became one of the most famous of all. (Mentioned in some catalogues as neeeding "a cool greenhouse in most parts of the country" its flowers are not only a delicate sulphur-yellow but also exquisitely tea-scented.)

The Vicar of Westwell must have been a man of great energy and industry, travelling to shows both here and on the Continent, giving advice or encouragement as required, and soon having correspondence with rose-growers from all over the world.

The Rose Society now publishes a rose annual which gives a long list of presidents, awards (The Dean Hole Medal is an annual award), arrangements for shows up and down the country and notices of

admission to display gardens (amongst many others) at Cardiff, Edinburgh, Harrogate, Southport and Taunton as well as to the Society's
gardens at St Albans.

Another letter to Caroline, this time from Reading and dated 11
February 1878:

> I have just come in from addressing 300 men in the Great Western
> Works, a very interesting scene. The work is hard and anxious. It is
> so very very sad to hear histories of sin and suffering from those who
> come to us for counsel, and, now and then, for confession. But God
> seems *always* to send them comfort through His priests . . . and now
> to work—Your fond and affectionate, Reynolds. ps. If you had seen
> Father Chad trying to light his fire when we came home one morn-
> ing from Holy Communion at 5 a.m. (it was a sight to see the
> working men) on his knees with a candle and some old clothes pegs,
> I think you would have been pleased!

It was in the year of this letter that accusations began to raise their
ugly heads. There was no disputing the fact of Hole's appeal to the
men and women from the industrial areas, exploited as they so often
were by their employers, some of them living under difficult if not
impossible conditions. He felt for them as though he were himself one
of them, and for this reason he often tried to interest them whenever
possible in the healing process of growing plants or vegetables in their
allotments. He was above the divisions of opinion between the different
branches of the Church—the lessons learnt from the Oxford Movement had shown him how little these counted in the religious life.

An example of his feeling as an Anglican churchman towards
Dissenters (at that time not a situation overflowing with Christian
charity and understanding) is told in his own words: "When I first took
Holy Orders and returned home . . . as the new curate, I went to call
upon a very old man who was the head of the Wesleyan body in our
village. I have never forgotten the interview, and remember his
words:

> " 'They told me,' he said, 'that your reverence would never come
> to see old Joe Green, the dissenter, but I have known you from the
> time that you were a baby in arms and went birds nesting with your
> grandfather, and I knew that you would come. I am anxious to say
> a few plain words to you before I die and I hope that they will make
> you think kindly of me and of our society when I go hence.' "

He then went on to explain what had happened when a Wesleyan went to "ask counsel and sympathy" from the curate. He was told that he must be physically sick and should consult a doctor. This was a time when "there was no heart in the worship and very little Gospel in the sermon. We wanted to hear a little less about the Church and more about Christ, less about the prayerbook and more about the New Testament, less about the Thirty-nine Articles and more about the two great commandments of the Law."

The results of this interview were beneficial to both parties. Reynolds Hole "became more anxious to repair the wrongs which had been done . . . and my companion expressed his belief that if the spirit of the Oxford Movement had breathed over the dry bones in John Wesley's time, neither he nor his disciples would have gone outside the Church."[9]

The accusations were twofold. First, that Canon Hole approved of Ritualistic practices; and, second, that he introduced a spirit of frivolity into serious religious arguments.

On the question of Ritualistic practices it might be as well to turn to Dr Arnold for a sermon in which he took as his text the third verse of chapter four of *Ephesians*: "Endeavouring to keep the unity of the Spirit in the bond of peace".

I would that all of us held the same *opinions* in all matters relating to Christ's gospel; but far rather that we all had the same principles, and lived in the same spirit; and if we did this, our differences of opinion would be of small concern. Such, indeed, there must ever be among men: from this very place, in this very church, it may happen, perhaps, that different sentiments and different feelings are expressed by the different ministers who preach here; but what matters this, if in our principles and spirit we are united; . . . For there are diversities of gifts, but the same Spirit; and there are differences of administrations, but the same Lord; and there are diversities of operations, but it is the same God that worketh all, and in all; . . .[10]

Dr Arnold was not putting forward a new idea. The Holy Roman Emperor, Maximilian II, expressed the same belief in a different way:

During the 1560s, while religious attitudes all over Europe grew increasingly harsh and intolerant . . . in the lands under Maximilian's immediate rule, in Austria and Bohemia, the religious climate remained mild, astonishingly temperate. . . . While Philip of Spain was proclaiming that he would "rather lose all his lands than permit freedom of belief", Maximilian was explaining to the papal legate that he was "neither Papist nor Evangelical, but *Christian*".[11]

These are almost the same words that Canon Hole wrote of Bishop Wordsworth: "He was neither papist nor puritan, but one who believed in his heart that 'before all things it was necessary to hold the Catholic faith'."

Many people are now familiar with the correspondence, on this question of Ritualism, published in *The Newark Advertiser* between Canon Hole and Canon Ryle in November and December, 1878.

Canon Ryle had, in a speech at Whitby accused the High Church party of fulfilling the accusations of Latimer—"that the first thing which the devil says when he gets into a church is, 'Up with candles and down with preaching' . . ."—to which Hole replied in a speech to the English Church Union on "The Catholicity of the English Church" early in November as follows:

I fear that I must trespass to-night on the kindness which I always meet at Nottingham, because having just come home from a ten days' mission I have not had at my disposal that time for thought which my subject and my audience deserve. This I foresaw when my dear brother . . . asked me to speak at this meeting; and I told him that I would add a few words in support of another speaker, but that I could not undertake a speech. . . . Once upon a time— (but it is a true story)—during the assizes held at Lancaster, an honest Lancashire lad was examined as a witness. A young conceited barrister, with a turn-up nose and a new wig, was brow-beating and bullying him in cross-examination, and doing all he knew to make him contradict his own evidence. But honesty was too much for him, and at last in his angry excitement he was carried by his zeal beyond the boundaries of trick and discretion to say, "Why, witness, half an hour ago you stated so-and-so," on which honest Tom Bobbler could not stand it any longer, and looking his accuser in the face he answered, "Why, ye powder-yedded monkey, I never said now't o't'sort; I appeal to the company." Mr President, ladies, and gentlemen, it seems to me that we, too, as members of the English Church Union, have been so baited and rated and falsely accused by the counsel for the prosecution that it is high time for us to make our indignant denial, "We never said now't o't'sort" . . . The counsel for the prosecution says (I have heard Canon Ryle, who seems to be their leader, say) that we who call ourselves Catholics are getting up a conspiracy to Romanize the Church of England. I defy them to prove it, for we "never said now't o't'sort". We know, of course, that there have been desertions from our ranks to Rome. They went out from us, but they were not of us. They were honest men, at all events, and did not eat the bread of the Church while they disparaged her

doctrine and evaded her discipline. . . . Where on earth does the
conspiracy exist? It has been my privilege to preach in many churches
where there has been what is called high Ritual; it is my privilege to
count among my friends many champions of the Catholic cause, we
have opened our hearts to each other, but never in my life have I
heard one word of this conspiracy, and if Canon Ryle will tell me
where these conspirators meet, I will go with him hand in hand, like
a brace of twin Guy Fawkes, and blow them up with a hundred-
weight of Roman candles. Apropos of candles, our accusers may say,
"Oh, we don't mean any organized, avowed conspiracy to Romanize,
but it exists in all your teaching and practice." What do you think
Canon Ryle told us at Whitby? I wrote down these words from his
mouth: "When the devil gets into a church the first thing he says is
'up with candles and down with preaching'." How does the Canon
know? Where did he get his information? I call upon him to verify
his quotation . . . a man may consider himself bound by the teaching
of his church to have two lights upon the high altar for the significa-
tion that Christ is the very light of the world and at the same time
preach that very beautiful doctrine as heartily as Canon Ryle. The
most impressive preaching I have ever heard or read of was that
which filled the Cathedral Church of Manchester with all sorts and
conditions of men four times a day during the Manchester mission!
There are lighted candles on the altar at St Albans by which the
preacher stands . . . give back the non-resident pastors the locked,
dirty, deserted churches, the prayers which were rarely used, the font
which was never, the miserable altar—(I must apologize for using
this word to our accusers, but prefer St Paul and the Fathers to these
foreign Reformers who mainly excluded it from our Prayer Book)—
when the altar was used quarterly and the sermon was all in all. And
we, forsooth, who have restored God's house and His daily worship,
sacraments, and scriptures (to read four lessons from them daily), we
are conspirators, and they who but go into their churches one day in
seven are the heroes of Christendom. . . . Firstly, we are English
Catholics, and intend to remain so, holding the faith of the Undivided Church as it was held "always, everywhere, and by all".
Secondly, we are satisfied by history and our own experience that we
have the Apostolical succession, and upon the Divine principle, "By
their fruits ye shall know them," we are ready in all humility (but it
does not require much) to have our priesthood compared, as to their
lives, conversation, and work, with that of any other nation. . . .
Thirdly, we shall continue to hold the Catholic doctrines of the Real
Presence and the Eucharistic sacrifice, but not Transubstantiation,
nor the "mere memorial" untruth. Fourthly, we shall continue to

receive confession, even from Roman perverts who desire reunion
with the English Church (two instances have recently come within
my own experience), but we shall not treat it as compulsory, or as
anything less or greater than our church declares it. Fifthly, we shall
love and reverence the holy and blessed Virgin as the mother of our
Lord and the Queen of Saints, but we shall never pray "Sweet heart
of Mary, by my salvation," "Hail, Holy Queen, Mother of Mercy,
our life, our sweetness, and our hope;" because in our case, and we
believe in hers, such words would be blasphemous. Sixthly, we shall
pray with the saints, and ask their prayers, but we shall not make
pilgrimages to pray before their bones; the process is too circuitous
for a truth faith, and duplicates of the same bone rather too numerous.
We shall honour those who have the gift of continence, remembering the Master's words, "He that is able to receive it, let him receive
it;" but we shall hold by the same authority that "marriage is
honourable to all", that except in rare cases, "it is not good for man
to be alone," and that if God gives the priest a help-meet for him,
she may do so much beautiful work for Christ among the poor and
elsewhere, which otherwise would not be done. I might multiply
these instances, in which, as we believe, we possess the ancient faith,
but what I have said or can say amounts to this—we are neither Protes-
tants nor Romanists; we are Catholics. We have received the doctrine and the discipline of the Church of England as a sacred heritage
from our Lord and His Apostles, from the Fathers and Councils of
the undivided Church, and as such we will keep and defend them, so
that we may transmit them to our children, neither despoiled by
the abstractions of schism nor disfigured by the novelties of Rome.

In a characteristic letter which *The Newark Advertiser* printed, Canon
Ryle responded:

Sir,—My attention has been called to a speech delivered by Canon
Hole at the recent meeting of the English Church Union at Nottingham, as reported in your paper of November 8, in which my name
is freely handled. I beg to thank the speaker for directing public
notice to the proceedings of the Church Association at Derby. I
believe he has thereby, though perhaps unintentionally, done good
service to the Church of England. I now ask permission to make
two, and only two, remarks in reply.

Canon Hole does not like an expression which I used at Derby
about the Ritualistic movement. I called it *"an organized conspiracy"*.
I beg to inform your readers that the expression is almost exactly
parallel to expressions used by bishops of the Church to which Canon

Hole belongs. In 1873 the Bishop of Bath and Wells called the Ritualistic movement "a deliberate conspiracy". In 1866 Bishop Waldegrave, of Carlisle, called it "an organized combination, the object of which is the reinstatement amongst us of those distinctive observances and doctrines of the Church of Rome, which were cast forth at the time of the blessed Reformation". Your readers will find this language in a volume entitled *Facts and Testimonies about Ritualism* by Oxoniensis, p. 11 and 12 (Longmans, 1874), a volume which I strongly advise all loyal Churchmen to buy and read. In the same chapter they will find some equally forcible condemnation of Canon Hole's party by the Archbishops of Canterbury and York and by the bishops of Winchester, Gloucester, Peterborough, Llandaff, and St David's, and by the *Athenaeum* and the *Quarterly Review*. If I erred in speaking of an organized conspiracy, I erred in very good company.

Canon Hole objects to an expression I recently used at Whitby, in a lecture delivered there upon "James II and the Seven Bishops," about candles and preaching. Unfortunately he did not observe that I definitely told the audience that the expression was borrowed from a sermon of Bishop Latimer, and was not original. I will now give your readers the passage in its entirety. "Where the devil is resident or hath his plough going, there away with books and up with candles; away with Bible and up with beads; away with the light of the Gospel and up with the light of candles, yea, even at noon-day. Where the devil is resident, that he may prevail up with all super-stition and idolatry, censing, painting of images, candles, palms, ashes, holy waters, and new services of man's invention." (Latimer's Works, Parker Society, vol. i., p. 70.) Once more I thank Canon Hole. He gives me an opportunity of recommending all loyal Churchmen to buy and read "Latimer's Sermons".

With regard to other matters in Canon Hole's speech I could say much. But I am content to leave him to the judgment of the public. I am sure we ought to be much obliged to him for his very candid exhibition of his opinions.—Yours faithfully, J. C. RYLE, Vicar of Stradbroke. 11 November, 1878.

The controversy continued as the newspaper printed Canon Hole's reply:

Sir,—Canon Ryle's trumpet gives an uncertain sound. He sends me an evasive answer—the usual process when a speaker has made a statement which he cannot prove. Canon Ryle distinctly affirms that "there is an organized conspiracy to Romanize the Church of

England". I distinctly affirm that "there is no such thing"; and when I ask for proof, he writes that the Bishop of Bath and Wells and other bishops and the *Athenaeum* (!) and the *Quarterly Review* have said very much what he says. But I do not want the opinions of prelates and periodicals, though I respect both. I want *facts*. I want to know where this organized conspiracy exists? Where are its head-quarters? What is the name and number of the street in which the office may be found? Who is the chairman? Who are the subscribers? Where can I obtain the rules?

Canon Ryle informed us at Whitby (I took the words down as he spoke them), that "the first thing which the devil says when he gets into a church is, 'Up with candles and down with preaching,'" by which he meant that the High Church party, under an evil influence, preferred ritual to preaching. My reply is that the Catholic party preach more frequently and more fervently than the Protestant party in the Church of England, and if Canon Ryle, instead of giving us inappropriate quotations from Latimer, will produce from the roll of the Church Association the names of such preachers as Pusey and Liddon, Carter and King, Gregory and Ashwell, Wilkinson, Knox-Little, and Body, it will be an interesting surprise.

The condemnatory form of procedure by which he commits me "to the public", may seem to him conclusive and sublime, but it does not frighten me a bit. The venerable old dodge is worn out, and scares me no more than the growl of an ancient and toothless terrier alarms a full-grown fox. Moreover, it is my chief desire that this discussion should be submitted to the public, because I believe that men of all parties will agree in this, that no deliberate statement should be made by a public speaker which he is not prepared to prove.—I am, sir, your obedient servant, S. REYNOLDS HOLE, Canon of Lincoln.

Now we must consider the second criticism—that he could be "frivolous" about Church matters. He had certainly made the discovery that a joke introduced at the right moment could accomplish wonders and that the attention of a large congregation could be held by the hope that there might be something worth listening to in the next sentence. But it was his personal sincerity which won people over.

What he had to say was of such importance to him that he might sometimes feel the necessity for a lighter touch. (His nephew, William Francklin, remembers that when he was preaching he would often lean over the pulpit, swinging his cassock out of the way with his arm, and he would laugh or cry with the people he was talking to, if there was something to laugh at or to cry about.) Other men have known an overpowering necessity to treat a subject with a levity that might seem irreverent to outsiders. When asked to submit plans for the Roman Catholic cathedral of Christ the King (Liverpool), Edwin Lutyens wrote to a friend: "*Au fond* I am horribly religious, but cannot speak of it and this saves my work."[12] No one was surprised or shocked when, in serious conference, a clockwork mouse was set loose over the Cathedral plans. He was delighted with the first words of the Archbishop when they met to discuss the plans: "Will you have a cocktail?"[13] At another first introduction, this time to Father Ronald Knox, Lutyens opened with the query: "Do you know it is a scientific fact that when you cut a carrot its temperature drops?" Father Ronald Knox was quite equal to the occasion. He replied at once: "Yes, and when you cut a friend his temperature rises!"[14]

Perhaps one of the best answers to this particular criticism was the trouble that Reynolds Hole always took about letters to those who had been bereaved. The following was written to George Powell who worked in a factory in Derby. For many years he and Hole corresponded and this letter was written on the death of Powell's son who was killed in a dreadful factory accident. It is dated SS. Simon and Jude 1887, from Caunton.

My dear Brother in Christ, I have been on my knees more than once since I received the tidings of your terrible bereavement, praying that the only Comforter may come into your poor bleeding heart. Vain is the help of man, however kindly it be offered, in such an overwhelming sorrow, but "God is our Hope and Strength, a very present help in trouble". . . . the burden seems greater than you can bear, but it is the Cross.

Dear Brother, do not be disheartened, because you cannot pray as you would wish, or because your natural grief seems to overpower your spiritual faith, or because all things seem to be confused, and you are bewildered, and almost in despair, only do your best to be resigned, to "be still and murmur not", and God in His good time will set the rainbow of hope upon the black cloud of your sorrow, and "the times of refreshing shall come from the presence of the Lord".

And tell your dear wife, that, as surely as our Lord Jesus restored her son to the weeping mother at Nain, so will He give her back her boy, at the Resurrection . . . Think of him as safe on the shore . . . May the Lord be with you both, and with your loving brother in Christ, S. Reynolds Hole.

Other answers might be found by glancing through his *Addresses*

Spoken To Working Men[15] which were later collected together and published. These were addresses or sermons delivered for the most part on his many missions and come under various headings such as "Christianity and Common Sense", "Unbelief", "Who is a gentleman", "The Church and Dissent"—all practical problems dealt with honestly and with common sense and kindliness. Here are a few quotations taken at random:

> Do you read The Bible?: The Church . . . teaches that Holy Scripture contains all things necessary to salvation, but she does not teach that in matters of minor importance there are no mistakes. (In this chapter he quotes Ruskin—"Live your Bible, and your doubts will cease", St. Augustine, Dickens, among others.)

> Christianity and Common Sense: What do we mean by common sense? With a considerable number of persons common sense means uncommon nonsense; it means, "If you don't think as I think, say as I say, do as I do, you must be a born fool", and this they call free thought, liberty of speech, independent action. . . . The common sense of humanity craves for happiness . . . and considering the varied circumstances in which we are placed, it differs little in its idea of happiness—health, plenty, independent freedom, successful work, the love of those around us. . . . "A man's life", our Lord declares to us, "consisteth not in the abundance of the things he possesses." His real, true, happy life consists in being satisfied with what he has, and making the best of it. . . . One morning as I was going into church for our daily service, an old man whom I had known and esteemed for many years as a most sincere, consistent, humbleminded Christian, always bright and cheerful, though infirm and very poor, came to me leaning on his two sticks and said: "If you please, sir, could you say that thanksgiving prayer this morning, for I'm eighty years old today, and I should like to give thanks to God for all the mercies he has sent me." Not many weeks ago that old man died, and the last words he spoke to me as I sat by his bedside were these: "I'm not dying in darkness; I'm dying in the Light of Life."

> Common sense suggests another element of happiness—the goodwill of our fellow men. A man may profess to disregard it, and may set his hat on one side and put his hands in his pockets, and sing with the Scotch miller, "I care for nobody, and nobody cares for me"; but he is a gregarious animal, and must have sympathies. To be happy he must love and be loved. But you cannot buy love . . . you may buy admiration, praise, adulation; but you cannot buy love. Common sense longs for it, but cannot find it. Philosophy never

defined it. Philanthropy lives in the precincts, but has not entered the shrine. Only religion, Christianity, tells us what it is and bestows it.

Work: There is no record of great men whom we admire in history, there is no remembrance of anything in our own lives which we retain with gladness, which does not assure us that no addition was ever made to the greatness of a nation, to the honour and happiness of a life, without hard work. No discoveries of science, no master-pieces of art, were accomplished without patient labour. And this applies to every individual soul.

True Education: The Duke of Wellington years ago forewarned those who would expel a definite religious teaching, that an educa-tion without Christianity would make a nation of clever devils.

Conversion: Assuredly we need conversion, all of us and always; for what does conversion mean? It means, in the language in which the blessed gospels were written, simply a turning to God. . . . And as our duty to Him consists in small but constant proofs of our love, so our duty towards our neighbours is performed through little acts of kindness and consideration which are in the power of all.

The Gentleman In The Loose Box: Once upon a time a clergyman kept a horse, and the man who groomed him discharged a great variety of other duties, including that of collecting weekly the alms of the congregation. On one occasion he had given up the plate and was going back to his place, when a sudden recollection caused him to return and to whisper to his master, "If you please, sir, you must let me have it again, for I've forgotten the gentleman in the loose box," indicating with his thumb an individual who monopolized a spacious apartment, lined and cushioned and carpeted, and looking like a brand-new sleeping car, with one passenger, in the middle of a train of third-class carriages filled with people!... With all my heart do I pray and hope that he may soon be forgotten by us all. . . . He (I am regarding this gentleman in the loose box as representing the Pew System) has done immeasurable harm—to religion, generally; to the Church of England, specially; and to social sympathies and intercourse. . . .

The Friends of the Working Man: True friends of the working man are they, who are proving to those who will see out of their eyes, or think with their brains, that it is as unnecessary and unprofitable, as it is unhealthful and unjust, to darken the light and pollute the air which God designed for us all. True friends who, like Mr Carpenter by his lectures, and Mr Herbert Fletcher of Bolton, by his smokeless chimneys, and Mr Samuel Elliott, of Newbury, Berks, by his recent practical experiments on the Thames Embankment, have proved that this smoke nuisance may be easily and inexpensively abolished. . . . Some of you have asked me what I think about strikes. I have thought a great deal about strikes, read about them, talked about them, made enquiries about them, and have collected a large amount of information, which would absorb our interest and determine our verdict were it not for the embarrassing fact that one-half of it contradicts the other, with a positive and hopeless defiance. *Now* I am assured that the mine-owners and coal-merchants are rolling in riches, and *then* I am told by the proprietors and purveyors themselves that they are on their way to the workhouse. They are like those commercial gentlemen at Coketown, of whom Charles Dickens writes in *Hard Times*, and who always announced themselves to be insolvent when they were asked to do anything unpleasant . . . they were ruined when inspectors were appointed to look into their works; they were ruined when such inspectors considered it doubtful whether they were quite justified in chopping people up with their machinery; they were utterly undone when it was hinted that perhaps they need not always make quite so much smoke.

Who is a Gentleman?: It is in the power of every one of you to be included in the number of God's gentlemen. They are not made by pedigrees, titles or estates, by learning or accomplishments. The only perfect Gentleman lived in a poor cottage and worked with saw and plane. . . . St Paul describes God's gentleman—"Abhorring evil, cleaving to that which is good, kindly affectionate, not slothful in business, rejoicing in hope, patient in tribulation, continuing instant in prayer, rejoicing with them that rejoice, and weeping with them that weep, not minding high things, not wise in his own conceits, as much as lieth in him living peaceably with all men."

Gambling and Betting: I have made enquiries and read reports from governors and chaplains of prisons, some of which I have personally visited, the last at Chatham, one of the largest in the kingdom, and these officers are unanimous in their declarations that an infinite number of prisoners, convicted for the first time of false entries, forgeries, and actual theft, have attributed their guilt to the results of gambling and betting.

The Church and Dissent: And, again, it must be remembered that in addressing Dissenters you accost them by a title which they do not own. They will tell you that they are constant to a religion in which many of them were born, and that they believe in it as firmly as you believe in yours.

12

Achievement

1879—1889

IN THE WINTER of 1879–80 Mrs Hole had been seriously ill and, as Canon Hole had also been overworking, their medical adviser suggested rest in a warmer climate for a few months. In a letter written on Sexagesima Sunday 1880, to Bishop Benson from a hotel, *"Près de Nice"*, explaining their visit, Hole says:

My wife was seriously ill last winter, from some "thickening of the bronchial tube"; the doctors urged a more genial climate, as likely to release her from the weakness; and I, having ascertained the length of my physical rope, and somewhat strained it, was glad on all grounds to obey their prescription. And now, with a sky above us,

"So cloudless, clear, and purely beautiful,
That God alone is to be seen in heaven,"

with the olive-clad, vine-clad mountains around us and the blue Mediterranean before us, we can sing "Non nobis" for health and strength and other manifold mercies. . . .

While staying near Nice he made notes of his surroundings, impressions, et cetera, visited wherever possible nursery gardens or famous Riviera gardens, such as the well-known Hanbury garden, La Mortola, Ventimiglia. He also mentions the rose nursery of Monsieur Gilbert Nabonnand at Golfe Juan, to whose memory there is now a formal public garden in the centre of the town with a specimen tree, Cinnamomum camphora, *"planté par G. Nabonnand"*. The plaque in the garden records that *Gilbert Nabonnand, Jardiniste—Botaniste, 1823–1903, fut aussi un rosieriste de renommée mondiale*. Another and different place of pilgrimage was to the burial-ground of the Trinity Church at Nice where he saw the grave of an old friend's father, H. F. Lyte, priest and poet. "He died at the Hotel de Grande Bretagne in Nice, receiving the last consolations of his Church from a brother clergyman, the Rev. E. Manning, now Cardinal of Rome."[1] He must have given comfort to many with the words of his much-loved hymn, *Abide with me* . . .

In August 1880, Hole's *Hints to Preachers with Sermons and Addresses* was published with a dedication which read "To the Right Honourable W. E. Gladstone, this endeavour to promote an object which has his sympathy, is respectfully dedicated by his kind permission."[2]

The reviews were glowing and there is no doubt that his method of preparing a sermon, together with the material he used, was of value to those who found sermons a problem. This book shows that the final result whilst seeming easy and natural was, in fact, the product of hard work and deep thinking beforehand. But the ease of his sermons was partly due to the warmth and sincerity of his manner and the fact that his delivery was excellent enough to reach a large congregation at St Paul's.

He always made it clear that he knew what he was talking about, for example, when asking for help with sick children:

How shall we help? Reason tells us first of all . . . that if we would diminish the number of sufferers, we must find out the cause of suffering, and make our main effort there. I have sought this information, as was my duty, before I preached to others on the subject, not only from printed statistics and from correspondence but from a personal inspection of the largest hospital for children in England, intended when complete for 168 beds, at Manchester.[3]

He goes on later to discuss the living conditions which have produced many of these cases:

The medical officer of the Dispensary of the Children's Hospital at Manchester notices a gradual diminution for some years past in the number of out-patients; and to what does he attribute it? *First*, to the action of the Health Committee of the Manchester Corporation in closing cellar-dwellings in the streets and courts in the neighbourhood of Deansgate; and, *secondly*, the clearing away of other crowded dwellings and narrow streets and courts, necessitated by the erection of a great central railway station. Whereas in places where no such improvements have as yet been made, the death-rate of infants and young children is appalling; in one instance 292 per thousand. "How is it likely", asks a great statesman, pleading for a Children's Hospital, "that a little child shall live in an atmosphere which would kill an oak?"[4]

(Perhaps the "great statesman" was Gladstone; in any case, his dedication of the book seems appropriate.) Reynolds Hole was the Charles Dickens of the pulpit and, like the author, he took trouble over his research before he brought his facts before the public.

It was also during this year of 1880 that a German edition was published of *A Book About Roses*,[5] and two meetings with rosarians took place—the visits to Caunton of Miss Jekyll in July and the Rev. H. D'Ombrain in November.

In December came the honour of preaching in St Paul's Cathedral for the first time—which proved to be the first of many sermons there (at least fifty), until he began to feel too old. He stayed at Halstead Place, near Sevenoaks, Kent, with his sister and brother-in-law and wrote from there to Caroline.

I am up "early in the morning", before Walter has been to call me, that I may send a letter to my best beloved by someone who is going to London by train. I should have written yesterday but was on my legs, except at breakfast and luncheon until I left Halstead, going all over St Paul's with Canon Gregory, interviewing my publishers, and Robinson,* and then off to Chelsea. . . . I was thoroughly delighted with St Paul's, such a dignified service, and such sublime music . . . the congregation in the evening literally filled that immense church from the choir to the western door. How far my voice went I know not, but they seemed to be listening in the horizon! I was not nervous in the least degree in the reality, though I had been in anticipation, because He, Who sends, always supports; and the more one is conscious of utter weakness and unworthiness, the more one seems to hear a voice saying, "If I condescend to use you as an instrument, your personal failures and feelings cannot interfere" . . .

He referred especially to Dr Stainer, "who is the chief source and strength, (and) is so humble and unselfish. He was a chorister, and a kind old lady paid for his first lessons on the organ."

During 1881 the notes he had written on their visit to the Côte d'Azur came out in book form under the title of *Nice and her Neighbours*. He dedicated it to his old friend from Scarborough days, Edward H. Woodall, Esq. This was a particularly apposite dedication. Although Edward Woodall lived for many years at Scarborough and during that time presented to the public gardens there, "gifts of rare and new specimens of plant life"—so writes Mr J. Clark who took up the post

* William Robinson.

of Parks Superintendent in 1922—, he also spent winter months in his house near Nice, for health reasons. There he had a fine garden and from his experience wrote a chapter titled "Roses in English Gardens on the Riviera" for the book, *Roses for English Gardens*, by Gertrude Jekyll and Edward Mawley. (Mr Mawley was the joint Hon. Secretary of the National Rose Society; and it was Hole who first introduced Edward Woodall to Gertrude Jekyll.) The visitors' book at Caunton shows that he stayed there in May 1882 and July 1883. Five years later, in November 1888, he was a guest at Rochester.

From Florence, in May 1881, came a letter from Edward Lear, thanking Canon Hole for a copy of the Nice book, and full of kind messages to Mrs Hole. Lear suffered from an attack of giddiness after he got back to San Remo that year and was warned that he had been "over-drinking" and working too hard. He did not care to cut down too much on the drinking—usually marsala and water—but

He did think though that he should perhaps cut down on the number of letters he had to write and he told Hubert Congreve, "I am about to make a new arrangement at the end of 1881, i.e. to correspond only with those I have been in the habit of writing to since 1850." But this was an impossible threat, for his correspondence was such a joy to him. "He really *lived* upon the letters of his distant friends more than any man I have ever known," Lushington wrote after his death."[6]

> Hotel Washington,
> Firenze.
> 10 May: 1881.

Dear Mr Hole,
The enclosed envellope will shew that I had intended some time back to write to Mrs Hole. But, unluckily, I had mislaid your address, & nowhere could light on it. My reason for writing was to thank you for a "Book about Roses", wh. I brought out with me this last autumn, but which I did [*sic*] know till I came to look at it,—was written by the particular Mr Hole I knew.

And now I have to write rather suddenly & while on a journey—lest a Nopportunity should not readily occur again. For, just before I left Sanremo, the Book post brought me your "Nice & her Environs", wherein—at page 61, I find you speak so very kindly of me, & of the small work I have been allowed to do for the pleasure of my Phellow Mortles. Please thank Mrs Hole also from me, as she ought to have half the ringsurgiamenti. For all that, I wish you had

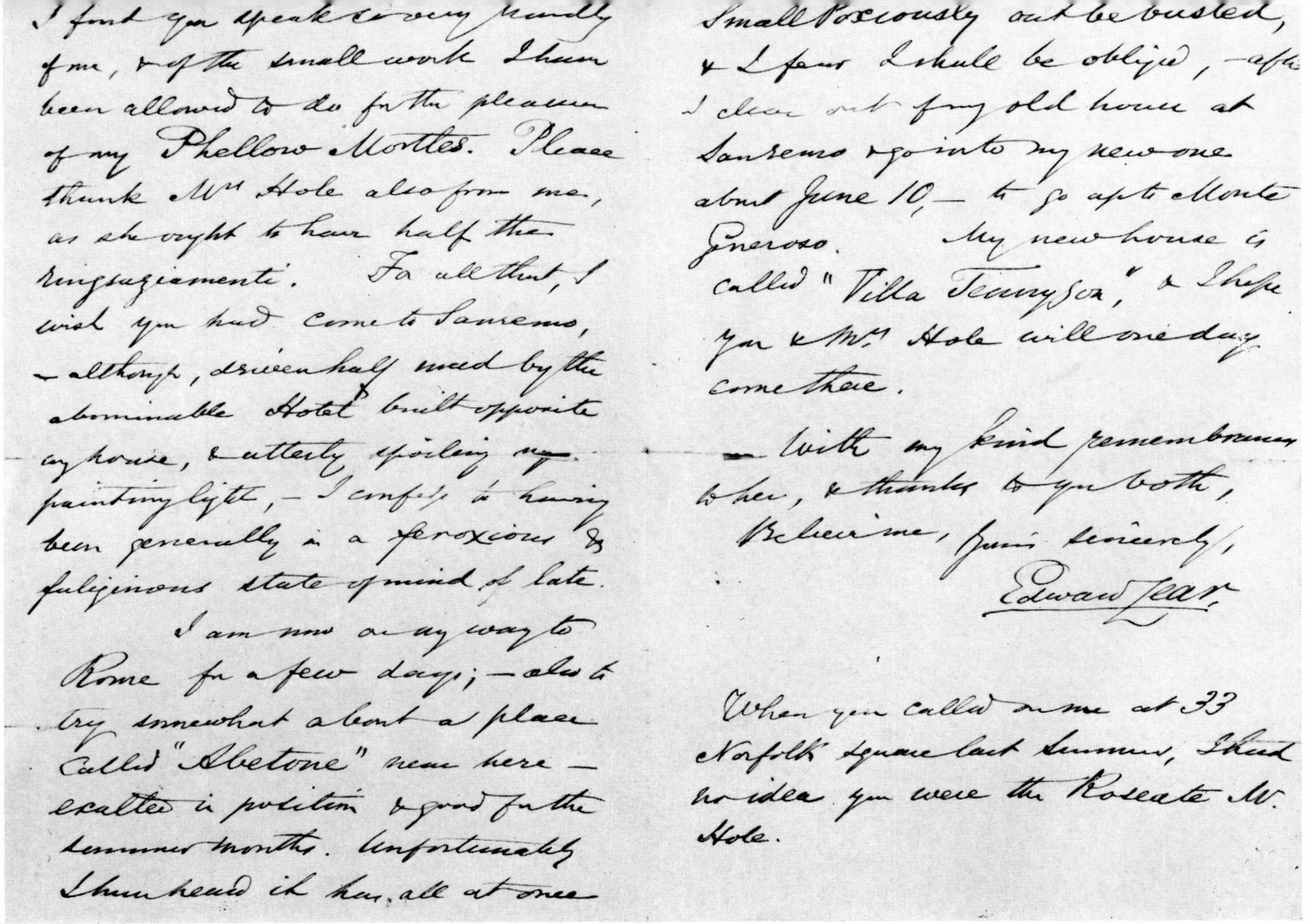

Letter from Edward Lear to Reynolds, 1881

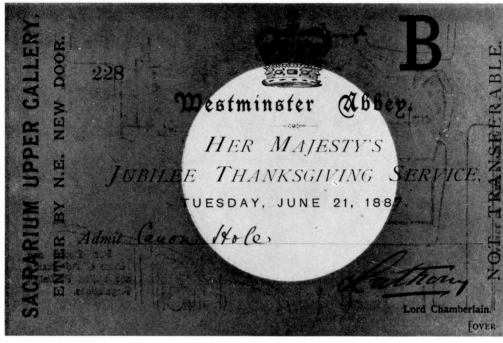

228

B

Westminster Abbey.

HER MAJESTY'S

JUBILEE THANKSGIVING SERVICE,

TUESDAY, JUNE 21, 1887.

Admit Canon Hole

Lord Chamberlain.

[OVER

Invitation to H.M. Jubilee Thanksgiving Service, 1887

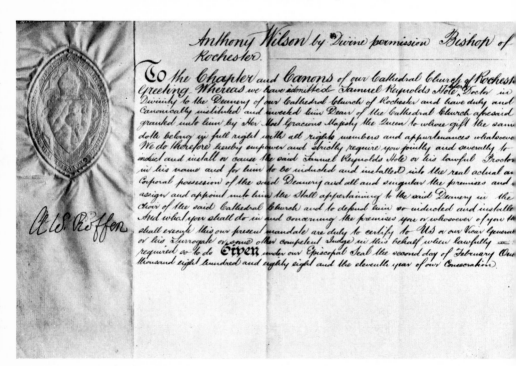

Anthony Wilson by Divine permission Bishop of Rochester.

To the Chapter and Canons of our Cathedral Church of Rochester Greeting Whereas we have admitted Samuel Reynolds Hole Doctor in Divinity to the Deanery of our Cathedral Church of Rochester and have duly and Canonically instituted and invested him Dean of the Cathedral Church aforesaid granted unto him by Her Most Gracious Majesty the Queen to whose gift the same doth belong in full right with all rights members and appurtenances whatsoever We do therefore hereby empower and strictly require you jointly and severally to induct and install or cause the said Samuel Reynolds Hole or his lawful Proctor in his name and for him to be inducted and installed into the real actual and Corporal possession of the said Deanery and all and singular the premises and assign and appoint unto him the Stall appertaining to the said Deanery in the Choir of the said Cathedral Church and to defend him so inducted and installed And what you shall do in and concerning the premises you or whosoever of you to shall execute this our present mandate are duly to certify to Us or our Vicar General or his Surrogate or some other competent Judge in this behalf when lawfully required so to do Given under our Episcopal Seal the second day of February One thousand eight hundred and eighty eight and the eleventh year of our Consecration

A.W. Roffen

Authority appointing Reynolds Hole to be Dean of Rochester, 1888

come to Sanremo—although, driven half mad by the abominable Hotel built opposite my house, & utterly spoiling my painting light, —I confess to having been generally in a feroxcious & fuliginous state of mind of late.

I am now on my way to Rome for a few days;—also to try somewhat about a place called "Abetone" near here—exalted in position & good for the summer months. Unfortunately I have heard it has all at once Smallpoxiously outbebusted, & I fear I shall be obliged,— after I clear out of my old house at Sanremo & go into my new one about June 10,—to go up to Monte Generoso. My new house is called "Villa Tennyson", & I hope you & Mrs Hole will one day come there.

With my kind remembrances to her, & thanks to you both,
  Believe me,
    Yours sincerely,
      EDWARD LEAR

When you called on me at 33 Norfolk Square last Summer, I had no idea you were the Roseate Mr Hole.

The reference to Lear on page 61 of the Nice book, runs like this: "Edward Lear, painter, poet, musician—who has not admired his pictures, laughed over his nonsense verses, and sighed over the pathetic melodies which he has composed for the songs of the Laureate?— showing as a fixed star at San Remo; . . ."

In a letter written to Mrs Hole much later a friend writes of the memories he has of visits when they were all together, and Edward Lear sat down at the piano to compose an accompaniment to one of Tennyson's poems.*

Nice and her Neighbours gave Reynolds Hole an opportunity to praise the plane tree in an avenue at Nice—a favourite—and also to quote from his friend Robinson on the subject: "Hence into that beautiful boulevard, more than a mile in length, the *Avenue de la Gare*, which leads to Nice. Well might Xerxes crown the plane with a golden circlet, for indeed that gracious tree is a royal benefactor amid the hot haunts of men. . . ." and the quotation from William Robinson's *The Parks, Promenades and Gardens of Paris*:

The best of all trees for European cities is the western plane *(Platanus occidentalis)*. It may be seen in many places, from the heart of the city of London to the shores of the lakes of Northern Italy; in the towns

---

* For further reference to this incident see *Life and Letters of J. E. Millais*, vol. II, chapter XVI, by J. G. Millais, Methuen, London, 1899.

of cold, central France; in the numerous new boulevards of Paris
... and everywhere it is by far the noblest city tree.[7]

(About one hundred years earlier, in a didactic poem by R. P.
Knight, addressed to Uvedale Price, Esq., 1794, in the opening lines of
Book II there is an appeal for an avenue of trees:

> Oft when I've seen some lonely mansion stand,
> Fresh from th'improver's desolating hand,
> 'Midst shaven lawns, that far around it creep
> In one eternal undulating sweep;
> And scatter'd clumps, that nod at one another,
> Each stiffly waving to its formal brother ...
> To Heaven devoutly I've addressed my prayer— ...
> Replace in even lines the ductile yew,
> And plant again the ancient avenue.)*

Later in 1881, a correspondence re-opened with the household of
Dr Brown in Edinburgh, or more correctly with David Douglas, the
publisher, in relation to the essays that Dr Brown was hoping to have
re-published in one volume, beginning with the one on John Leech.
(Owing to Dr Brown's illness and depressions there had been a silence
from Edinburgh of about twelve years, although he had been to
Caunton to visit the Holes and there had been friendly notes between
them, with references to the canon's favourite horse: "How is Bene-
dictus? that noble, leisurely, capable fellow?" and "My regards, too,
to the big thoroughbred".) It was Mr Douglas who was breaking the
silence and there now follow excerpts from three of his letters written
during October.

> No. 9 Castle Street
> Edinburgh   Oct. 7th 1881.

Revd Sir,
I take the liberty of sending a rough proof of an article on *John
Leech* by Dr John Brown which originally appeared in the *North
British Review* in 1865. It was, as you are aware, the author's intention
to have written a memoir of your friend and he had got together
some material when ill health came in the way. Dr Brown is so
well at present that I have thought it would not only interest and
amuse him, but do him good to revise his scattered papers on various

---

* See also *Mansfield Park,* chapter VI, Fanny Price quoting Cowper: "Ye fallen
avenues, once more I mourn your fate unmerited."

subjects and gather them into one volume. He commenced with Leech and intended to write to you on the subject, but I can see from his putting it off from day to day that he finds it difficult to break the silence of a dozen years. I therefore send you the sheets without his knowledge in order that you may read the article . . . if you do not disapprove perhaps you will say so frankly to himself telling him that I sent you the proofs. . . . I am Revd Sir, Your very faithful David Douglas.

No. 9 Castle Street, Edinburgh.   Oct. 11, 1881

. . . Since I wrote you several of the Doctor's friends have urged me to include some half-dozen of his own quaint designs of dogs to illustrate some of his other papers in the volume.

I have no doubt were there time and Dr Brown had the necessary strength, plenty of Leech's illustrations could be got to fill the place of those so pleasantly supplied by Bradburys in 1865 and now in 1881 refused by the new firm. I have only to ask Mr Bentley I am sure to obtain permission to use any of those that appeared in his publication, but I am desirous of pushing on the volume with the materials in hand as I fear by delaying its publication for another reason our dear friend may positively forbid it: he is really wonderfully well at present were it not for a morbid sensitiveness which makes him shrink from anything like publicity. . . .

I am Dear Sir, Yours very faithfully, David Douglas.

No. 9 Castle Street, Edinburgh.   Oct. 21, 1881.

Dear Sir,
Your obliging letter arrived two days ago and I quite understand and agree to the conditions upon which you permit your paper to be used by Dr Brown. I have left the letter with him today hoping that it may incite him to write you but poor fellow he had a sleepless night and was very wretched when I saw him. . . .

I am dear Sir, Yours very faithfully, David Douglas.

A later one in May of 1881 tells of Dr Brown's death.

No. 9 Castle Street, Edinburgh.   May 12, 1882.

Dear Sir, I have to tell you the sad news of Dr John Brown's death. It took place yesterday morning. His mind clear until the final separation and he was able to take an affectionate farewell of his friends on Wednesday night. . . . He was out on Friday as usual but somewhat depressed. . . . On Saturday morning . . . he thought himself ill and requested that an old favourite nurse might be sent for. She came on Monday and he said when he saw her, "Come away, Mrs Scoll, you know you 'trysted' to be with me at my death." On Wednesday afternoon all hope was given up. . . .

Now I tell you all this knowing the regard you had for him and to thank you on the part of his Edinburgh friends for being the means of rousing him from his apathy by writing him so cordially in October last regarding "John Leech". I look upon your writing to him as the turning point from great depression to a state of mental vigour such as he had not shown for 20 years. After getting your encouragement he entered heartily in the correction of his papers and quite enjoyed the praises of a new generation of critics. He has been very happy since Xmas last in various ways.

I am Dear Sir, Your very faithful David Douglas.

Whilst staying at the Derwentwater Hotel, Keswick, Reynolds Hole met Canon Rawnsley. In an undated letter to his wife he says, ". . . I had a busy day after you left. Mr Rawnsley (who was pleased that you liked his book), went part of the way with me to Mrs Howard . . . There I met Robinson at luncheon, saw Mrs Howard's garden (only the beginnings of a pretty place) . . . Just got home in time to dress for dinner, and went with the Rawnsleys to dine with the Provost★ [of Eton] and to meet the Master of Balliol . . ."

Canon Rawnsley was beginning his activities in preserving beautiful areas of the Lake District, and at a meeting of the Commons Preservation Society, held at Grosvenor House in June 1883, Octavia Hill had called on new members to take their place with "a few unknown heroes fighting an uphill fight for a great cause . . ."[8] One of the "unknown heroes" was Canon Rawnsley who had been introduced to Octavia Hill by Ruskin, and who later joined Octavia Hill and Robert Hunter as the founders of the National Trust. At this time he was working to retain access for the public to the view from Latrigg Fell (1,200 ft.), sometimes called Skiddaw's Cub; the view across Derwentwater and Bassenthwaite thought more beautiful than that from Skiddaw itself. In fact, it was partly on account of Canon Rawnsley's despair over the fate of the Lodore Falls which came on the market about ten years later, and his realization that a body must be formed to deal with such a situation, that prompted the founding of the National Trust. "The Lake District was in danger . . . Almost overnight the long-cherished aim to create a 'National Trust' seemed realizable."[9]

★ Dr Hornby, Provost of Eton, 1862–1884.

In March 1883 Canon Hole replied to a letter from the Archbishop of Canterbury inviting him to be one of his chaplains.

... With all my heart, I accept an invitation which is alike irresistible from its authority and from its sweetness—a Royal mandate, set to music; and with all my prayerful hope, that He, Who sends the message, will not permit the unworthiness of His servant to mar its import, I will come to Lambeth and St Paul's. ...

A stringent comment on this appointment appeared in the *Church Review* of 26 May:

The Archbishop of Canterbury has appointed Prebendary Hole to be one of his chaplains. This is the gentleman whom the *Guardian* described as the "stalwart champion of Ritualism". We wonder what will happen when he meets Prebendary Cadnam, another of his Grace's chaplains? We suppose they will at once proceed to knock each other down.

His duties in the Church had now become almost overwhelming; his timetable was so full it was difficult to find the time necessary for all the work to be done. Certainly the rose took its place in the background of events, although it was still very much in his heart. In a letter from Caunton dated 18 June 1883, to T. B. Hall (a well-known rose-grower of the time with acres of roses, many of which he showed all over the country), Canon Hole wrote:

My Master, the Archbishop, wishes me to speak at the Annual Meeting of the Church Defence Society in London, on the 9th of July, and as this is his first invitation to duty since I became his Chaplain, I cannot plead pleasure as an excuse. Regarding the Fête des Roses at Larchwood as the *most joyful holiday* of my year, from my first entrance into that pleasant home until you chaperon me to the omnibus at the gate of the Show ground, I need not enlarge on my disappointment. The less said the better.

"When Dido found Aeneas did not come
She mourned in silence and was Di do dum."

Some months later he is writing to Mr Hall again in a letter dated S.ii Epiphany, 18 January 1885, this time not so much about roses as religion:

The Protestant protest is so unwise and so unjust that I have sent a few words of remonstrance to the *Liverpool Courier*, which will appear, I suppose, on Tuesday. Just when Christianity needs all its auxiliaries to battle against sin and unbelief, there is something very sad in a number of clergymen coming forward as accusers of the brethren, because they do not work in the same yard, or use precisely the same tools, as themselves.

I must hurry home from Liverpool for I am working against time. I conduct the mission at St Paul's, Knightsbridge, Feb. 7 to 17, giving an address at 12 and sermon at 8. I *greatly admire* the Penny Dinners. . . .

and about a week later, again to Mr Hall:

I have to speak at a Meeting of Working Men in Derby on Thursday evening, and hope to reach Liverpool at 1.20 p.m. on Friday, so that I may have the afternoon for work. It would be a great pleasure to grasp your hand, and have a smile from your beaming eye, if you can kindly realize your suggestions and meet me at the Central Station. I was preaching at Macclesfield on Wednesday and heard high praise of your new Bishop. He had greatly encouraged the Church people by a most unmistakeably Catholic sermon. . . .

Another rose contact; this time was with Francis Rivers. Writing from Caunton, 6 August 1886:

Dear Mr Rivers, I propose to write, if I can find the time, an article on Roses for The Quarterly Review. . . . Will you kindly inform me when "The Rose Amateur's Guide" was *first* published by my beloved friend, your father? I have "A new descriptive catalogue of Roses, cultivated and sold by Thomas Rivers and Son", and issued in 1834 (Probably the first important catalogue ever published): but I have only the Third Edition of the book . . . and do not know the date of their predecessors. . . .

Francis Rivers must have sent him the first edition, as on 9 August he acknowledges its safe arrival. "To that little book we owe the great development of Rose-love and Rose-lore which has gradually increased in this country since it was published." In a further letter dated 28 September 1886, Canon Hole returns the precious first copy:

. . . What innocent happenings that book has diffused throughout the land. It is more than forty years since I devoured it, little thinking that the author would ever sign himself, in writing to me: "Once your Master, now your Pupil". Kindly said by the dear old man, but he had forgotten more than I ever knew. How I loved and love him! Gratefully and sincerely yours, S. Reynolds Hole.

In February 1887, he is writing once more to his wife on mission work, this time from Wolverhampton:

There is to be a grand gathering of working men tonight, and the Bishop of Lichfield has just paid me the compliment of asking me to speak last, "because", he says, "they won't listen to anybody afterwards." It's all very nice, but only makes me wish that I could do more practical work for the men. I must attend to my speech and sign myself—lovingly yours, S. Reynolds Hole.

On Tuesday, 21 June 1887, Her Majesty's Jubilee Thanksgiving Service was held in Westminster Abbey, to which Canon and Mrs Hole were invited. Caroline was writing to her son, wishing that he "could go in her place". On 15 October she is writing to him with "my best wishes for your 25th. birthday". She sends blessings and his father's good wishes. "I have been working so hard all day, picking apples, and pulling up rubbish in my fernery. I wish I had a daughter to help me, for my old back is quite stiff with stooping so long." She signs herself... "Heaps of love from your old Mother, Caroline Hole." She could only have been about forty-six years old, but this was not a grumble merely a statement of fact. In her own way at home she worked as hard as he did and much of it was done to help with the finances.

Now comes his appointment as Dean of Rochester, and it seems significant that one of the first letters he should write on the very day of receiving an official notification of his new post should be to Joe Birley. It is addressed from Caunton Manor, dated 10 December 1887 and begins:

Dear Old Friend, It gives me special pleasure to write, because I know that it will give you special pleasure to read, that I have a letter from the Marquis of Salisbury this morning, in which he says that "the Queen has been graciously pleased to name me for the Deanery of Rochester".... I hope by God's grace to do some service for my Divine Master, among the soldiers, sailors, dockyard labourers and other working men. You must come to Caunton before we leave— I should think in two or three months. I trust that your health improves and that your wife and family are well. Yours always truly, S. Reynolds Hole.

Shortly after 13 December he received the following from one of his co-workers for the Rose Society:

Horticultural Club, 1 Henrietta Street, Covent Garden, W.C. Dec. 13, 1887.

My dear Hole, Altho' I am an Evangelist of the old school & you a High Churchman of the new order, yet I do most heartily congratulate you on your appointment to the Deanery of Rochester, and delighted that we shall have you in the County altho' not in my diocese—and I am sure you will endeavour to promote all that is good. I trust God's blessing may be with you. Your Ever affly., H. Honywood D'Ombrain.

It must have been one among many as he wrote to T. B. Hall on Christmas Eve:

My dear Hall, I have a sure conviction that of all the congratulations which I have received, some hundreds, none have been *more* hearty, *very few so* hearty, as those from my beloved friends at Larchwood. I know those bright eyes of yours would sparkle when they saw the news, and that you would read it, even more joyfully, in your unselfish sympathy, than the "First Prize and Cup" so dear to the Rosarian's gaze. We have been to inspect Rochester, and met with a most kindly reception. The Deanery is a large rambling old house, and there is a spacious garden, with no signs of horticulture! We want a gardener . . .

William Francklin, the Dean's nephew (since died), of Gonalston, related a small incident about this first visit. He was being taken round by Miles, the Verger, and in the Deanery garden they came to rather a large post in the ground. The Dean asked if this could be removed as it was in the way and appeared to have no purpose, and Miles replied: "Oh, that's only removed for the Dean's funeral." The Dean's comment afterwards was: "What a nice introduction!"

There were, of course, many references to his appointment in the current press. The *Church Times* reports the event "with very great satisfaction" and goes on:

There is probably no clergyman in the Church of England better known or more respected, and his appointment to the deanery will be acknowledged by all parties as a recognition of the great services he has rendered the Church, both as a mission preacher and a defender of her rights.

Other papers mentioned his books, his various clerical appointments such as his becoming Rural Dean of Southwell in 1873, a Prebendary of Lincoln in 1875, Select Preacher to Oxford University, 1885–1886, and 1885–1886 Proctor in Convocation for the archdeanery of Southwell. And all emphasize his work "as an able preacher and an earnest parish priest. He was a philanthropist, an earnest worker in every movement, either moral or physical of those amongst whom he lived . . . and was one of the best known and popular clergymen in the diocese."[10]

Farewell presentations were made to the new Dean and Mrs Hole, at Southwell and at Caunton, the latter being especially touching. It was understandable that qualities which had brought about these various appointments and promotions during the years should now culminate in his appointment as Dean of Rochester, yet it was these same qualities which had endeared him to Caunton, "and their sorrow and regret in thus losing him and Mrs Hole from their midst was very great. . . ." The Dean replied with some difficulty—he was much moved by their affection for him and his wife.

He would not say farewell, he hoped often to see and meet them again and trusted from time to time to preach to them in their dear old church. . . . Many he had baptized—many he had married & their children baptized . . . and he did not think there was a bedroom in any house in the parish in which at some time or another he had not knelt in prayer by a bedside. . . . He would remember them in his prayers. For years past he had prayed, if not twice, certainly once a day for them, and he begged them to remember him and his dear wife in their prayers.

This feeling of loss in the parish of Caunton was very real. It was known that people walked the five miles to and from Newark to hear him preach on a Sunday evening and his interest in every parishioner and readiness to help in their needs had become their great support. He was a true shepherd of his flock.

But the mood was not all of sadness and many of the messages of congratulation from friends who knew him well showed a lack of formality; they knew a lighter note would not be misunderstood. "I hope he will make a good Dean and behave as Deans should . . .",[11] "How I should like to see you in a shovel hat and gaiters!",[12] and

There once was a Dean of Rochester
Who measured four feet round the chest, sir,
   He said mass in red
   With a thing on his head,
That Ritualist Dean of Rochester.[13]

Once established at Rochester he plunged straight away into various activities, such as special Sunday evening services, much public speaking for local charities, et cetera, and preaching in various churches of the diocesan area. Many of these were fully reported by local newspapers, commenting as often as not on the size of the congregation. "Dean Hole preached to a large congregation at Rochester Cathdral on Sunday morning from the words, 'Beloved, let us love one another, for love is of God'. . . ."

The Dean of Rochester, the Rev. Dr Hole, addressed a powerful sermon to a full congregation in Chatham Parish Church on Sunday evening on the subject of the education, and especially the religious education of children . . . [23 June 1888]

Notwithstanding the exceedingly wet and unpleasant weather, the nave of the cathedral was again crowded on Sunday evening, when the Dean of Rochester delivered an eloquent sermon upon the words, "A certain man had two sons; and the younger of them said to his father, Father give me the portion of goods that falleth to me. And he divided unto them his living [14 July 1888]

Spite of the wet evening, the nave of Rochester Cathedral was again filled at the special service on Sunday evening five minutes after the gates were opened. A crowd had collected outside and when the bolts were slipped there was quite a rush for seats. [28 July 1888].

The nave of Rochester Cathedral was again crowded to its utmost limits on Sunday evening last (fully 1,000 persons being present) when Dean Hole continued his series of discourses upon the career of the Prodigal Son. [5 August 1888]

The Dean was President of The Industrial Home for Friendless Girls, especially for girls with no home background at all or where the home influence was a bad one, and frequently chaired their meetings. Another concern close to his heart was the Prevention of Cruelty to Animals and, at a meeting in June 1888, he spoke at some length about cruelty to horses, ending with this story:

Some time ago in his (the Dean's neighbourhood) there was a great deal of cruelty on a certain road, and a lady who was sorely grieved to see it, did not go to a male champion but herself took out a summons, appeared in the witness box and got the offender convicted and fined a couple of pounds, and from that time to this complaints had been very rare and infrequent. That lady he (the Dean) was thankful to say was his wife, and had she been in Rochester she would most certainly have attended the meeting.

Mrs Hole had not yet moved to Rochester as she had had to close up the house, arrange the sale of some of the furnishings and effects which was held on 17 May 1888, and organize the move of all the livestock to Kent from Nottinghamshire which included a certain number of pigs. It is suggested that these were kept to help to increase the family budget and evidently caused quite a stir when they arrived in the Deanery garden.

Dame Sybil Thorndike, much of whose childhood was spent at Rochester where her grandfather was a canon of the cathedral, recalls that Caroline had a pet one, called Ianthe, which followed her about the house, and that when she arrived at the Deanery there was a general enquiry: "What is the new Dean's wife like?" To which came the reply: "Oh, she's a great farming woman and brought her pigs with her." In fact, Caroline had known nothing whatever about pigs and had learnt all she knew from the old shepherd, Luke, at Caunton. However, the populace got it into their heads that she was an expert, and so directed their conversation into channels relative to pigs for some time to come. "What is the matter with these people?" Dame Sybil remembered her saying. "They think I can only talk about pigs."

It was Caroline who did most in the Deanery garden, with the help of one full-time gardener, Etherton, and a boy. But, as William Robinson was one of their first visitors—on 25 July 1888—it is highly probable that he advised on the large-sized garden "with no signs of horticulture". In a letter, which must have been among the first written from the Deanery at Rochester, and dated 5 November 1888; Dean Hole refers to the state of the garden.

Yes, my dear Edward [Woodall?], mine *is* a busy life; but I do not forget my genial friends, and much appreciate the refreshment which I have in their kind remembrances of me . . . Our predecessors "did not like a garden"—(I remember a servant of ours, who "didn't think much of the sea"), and so we have hard times before us. We begin with a long border of hardy flowers, backed by a wall of roses (the Dijon family, Hyb. Bourbons and Boursaults, Sempervirens,

and *Teas* galore); and tho' they tell me I can't grow roses, I have satisfied myself already (as you on your cliff) to the contrary ...
PS: Carnations grow here beautifully. Of course you have seen "Mrs Reynolds Hole" and our friend Robinson sent a lovely seedling to be called "The Dean".

The Dean was writing, as usual, to his "best beloved" when he was away from home, and on the first big mission he undertook as the Dean of Rochester, he wrote to her from the north of England.

Preston, Saturday, October 6th.
Own dearest, I flatter myself that you will like to hear that, tho' one of my legs gently intimates that I have had enough tramping on the Manchester pavements, I am quite well, after 10 sermons or speeches in 10 successive days.

The Congress has been a grand success, and no one has enjoyed it more than I have. It was so very pleasant to be with the Bishop of Manchester, a grand man ... I went one night to a great meeting of working men, about 3,000, in the Free Trade Hall, to listen and to rest, without a thought of speaking; and suddenly, to my astonishment, there came a cry of "Canon Hole", "Hole", "Hole", from all parts of the Building. The Bishop rose and said: "If you working men would rather hear Dean Hole than speak yourselves, or hear the other speakers, I have no doubt the Dean will find something to say to you;" on which they cheered, and the Dean made a very poor speech, but they seemed quite satisfied. The fact is, they know that my heart is with them, and they reciprocate.

I am going to Liverpool this afternoon, for 3 sermons and a speech and then shall bring what remains of your old man to Rochester on Tuesday. Archdeacon Farrar* and Knox Little were my companion speakers at a meeting of working men, over 3,000, held here last night. Farrar gave an excellent address but dear Knox Little is not what he was. The London Guardian has a complimentary leading article on my speech on "Gambling and Betting". . . .

---

* Later Dean of Canterbury and author of *Eric; Or Little by Little*. He officiated at the marriage of Hugh Hole to Geraldine Markham in April 1889.

13

Three Gardening Friends

IN THE OPENING chapter of *Our Gardens* Dean Hole asked various
people of different tastes and ages what they felt was the purpose of a
garden. A schoolboy replied instantly: "strawberries". The boy had a
younger sister who said "croquet" and an elder who said "garden
parties". A young man up at Oxford plumped for "lawn tennis and
cigarettes" and a senior tutor of the same establishment declared that
"a garden was designed for botanical research, and for the classification
of plants". The Dean then asked "a middle-aged nymph, who wore a
feathered hat of noble proportions" and she replied: "What is a garden
for? For the soul, sir, for the soul of a poet." An elderly gentleman
confessed that "nothing in horticulture touched him so sensibly as
green peas and new potatoes", and a morbid millionaire "declared that
of all his expenses he grudged most the outlay on his confounded
garden".

But the Dean sums up with "the unkindest cut of all, so common
that it makes one callous", and this comes when visitors declare how
much they "would be delighted to see our garden!" and they come and
see and forget to be delighted. They "admire the old city walls which
surround it, they like to hear the cawing of the rooks, they are pleased
with the sundial and the garden-chairs, but as for horticulture they
might as well be in Piccadilly!"

It is really only the visitor who, like the last-mentioned, asks to see
the garden with a *pretence* of interest who casts the gloom. The gentleman looking forward to his new potatoes or the boy to his strawberries
belong to a much less formidable category—both, in their own way,
worthy subjects for interest.

The book from which these instances are quoted was dedicated to:
WILLIAM ROBINSON, "author of *The English Flower Garden*, with
admiration of his genius, congratulations on his success, and pleasant
memories of his friendship".

Known as the originator of the herbaceous border and champion
of the wild garden, William Robinson was also the vanquisher of the
Victorian formal garden, especially as practised at the Royal Botanic

Gardens, Kew, under Sir Joseph Hooker. When he was born in Ireland in July 1838 the formal garden in England was well on its way to success; when he died, at the age of ninety-seven, the picture was a very different one. "But", wrote Mr Ralph Dutton in *The English Garden*,

> long before the close of Queen Victoria's reign better influences were at work under the leadership of William Robinson, who in the course of his long life brought an overwhelming improvement in the standard of gardening and, as the virtual introducer of the herbaceous border, may be said to have created a greater change in the English garden than any of his contemporaries.[1]

Little is known of his boyhood except that he started his gardening career on the estate of an Irish baronet, Sir Hunt Johnson-Walsh, at Ballykilcannan. He must have acquitted himself well because at twenty-one he was already in charge of the large range of greenhouses. Then comes the story of his bitter quarrel, either with his employer or with the head gardener—there seems to be some doubt about the exact details. The fact emerges that on a cold winter night the fires for heating the greenhouses were either drawn out or allowed to die out and some accounts say that the windows were opened wide. Meanwhile Robinson was on his way by foot to Dublin, where he arrived early the next morning. Those greenhouses at Ballykilcannan had been full of tender plants, most of them raised from seeds, and cuttings from these had been taken, probably by the young man himself, representing hours of loving care and attention. Thus it seems unlikely that Robinson would destroy the fruits of his own labours. However, there is another version of this story which says that Robinson was well on his way to Dublin before he remembered that he had not stoked up the fires. This seems the more probable and certainly the kindlier of the two to believe.

On his arrival in Dublin he went at once to see Dr David Moore, head of the Botanical Garden at Glasnevin who was an old family friend, and poured out his story and asked for help and advice. Dr Moore must have felt that there was some justice on his side as he gave him an introduction to the Curator of the Royal Botanic Garden Society in London. He was given work, rapidly rising to foreman again, but for obvious reasons he was not put in charge of the glasshouses. Instead he was given the hardy herbaceous plants to care for, which included wild flowers found in England. These two things must have influenced his future career considerably. He became the founder of the herbaceous border and wrote fervently in praise of a wild garden. Naturally enough he ever afterwards disliked greenhouses, and abolished them all from his home at Gravetye.

In 1867 Robinson became horticultural correspondent for *The Times* and in 1868 published his first book, *Gleanings from French Gardens*, a signed copy of which he presented to Dean Hole, inscribed 18 May. As he explains in the Preface: "Some of the matters treated of in this book have lately been the subjects of much discussion in *The Times*. . . . I went to France in January 1867, with a view to study the horticulture of the country so far as possible while continuing my connection with the horticultural press; . . ."[2]

After further visits to Paris, from whence he travelled to other gardens in France, and a journey into Italy via the Swiss Alps, Robinson paid his first visit to the States in the autumn of 1870.

This interest in America was not entirely focused on seeing gardens, as it had been in France and Italy, but rather on an energetic hunting for new trees and shrubs and for meeting the American people. Certain American gardens he visited and commented on—George Washington's old home at Mount Vernon being one of them—but it was the noble trees and flowering shrubs found on mountain slopes which meant most to him.

It was in this same year that *The Wild Garden* was published by John Murray, following on *Alpine Flowers for English Gardens*. The first edition of the former of these two books contains in Part IV an enchanting essay entitled "The Garden of British Wild Flowers". For some reason this was not included in later editions which deprives those not fortunate enough to possess or have access to the first edition of some of his best writing. Depending here on his own direct style, he discusses a water plant:

Not rare—growing, in fact, in nearly all districts of Britain—but exquisitely beautiful and singular is the Buckbean or Marsh Trefoil, with its flowers elegantly and singularly fringed on the inside with white filaments, and the round unopened buds, polished on the top with a rosy red like that of an apple blossom. In early summer when seen trailing on the soft ground near the margin of a stream, this plant is very beautiful and should be grown in abundance in every piece of ornamental water. It will grow in a bog or any moist place, or by the margin of any water.

So far the rather feverish approach of some of his later writing is not apparent. It is his genuine love of naturally growing plants, shrubs and trees which shines through the written words. In 1871 he founded his own gardening journal and the Rev. Reynolds Hole describes helping him to choose a title for it:

... I sat down with my friend, William Robinson, under a tree in the Regent's Park, and suggested THE GARDEN as a title for the newspaper which he proposed to publish, and which has been so powerful in its advocacy of pure horticulture of the natural, or English, school, free from rigid formalities . . .[3]

This description by Dean Hole enumerates the gardening aims of William Robinson as clearly as one could wish. He even here attributes the "natural" type of garden to the "English" school and describes it as being free from rigid formalities, et cetera. It is a measured declaration of a way of gardening under the leadership of the author of *The Wild Garden*.

The first issue of *The Garden* was published on 25 November and soon the contributors included many well-known gardening names: Dean Hole, in the first issue writing on "The Time Of Roses" and about six weeks later on "Roses and Rose Culture" and "The Six Of Spades"; Canon Ellacombe; James Britten, from 1871–1909 the Assistant in the Department of Botany, British Museum Natural History; Oliver Wendell Holmes, and Ruskin. There is little doubt that Robinson had read a good deal of Ruskin's work, and his writing shows this influence from time to time.

The Garden was not a financial success but it helped to establish Robinson more firmly in the world of journalism and provided a useful platform from which he could expound his ideas unhindered. His selection of authors and articles was often of general interest. For instance an article by Ruskin in the issue dated 3 February 1872 entitled "North and South" gave the physical characteristics of countries, birds and animals, and in 1879 he had an article by William Morris on "The Art of the Future", by the Rev. Wolley Dod from Cheshire on "A Substitute for Nettles", and from Reynolds Hole a series of articles on the "Tea-scented Rose". Other contributors included the Rev. H. D'Ombrain, Canon Ellacombe, Edward Woodall of Scarborough and Gertrude Jekyll.

In 1879 he launched another gardening journal, *Gardening Illustrated*, written largely for the wealthy dwellers of suburbia. This was such a financial success that he was able to invest money in London house property.

Published from The Garden Office, 37 Southampton Street, Covent Garden, in 1882, was a different venture entitled *God's Acre Beautiful or The Cemeteries of the Future*. Like Miss Burdett-Coutts, William Robinson was concerned about the state of urban churchyards, over-crowded, without dignity or beauty, lacking often even in rudimentary hygiene. This is a tastefully designed publication, with delight-

Caroline Hole, with the carnation that bears
her name, by Sir Herbert Olivier.

Gloire de Dijon, one of the roses most favoured by Reynolds Hole,
growing today in the Royal Horticultural Society Garden at Wisley.

ful illustrations in sepia, many of them showing early Greek and Roman urns. One full-page consists of "marble, porphyry and terracotta cinerary urns and chests" drawn from specimens in the British Museum. Something of the same kind could be incorporated into what would be, in effect, a natural garden, with stretches of grass and plantings of trees. The scheme for "Cemeteries of the Future" would ensure an atmosphere of peace and restfulness which would also be economical in upkeep. A vista of grass, the dignity of well-chosen trees—these would take the place of headstones, toppling or sloping as the years go by, of untidy grass verges which are almost impossible to cut owing to protruding stonework, or the sadness of floral tributes perished and dishevelled.

Like his friend, Dean Hole, he had always been an advocate of grass and the Dean quotes him in *Our Gardens*: "The lawn", writes Mr Robinson, "is the heart of the garden, and the happiest thing that is in it." The Dean goes on: "Flowers may come and leaves may go, the lawn goes on for ever. It refreshes the spirit through the eye, which never tires." When William Robinson looked at the depressing sights of some of the London cemeteries of the period, his imagination must have conjured up the smooth and dignified effect of a stretch of grass.

When the announcement of his death was inserted in *The Times*, it was one of three amongst a long list where the funeral service was announced as being followed by cremation.

His next, and perhaps most important, publication came in November 1883—*The English Flower Garden*,[4] "Design and Arrangement shown by existing examples of Gardens in Great Britain and Ireland followed by a Description of the best Plants for the Open-air Garden and their Culture". It was published by John Murray and dedicated to Canon Hole.

He writes in the Introduction to the fifth edition of June 1896:

The English Flower Garden consists of two parts: the first dealing with the question of design—the aim being to make each place at various seasons an epitome of the great garden of the world itself. I hope to prove that the true way to happiest design is not to have any stereotyped style for all flower gardens, but that the best kind of garden grows out of the situation, as the primrose grows out of a cool bank.

The second part includes most of the plants, hardy and half-hardy, for our flower gardens, and it is illustrated with a view to show the beauty of many of the plants, as few know the many flowers worth a place in our open-air gardens, and it is useless to discuss arrangement

if the beauty of the flowers is hidden from us. . . . At present, too
often there is no art, no good grouping, no garden pictures, no
variety—little but repetitions of ugly patterns. The choke-muddle
shrubbery, in which the shrubs kill each other, shows betimes a few
ill-grown plants, and has wide patches of bare earth in summer, over
which pretty green things might crowd. Yet the smallest garden may
be a picture, and not only may we have much more variety in any
one garden, but, if we give up imitating each other, may enjoy
charming contrasts between gardens.

For this second half of the book he acknowledges the use of articles
taken from *The Garden*, and also the help of many contributors who
had written on specialist subjects. Amongst these was, of course, Miss
Jekyll and except for the first few paragraphs, the chapter on "Colour
in the Flower Garden" is all her work. Others include her friends Miss
Ellen Willmott, Edward Woodall and G. F. Wilson. France is represented by Maurice de Vilmorin and an acknowledgement goes also to
Mr H. G. Moon, a painter of flowers whose work was much admired
by Mr Robinson—he had a collection of his flower pictures at Gravetye
Manor.

His home, Gravetye, near East Grinstead in Sussex, is a fine Elizabethan manor which, owing to the success of his *Gardening Illustrated*
and his investments in London house property, he was able to purchase, together with several hundred acres of rich pasture and woodland, in 1884. The following letter with the enlarged heading on the
writing paper, although from the same office, reflects the growth of his
journalistic activities.

(any reply to this to be marked private on envelope)
W. ROBINSON,   ·   37, Southampton Street,
The Garden   Strand, London, W.C.
Gardening Illustrated
Farm and Home
                                        Dec. 28th. 1887.

Dear Dean Hole,
Frank Mills has sent me a long letter without any signature. It is the
most inconsequent thing ever sent to me. I do not send it fearing you
will now have too much correspondence. I know no one "nearer" to
him than you. He speaks of his marriage and of your marrying him.
The curious letter leads me to fear that something may be wrong
with his mind. I sincerely hope I may be wrong! Thanks for kindly
note. I am really glad you are coming nearer us but what will

Caunton say to it and how are you going to leave the old home and parish! It must be more than a home to you!

always truly yours,

W. Robinson.

In a letter to his wife dated 12 September 1889, the Dean wrote describing a visit to the manor house:

Dearest Own,

Delightful day with Robinson at Gravetye Manor yesterday, and you must take Isa to see it, before the beauty of the garden is gone. The only drawback is the tedious tardy journey by rail, and you must not arrange to give only one day to the visit: in fact, it would not be practicable. You must go from London and return for the night. Victoria is the station and the Hotel Windsor might be your place of sleep.

Think of Robinson, the working gardener, Lord of the manor of Gravetye and 700 acres of land!

The house is Elizabethan, of gray stone, as pretty and comfortable a home as man could desire, surrounded by woods, green fields, hills, slopes, and distant views, with 7 acres of lake. The stables cost £2000. I asked him if he had any horses and his reply was "30". He does not live in the Manor House, at present unfurnished, but in a smaller house adjoining. The plan is of course in process of formation and will ultimately be, on a small scale, one of the most attractive abodes in the land.

I brought back a huge bouquet of tea roses. . . .

Some years later William Robinson laid paving close to the house so that he could get round and see his plants from his wheel chair—from the age of about seventy he lost the use of his legs—and Miss Jekyll used to remark that, in spite of all his claims to "natural" gardening he had, in fact, a piece of formal gardening made to his own design at Gravetye.

His journalistic writings, due to his "ferocious" style, strained many friendships including that of the kindly Canon Ellacombe who found some difficulty in bearing with Robinson's outbursts. Latin plant labelling came under his fire as also the railings round London parks. On a visit in the summer of 1898 with Dean Hole to Pope's garden at Twickenham he did not hesitate to express indignation at the alterations perpetrated by Sir William Stanhope.

In *Our Gardens*, there are the following references to Robinson: "Three friends, three famous friends—Mr Robert Marnock aforesaid, Mr William Robinson, and Mr William Ingram . . . came to give *me* not advice merely, but personal, practical help."; ". . . and when in the summer of 1898 I went with my friend Mr William Robinson, the author of the *English Flower Garden*, on a pious pilgrimage. . . ."; and, discussing progress in the design and beauty of rock gardening—"Mr Robinson has been foremost in this, as in so many other branches of hardy floriculture, to encourage and to teach, by his exhaustive volume on 'Alpine Flowers' and his commentary in the *English Flower Garden*[4]. . . ."; and referring to the planting of a wild garden "And then I should go, and I advise my readers to go, to the supreme authorities; to Mr William Robinson, who in his *Wild Garden* (inscribed to his proud friend, the Dean of Rochester) revived the idea of a supplemental garden. . . ." It was a friendship which extended over many years.

In 1899 Robinson gave up the editorship of *The Garden* to Miss Jekyll, with whom he had one of his more peaceful friendships lasting for many years. He had often visited her garden at Munstead and when she died in December 1932 he travelled thirty miles by road to be present at her funeral. They lived over much of the same period of time and they fought together for the natural garden which was their creation.

Although he waged the battle against formal design throughout his life, not all his writing was dogmatic and he became almost lyrical when writing about the wild flowers of the English countryside and especially the cottage gardens. In the *English Flower Garden* he wrote: "Those who look at sea or sky or wood see beauty that no art can show; but among the things made by man nothing is prettier than an English cottage garden."

Gertrude Jekyll shared Robinson's affection for the cottage garden. She acknowledged her debt on many occasions to the plantings seen in small roadside gardens: "Some of the most delightful of all gardens", she wrote in her first book, *Wood and Garden*,

> are the little strips in front of roadside cottages. They have a simple and tender charm that one may look for in vain in gardens of greater pretension. And the old garden flowers seem to know that there there they are seen at their best; for where else can one see such wallflowers, or double daisies, or white rose bushes . . . I have learnt much from the little cottage gardens that help to make our English waysides the prettiest in the temperate world. One can hardly go into the smallest cottage garden without learning or observing something new.[5]

But Miss Jekyll had other ideas in common with William Robinson and one of the most important was the introduction of natural gardening as opposed to formal bedding-out. Whereas his interpretation of natural gardening was based on practical experience from his boyhood upwards, Miss Jekyll's was largely due to an art training she had as a young woman.

Born in 1843 and given an intelligent upbringing which included the study of Greek, German, painting and music, she went to the Kensington School of Art. At the age of nineteen she was fortunate enough to travel to the Greek islands with Charles Newton (the distinguished excavator of Halicarnassus and Keeper of the Greek and Roman Antiquities at the British Museum) and his wife, who was the painter Mary Severn, daughter of Joseph Severn the friend and companion of Keats. Mrs Newton had studied drawing at home—copying the engravings of Dürer and portraits by George Richmond—in Paris under Ary Scheffer, and later returning to England to paint the royal family.

The two young women painted in most of their spare time on this trip and especially made great use of opportunities for drawing on the island of Rhodes, where they stayed for three weeks. It may be true to say that this journey influenced her taste and ideas not only in her artistic studies but in the later development of her gardening talents. Miss Jekyll described Mary Newton as "one of the best and kindest friends I ever had"[6] and it must have been a sad blow when she fell ill with a severe attack of measles at her home in Gower Street in 1866, and died as a result.

Miss Jekyll's other close friend was Madame Bodichon, a founder of Girton and a painter of some standing. She made enough by selling some of her work to be able to contribute £1,000 towards a fund for the foundation of Girton. They were often fellow visitors to Oaklands, Sedlescombe, the home of Hercules Brabazon, the well-known watercolour painter, and it was from him that Miss Jekyll learnt her lessons in colour which stood her in good stead in her gardening many years later.

Every connection seemed at this time to lead towards painting. However, in middle life, her eyes began to trouble her seriously and she was advised to give up all close work, especially painting and needlework. One can imagine what this must have meant to an artist, but it is strange to think what it has since meant to the gardening world.

Fortunately for Miss Jekyll she had not followed her painting to the exclusion of everything else, and, as we have seen, she had already written gardening articles for William Robinson's journal *The Garden*, having visited his office as early as January 1875. Dean Hole was, of course, one of the contributors and it was he who eventually took William Robinson out to see Miss Jekyll's garden at Munstead near Godalming.

At this crucial turning point in her life there came a meeting at the house of Harry Mangles (expert in rhododendron growing) with a young architect named Edwin Lutyens. With him she was to form a partnership which would influence English domestic architecture and the planning of gardens in this country for years to come. They worked together with lasting results, some of which may be seen today in certain of the gardens which have been cared for in that tradition. One which comes to mind is the garden of Great Dixter, Northiam, Sussex. Miss Jekyll's influence may be seen in the juxtaposition of many of the plants and the general planning of the large border, which includes some of her favourite grey-foliaged plants. Deanery garden, Sonning, Berkshire, is another example of which Mr Christopher Hussey wrote: "Miss Jekyll's naturalistic planting wedded Lutyen's geometry in a balanced union. . . ."[7]

It was about the turn of the century when the Deanery garden, Rochester, was completed and so Miss Jekyll must have been on close terms with the Dean and his wife for many years before, according to a letter written from Munstead Wood and dated 9 March 1900, to Mrs Hole:

My dear Carry,
I cannot be forbidden to answer your most welcome letter. How I wish we were neighbours within dropping-in-to-tea reach. I am so glad of your good words about "Home and Garden". Yes, it is too hard that a real countrywoman like you should live in a town and away from the good simple things and clean air that we were certainly meant to live with. Those H [illegible] are grand things and if I did not say much about them it was because they are such rampant rooters that I have had to banish them from the flower border proper.
I wish I could think you were likely to be here some day in the summer.
                                        Yours affectionately,

Miss Jekyll was not the person to wish anyone living close enough to her to be on "dropping-in-to-tea" terms unless she was fond of them and felt on familiar ground. Her acute myopia may have been responsible for this rather reserved attitude to visitors—she had a natural vision of two inches—as well as the fact that she was anxious to fit into every available hour of time as much work as was possible. These precious hours grew less as she became more tired and she was not allowed as many working periods a day.

In spite of so much physical hindrance Miss Jekyll helped to advise or design at least 300 gardens; advice was sent all over England in the later years when travelling became difficult for her. Sir George Sitwell's garden at Renishaw, the Headmaster's garden at Charterhouse, the school's war-memorial garden at Winchester, Newnham College, Cambridge, were some of these, and smaller, more domestic, gardens included two in Hamilton Terrace, London, and a number in East Anglia, Northumberland, West Surrey and Scotland.

Miss Jekyll wrote books which are gardening classics including *Wood and Garden, Home and Garden*[8] (both about her Munstead Wood house and garden) and *Colour Schemes for the Flower Garden*.[9] She wrote one of the few gardening books for children[10] and also one of the first ever published in this country on flower arrangement.[11] She collaborated with Edward Mawley on *Roses for English Gardens* (it will be remembered that it was he who became Joint Hon. Secretary with the Rev. Honywood D'Ombrain of the National Rose Society in 1878, when Dean Hole was President) and also wrote a book on lilies,[12] one on wall and water gardens[13] and another on Old West Surrey.[14]

Dean Hole writes at some length in admiration of Miss Jekyll's *Wood and Garden*:

Miss Jekyll has given to horticultural literature the most perfect example of practical wisdom in combination with poetical thought. . . . It is her reverent appreciation of beauty which empowers her first to realize for herself, and then to impart to her readers, a sense of the grace and of the glory which surround us and which constrain us to join in the hymn of praise, "Oh all ye green things upon the earth, bless ye the Lord; praise Him and magnify Him for ever!" It is this divine affection which paints for us pictures far excellent than the photographs of her camera, though these too are excellent, as when she writes of January:

"The ground was a warm carpet of pale rusty fern; tree stem and branch and twig show tender colour harmonies of grey bark and silver-grey lichen, only varied by the feathery masses of birch spray. Now the splendid richness of the common holly is more than ever impressive, with its solid masses of full deep colour, and its wholesome look of perfect health and vigour. . . ." "June is here—thank God for lovely June! The soft cooing of the wood-dove, the glad song of many birds, the flitting of butterflies, the hum of all the little winged people among the branches, the sweet earth scents all seem to say the same, with endless reiteration, never wearying because so gladsome."

Long reign this Queen of Spades, as long, as happily, as Victoria, Queen of Hearts.[15]

Discussing later the wild garden planting ideas of William Robinson, the Dean goes on:

and Miss Jekyll will warn us that whatever may be our soil or our site, the attempt to improve nature, even in her rudest dress, is a very perilous process, and that there is need of the utmost anxious caution lest we disfigure that we would adorn. . . .

Unthinking persons rush to the conclusion that they can put any garden plants into any wild places, and that that is wild gardening. I have seen woody places, that were already perfect with their own simple charm, just muddled and spoilt by a reckless planting. . . .[16]

But nearer even to the Dean's heart than "natural" gardening, "wild" gardening or perhaps roses, was the small garden of the working man who had little time for gardening and no space to speak of where he could grow plants. Writing of the townsman who thinks "it worth a run upstairs to smell their mignonette or a descent to the back yard to contemplate their double wallflower",[17] he refers to an episode in Miss Jekyll's book with obvious admiration.

Miss Jekyll relates in *Wood and Garden* how a factory lad in one of the great Northern manufacturing towns advertised in a mechanical paper that he wanted a tiny garden in a window-box—would somebody help him? Somebody (I have my conjectures) sent him a box, three feet by ten inches, with little plants of mossy and silvery saxifrage and a few small bulbs. Even some stones were sent for, it was to be a rock garden with two hills and a long valley. "Somebody" seems to have known somehow of the boy's delight when the pure white of the snowdrop and the brilliant blue of the squill came forth in his attic window under that grey, soot-laden sky.[18]

(In fact, Miss Jekyll also reports that she had to dissuade the boy from overdosing his window-garden with stimulants.)

In his poem, "The Task", Cowper might have dedicated his lines to Miss Jekyll:

> Strength may wield the pond'rous spade,
> May turn the clod and wheel the compost home,
> But elegance, chief grace the garden shows
> And most attractive, is the fair result
> Of thought, the creature of a polish'd mind.

Another, who had, like Dean Hole, a deep affection for the rose, was "my friend Mr Shirley Hibberd".[19] He, too, has left a legacy of fine gardening books behind him.

Known best perhaps for his classic entitled *The Fern Garden* or *Fern Culture Made Easy*[20] first published in 1869, Shirley Hibberd was born in the parish of St Dunstan, Stepney in 1825. He was the son of a retired sea-captain, and it was intended that he should enter the medical profession. However, it was later obvious that medicine was out of the question. His father died young and this meant the boy following a trade. He was apprenticed to a Stepney bookseller.

The young man settled well into his work and soon became interested in writing himself. In a short time he was doing a certain amount of journalism, much of it devoted to various branches of horticulture. He had other enthusiasms—he was a vegetarian and a temperance advocate —but his interest in growing fruit, vegetables and flowers soon superseded everything else. He moved further out into the suburbs of London so that he could have greater opportunities for research and experience, most of which provided the material for his many books later on in life.

Like Miss Jekyll, William Robinson, Canon Ellacombe and others, he wrote from personal trial and error. In the preface to *The Amateur's Kitchen Garden* first published in 1877 he wrote:

> The book in the reader's hands has its defects no doubt—at all events, no pretensions are made to infallibility, or any near approach thereto —but it is no compilation: it is original in the fullest sense of the word, so far as it can be applied to such a work: and it embodies the results, in a comparatively small compass, of the work of a quarter of a century in gardens largely devoted to fruit and vegetable culture.[21]

It would be difficult to decide which were his special subjects in the fruit and vegetable world. He carried out various experiments on the potato and was consulted by the government over the potato disease in Ireland during the 'eighties. On the other hand, shortly before he died he had sent a letter to *The Times* entitled "Fruit Culture" which was later described as being written on his favourite subject.

As to the cultivation of fruit, every conceivable kind is fully discussed in *The Amateur's Kitchen Garden*. In the section on apricots it is interesting to note that the variety, Moorpark, heads his list of the best for "a small place", and that this is the variety which was obtained for the restocking of apricot trees at Aynho, Northamptonshire, and that earlier plantings "were the same or a very similar variety". Mrs Norris in *Mansfield Park* remonstrates with Dr Grant that his apricot tree in the

Parsonage garden must be good-tasting: "Sir, it is a Moor Park, we bought it as a Moor Park . . . and I know it cost seven shillings and was charged as a Moor Park". They had put it in against the stable wall and one feels that that indefatigable lady's verdict must also count for something.

In *Garden Glory* by Ted Humphris, there is the following reference: "MOORPARK is a hardy and vigorous variety—its fruit is very juicy and exceptionally large, particularly when the young fruit has been properly thinned."[22] From reading up some of the old fruit catalogues it would appear that the present-day Moorpark apricot is derived from the variety either raised or introduced by Lord Anson in 1760 at Moor Park, Hertfordshire. But this was not the first time it is said to have been introduced into this country. Sir William Temple introduced Moorpark from Brussels in 1652, but no one is quite certain whether he named it after his own garden Moor Park, then spelt More Park, at Farnham in Surrey, or another that he admired, Moor Park in Hertfordshire.

Going back to *The Amateur's Kitchen Garden*, Mr Hibberd has a cheerful piece of philosophy about the "enemies" of the kitchen garden: after instructions as to "Deep digging and liberal manuring" being the "surest preventitives" and exposing them (caterpillars, slugs, snails, et cetera) to "the keen eyes of the thrushes, and robins and nightingales" he settled for an optimistic disregard:

We must confess we do not trouble ourselves much about vermin, for life seems to be too short for such small things to interfere with our happiness. We mentally ignore their existence, and they probably sicken through loss of importance, for we so rarely suffer by their depredations, that we know of no better way than to persuade oneself that such things exist only in morbid imaginations.

Paul Valéry, talking about slugs, describes them as "that marvellous little population always in opposition".

In the pages after the index there are descriptions of some of his other books, including one on *The Ivy*.[23] Among many appreciative recommendations from contemporary journals there is the following from the *Scotsman*: "Mr Shirley Hibberd's 'Monograph of the Ivy' is a fine work and forms an enduring monument of his literary research . . . should the work become as popular as it deserves to be, ivy-hunting will become as favourite a pastime as fern-gathering."

As well as the book on Ivy and the one on the popular subject of Ferns, he also wrote another on roses[24] and yet another on field flowers.[25] Dean Hole, expounding on the desirability of pure air for rose-growing, mentions him as an example of what can be done in London: "I have seen good roses, it is true, which were grown within three miles and a half of St Paul's Cathedral, and were exhibited at the first Crystal Palace Rose Show by the grower, my friend Mr Shirley Hibberd."[26] This was at Stoke Newington and in *The Rose Book* Shirley Hibberd mentions this problem of impure air and how to overcome it with intensive culture and, sometimes, by the use of a glasshouse. Like Dean Hole he particularly praises the Gloire de Dijon.

But the book which may have had most to offer in the way of new material—based to some extent, no doubt, on the work of Sir Joseph Paxton—was *The Amateur's Greenhouse*,[27] which is full of practical details about the construction and costs of the actual buildings. In his introduction he writes:

Considering the treacherous nature of our climate and the length of the winter season, it cannot be said we have as yet attained to a full knowledge of the value of glass in horticulture. Nevertheless immense progress has been made since glass and bricks and timber were rendered free of duty. . . .[28]

The repeal of the glass tax in 1845 coinciding with the rise to power of the young gardener, Joseph Paxton, at Chatsworth had ensured that there should be adequate provision for the half-hardy plants arriving from abroad, the seal being set by the Crystal Palace of 1851. Shirley Hibberd also included a number of chapters on how to grow and care for some of these half-hardy plants, many of which were still at this time reasonably rare and of recent introduction into this country. His knowledge of orchids seems especially extensive.

In *The Fern Garden* there is a charming wood engraving showing the one built against his own house which had become a fern garden owing to a nearby construction blotting out the afternoon sun. This became Mrs Hibberd's care and delight about which he writes with understandable pride.

In the course of time, some building and planting took place a little way off towards the west, and the nice gleam of sunlight that enlivened the house from 2 p.m. till sunset was effectually blocked out, and the house became unfit for flowering plants. Instead of bringing an action against the neighbour who devoured my sunshine, I brought an action against myself, and the verdict was, that the shady house should be forthwith converted into a fernery.[29]

This approach to a problem which so often arises between neighbours in one form or another, shows good sense and tolerance as well as determination to turn what might have become a source of bitterness into a source of benefit and even pleasure, and throws a light on his character.

There is a reference in *The Fern Garden* to the state of the church-yards of the time and in yet another book, *Garden Favourites*, Shirley Hibberd comments on a stanza from Virgil where Aeneas scatters flowers on his father's grave:

> It is not surprising that a custom so highly poetical should have sur-vived to this day. In our new and beautiful cemeteries, which truly merit the German appellation of "God's Acre", compared with the old crowded town churchyards where it seemed a sacrilege to place the dead, we do but perpetuate a highly classic usage in our free use of flowers. The Christian fathers enjoined the decoration of graves as a duty . . .[30]

His claim that "gardens are unknown" in a great city seems to be an exaggeration if he has London in mind (and one imagines this to be so as he lived for many years within its environs). According to Thomas Fairchild, writing in 1722, there were already public gardens known for their collections of plants and, although some amateur gardeners found a certain difficulty in combating the smoke from the sea-coal, he writes: ". . . yet I find that almost every Body, whose Business re-quires them to be constantly in Town, will have something of a Garden at any rate. . . ."[31]

It is difficult to think of Shirley Hibberd without also recalling to mind the benefits of the "Wardian Case". He relates the history of its development, "being the invention of the late Mr B. N. Ward, an eminent surgeon, many years resident in Finsbury Circus, who died at a ripe age in 1868". Mr Hibberd reminds us of the importance of this Case, not only for the decoration of the home or the conservatory, but for its even greater value in making possible the transport of plants, shrubs and cuttings sent or brought from abroad by collectors at a time when sea travel was not only slow but also unreliable.

He writes of it first in *Rustic Adornments for Homes of Taste*, [32] perhaps the book which is most typical and indicative of his period: "Who would live contentedly, or consider a sitting-room furnished without either a Ward's Case or an Aquarium?" he asks. There are suggestions for ferns for the Wardian Case and fish for the Aquarium. Rustic seats for garden furniture, a "dark cave for the growth of mosses and ferns", sundials, arbours and beehives, all come to his notice. Describing the furnishings for a grotto he writes:

A rustic table, a rustic bench, and a locker would be useful, if ideas of picknicking came into one's head; and to enhance my own solitary and selfish enjoyment, I would have an inner chamber luxuriously furnished with a couch, a locker for whatever I might choose to put into it, such as a bottle of Burgundy and a box of cigars, and a few of the choicest books, quaintly bound, and arranged neatly in a recess. . . .[33]

Amongst other valuable information, this book gives a clear picture of the arrangement of flowers for indoor decoration in the mid-Victorian era. There is an illustration, for instance, of what he likes to describe as "a simple fireplace decoration". In the centre of the mantelpiece there is a large pedestal bowl supporting a heavy-leafed plant. Four others all contain flowers and below are three large vases, one full of foliage, another of flowers, and the third of grasses, flowers and leaves. This is not only an indication of the taste of the time, it is an example of the close link between the gardener and the flower arranger. No wonder Miss Jekyll wrote, about forty years later, "There comes a point where the room becomes overloaded with flowers and greenery. During the last few years I have seen many a drawing-room where it appeared to be less of a room than a thicket."[34]

Shirley Hibberd was taken ill on Sunday morning, 16 November 1890, and died within a few hours. On the previous Thursday he had attended the Chrysanthemum Society's dinner. He was a Fellow of the Royal Horticultural Society, a judge at the Guildhall Flower Show, and was considered to be one of the best authorities on the cultivation of fruit, vegetables and flowers of his time. He was the product of an age which provided unbelievable opportunities for industrious and detailed work, which encouraged it and expected it. Prolific in his literary output he was also a practical gardener trying out things for himself and with a great love for the natural countryside.

14

Letters and Lectures

1889–1900

"AND HE WROTE with a quill pen": Dame Sybil Thorndike remembering the Dean at Rochester, in the library, writing letters, writing books. How did he find time for his ever-growing correspondence, over which he took so much trouble? There was no dashing off a letter without care and thought—he would sometimes be so engrossed that he would forget engagements. Dame Sybil recalls the time that he was writing in his library. Whittaker, over seventy, old Samuel Hole's nurse, appeared. "The fly's at the door, sir." He went on writing: "Fly ... fly ... what should I want with a fly?" "Don't you remember that you're preaching at St Paul's and spending the night at the Deanery?" "God bless my soul—so I am." He rushed out, picked up his hat in the hall and off he went.

Letters were part of his life and there is correspondence, over a period of many years, with relatives, friends in the gardening world, members of the Church, members of his parish at Caunton and answers to enquiries about roses. Dean Gregory, the Archbishop of Canterbury, Canon Knox-Little, the Bishop of Argyll and the Isles, Dean Farrar, the Bishop of Rochester, Sir John Stainer (who wrote the music for some of the hymns written by the Dean), Sir Walter Parratt (Master of the Queen's Musick) and Canon Pollock are but some of the names connected with the Church, whilst the list of those writing about his books or especially about roses would be too long to enumerate. He enjoyed correspondence with most members of the *Punch* circle, especially, as we have seen with Henry Silver and, of course, John Leech. Letters from painters included Alfred Parsons, George Elgood and Charles Furse (who painted his portrait and also that of Mrs Hole).

A long correspondence went on with Joe Birley, James Blackney (a Caunton choir boy who went to work in the Railway Clearing House), Lord Halifax and Lord Salisbury, Conan Doyle, Edward Lyttleton and J. W. Maxwell Lyte. Occasional letters came from Edward Lear, the

Baroness Burdett-Coutts and Rudyard Kipling. But no matter from whom they came or to whom they were written, all received the same attention and consideration.

A more recent correspondent in 1888–9, was J. Henry Shorthouse, author of *John Inglesant*. In the preface to the 1881 edition the author explains that the book is an attempt at "Philosophical Romance". "Yes, it is only a Romance. It is only the ivory gates falling back at the fairy touch. It is only the leaden sky breaking for a moment above the bowed and weary head, revealing the fathomless Infinite through the gloom. It is only a Romance."[1]

The friendship between the two families was intimate and affectionate, humorous and lively. In a letter dated the first Sunday after Trinity 1891, Mr Shorthouse writes: "Mrs Hole deserves our grateful thanks for allowing you to write. I well remember how potent her influence for *good* is, as when she gently and sweetly persuaded us to go to bed, instead of injuring ourselves, by sitting up, smoking and drinking . . ."

Another correspondence, full of humour and fun and jokes was that carried on over some years with Dean Pigou. Francis Pigou stayed at Caunton in 1883 and later at Rochester. One of the Dean's shorter letters to him consists almost entirely of a rhyme and a joke:

> Dear Pigou
> Is *Truth* true?
> And are you
> Going to be
> D of C.? [Dean of Chichester]
> Personally I shall rejoice; but not to be too reticent, how about Income? But, as the lady said when congratulated on her daughter's engagement, "Ah, thanks; Jenny hates the man, but there's always a something." One thing I must impress on you; if you are going to be a Dean there is only one man in England who can make gaiters—all others are alligators. Come at once to Rochester. . . .

They used to buy really bad pictures together, and an especially terrible one of the "Death of Wolfe" was always kept by Pigou to hang above the Dean's bed when he visited him. "Someone—I imagine a surgeon—is dabbing a very large bath sponge in Wolfe's eye."[2] They bought it for five shillings [25p]. Then there was the joke about Lord Rothschild's purchase of *The Times* yesterday—"How much did he pay for it?" "He gave threepence," et cetera. In a letter dated November 1891, he writes:

Dear Pigou, Partly for my wife's health, partly for my own, and because I desire to see Naples and Rome and Venice, and may not have another opportunity, I have accepted the chaplaincy at Amalfi (in reply to an advertisement for an ecclesiastic of abnormal beauty and immense intellect) and shall be out of England in Lent.

I wish you had been with me on Sunday in a London Church. We had huge rainbows of tapers, incense as thick as a London fog (we were all specially censed), lace-edged cottas, copes, 20 banners, etc. You may guess how depressed your friend Moody felt, tho' I must say that there was real devotion, and the heartiest congregational singing. Rome is no longer "in it" . . . This was at evensong, so I suppose on greater occasions they have fireworks and artillery. Your affectionate frater, Decanus Hole.

Before leaving for Amalfi he had received the following letter from W. P. Frith the painter, and biographer of John Leech:

Ashenhurst, Sydenham Rise, S.E. Augt. 21, 1890.

Dear Sir, I am commissioned by Messrs Bentley to write the life of John Leech. You were one of his dearest friends & can—if you will—be of great assistance to me. You published "A Little Tour in Ireland" illustrated by Leech, have you a copy, & if you have & will kindly lend it to me, I need not say I would take the greatest care of it & return it to you in due course—I believe you had it in mind to write a life of Leech yourself as is shown by some most interesting fragments published by Dr John Brown, from which I have ventured to quote largely, & I am sure I shall find much that is valuable in the Irish Tour to say nothing of the illustrations some of which I should ask permission to reproduce. I shall be very grateful to you if you will help me in the way I propose, & if you have any letters of Leech which you would not object to see in print you would greatly add to my obligation if you would allow me to have them; to be carefully preserved & returned of course. In the hope of a favourable reply I am Dear Sir, Faithfully yours, W. P. Frith.

To the Right Revd. The Dean of Rochester.

Frith's biography paints an affectionate portrait of the man beloved by so many and presents his excellence as an artist with many examples of his work. Whether the Dean gave him any assistance is not certain but, as the *Life* was published in the year following this letter, time must have been running short: added to this, the Dean must already have been working on his own book, *The Memories of Dean Hole*,

Drawing of Miss Jekyll by Lutyens, c. 1896.

William Robinson, author of *The English Flower Garden*.

Shirley Hibberd (1825–1890.) seen walking away from his fern house. "In the cut the house is shown with a stage for flowering plants, as originally constructed. In the course of time, some building took place a little way off towards the west, and the nice gleam of sunlight that enlivened the house from 2. pm. till sunset was effectively blocked out . . . Instead of bringing an action against the neighbour who devoured my sunshine, I brought an action against myself, and the verdict was, that the shady house should forthwith be converted into a fernery . . . all I can say in concluding this part of the history is this, that I never did a better job in my life; . . ." (from *The Fern Garden.*)

which came out in 1892. He writes again to Dean Pigou in July 1892:

. . . I have so much work on hand and in contemplation here, that henceforth I must give up foreign service. [By this he means preaching for other churchmen, but not necessarily missions.] Moreover I have a book of Memories in preparation . . . In conformity with the announcements of the English Churchmen and other protestant accusers of the brethren I have been "over to Rome" and was bitterly disappointed with the same; always excepting St Peter's and the Vatican Galleries. We were all ill in that city of stinks, and my niece was in bed for a month with typhoid fever. Will you come with me to Chicago for the Exhibition? The Bishop of New York invites me to preach at the opening—expenses paid there and back. . . .

In November of the same year, he writes to his wife from a mission at Winchester:

You always make the best of yourself, and I can tell that, tho' you say that you are better, you are still far from well. The weather is hopelessly against invalids and here it is dripping and dreary from morn till night. Nevertheless you have a better air in Notts than at Rochester and I hope you will remain. . . . The perpetual rain is very unfavourable to the Mission which is being held throughout the city here, but we have good congregations. . . . I have made up my mind to retire from Foreign Service and wrote yesterday to Dean Gregory declining his usual invitation to St Paul's. I am too old to go scampering all over England, and there is plenty to do at home.

My Book is successful beyond my hopes, and has passed into a second edition before it has been published a week! The Liberal and Conservative, High Church and Low Church newspapers have alike most favourable reviews.

I go home on Friday. I shall sadly miss you, but don't come back until you feel stronger.

This last letter and the next few written to his wife indicate that she was making frequent return visits to her beloved Nottinghamshire in search of better health from the pure air of the country as opposed to the smoke-laden atmosphere of Rochester:

March 15th, 1893: I received your welcome little letter just before I left Halstead this morning, and hope that you have safely arrived among the old familiar places and faces. I enjoyed my London visit—

pleasant host and hostess, a beautiful church, with a congregation (morning) of 1000 people, chiefly men, and perfectly delicious weather. I arrived at Halstead about 4.30 p.m. and went next day to see Lamberhurst—such a pretty village, amid charming scenery of hill and valley, orchards and hop-yards. . . .

Sunday, February, 1894: My Best Beloved, I must send you a brief assurance that you are ever in my thought, and prayerful hope that you are fast recovering your health. . . . The Master of Trinity is a most agreeable host, and we have many mutual friends including Henry Nethercote of whom he tells me pleasant reminiscences. I preached in the grand old Chapel this morning, and we have a meeting this evening.

15th July, 1894: . . . I am much interested in your account of Caunton and longing for more. I should like to have been with you and Annie in Maplebeck Lane among the roses, if they were not over.

I can't help thinking about that poor tooth and shall heartily rejoice, when, like the Queen of Sheba, you have given up your ivory to the King. . . . Ever your fondly affectionate Reynolds.

At a Chapter-General of The Grand Priory of the Order of the Hospital of St John of Jerusalem in England, held on 9 August 1894, Dean Hole was selected for admission as a chaplain. The notification was dated 23 October and his declaration of Allegiance signed on 4 November.

It was during this year that there had come the invitation to lecture in America and, as he had already been approached by the publishers of *Memories* for a further instalment, he combined the two things, as he explained to a reporter: "—like the man who, having to write on 'Chinese Metaphysics', read up in the cyclopaedia under the letters C and M and combined his information."[3] Each separate chapter in *More Memories* was, in fact, a lecture for his tour. He had a good many different ones; "but", he remarked, "the people seemed to prefer 'Recollections of my Famous Friends' and next to that they liked 'Bores and Imposters', so I gave those mostly. They are taken from my second volume of 'Memories', which I wrote with the view of going to America."[4]

The lecture on "Bores" comes in chapter nineteen. As we know of his feelings for some of his "Famous Friends" but no idea at all of his reaction to "Bores" (unless from guesswork) excerpts from that lecture follow:

While I protest against these railing accusations, by which certain classes of the community are consigned to transportation for life, I would as earnestly denounce, and, in each individual and convicted case, condemn to exile or extinction, those bores, and imposters, and otherwise objectionable persons who infest and irritate society, like wasps at a picnic, or mosquitos—

"Oft in the stilly night, ere slumber's chain has found us,"

or gnats, when we have just made every arrangement to fish in our favourite pool. . . . .

. . . One would almost prefer to meet a herd of buffaloes in a blizzard than some of these stupendous bores. You feel a shrinking, a loss of vital power, as they approach. Like the rabbit, fascinated by the glittering eye of the weasel, you are powerless to escape. He gloats upon you as some famished spider upon an obese bluebottle, entangled in his mesh, and he tells you, that "you are the very man he most wished to see," just as a hawk might say in his swoop, "Of all the dear little sparrows in the universe, I love thee best."

He always chooses for his abominable and excruciating discourse some subject in which I have no interest whatever—a family quarrel, or a local meeting, his investments—or, of which I am profoundly ignorant, bimetallism, the last new thing in torpedoes, archaeology. I have no taste, I have no time, for archaeology. When an anti-quarian wrote to ask me whether I could give him any information as to the nailing of Danish skins to the great door of the cathedral, I was too much occupied with the bodies and souls of living Christians to inquire about the epidermis of the Danes. . . .

Oh that we could rid ourselves of the bore loquacious, who attacks us *viva voce*, as easily as of the bore epistolary, who assails us *currente calamo*! No; he holds you by the coat; he plays with you, as a cat with a mouse; he mouths you, and lets you go awhile, and, when you think there's an opportunity of escaping and make a movement accordingly, down comes his paw. As he goes prosing on, the brain seems to soften; as with the mouse, the position is altogether embarrassing. . .

If you raise your hand, as though to take leave, he has "just reached a point, which concerns you personally, or on which he must have your invaluable opinion" (not to be noticed for a moment, unless it coincides with his own), and then on he goes, "and so I said to my solicitor," etc., etc., etc., and you try to solace yourself, as you accept the inevitable, with Byron's lines—

"Society is now one polished horde,
  Formed of two mighty tribes, the bores and bored."

You can only deliver yourself from the bore by fighting him with his own weapons; you must return to him a portion of the annoyance which he has so abundantly bestowed upon you. . . .

I had a friend at Oxford, who, with many good qualities, had one foolish infirmity, by no means uncommon, an idolatry of titled folks. He sent me a letter, commencing with "My dear Countess," but he had drawn his pen lightly through the words, and had written over them, "Dear Hole." I lost no time in responding with, "My dear Prince Albert," copying his erasure, and substituting, in place of His Royal Highness, the salutation, "Dear Dick." A mutual friend said to me, "That Dick is an awful bore in London. He gets himself up regardless of expense, with a new hat at one end and patent leather shoes at the other, and thinks that he is the pink of fashion, and the mould of form, and he pretends to know the occupants of every swell carriage he sees, and looks as solemn as if he were in church; and if I want to gaze into a shop window he won't wait, but remarks scornfully, 'They'll think you've never been in London before' (as if I cared what *they* thought), but I generally get rid of him by putting my hat at the back of my head, and assuming an expression of mental debility, addressing the policeman as 'Sir,' and asking him to show us a nice little public-house, where we can be supplied at a small outlay with tea and shrimps. If these experiments fail, I begin to whistle some melody, beloved by the people, rattling my stick against the area railings as an accompaniment, and then he suddenly remembers an engagement to meet a Marquis."

The pessimist, the dreary, doleful, stern, gloom-pampered pessimist, . . . revels in disasters, and gloats upon malformations. . . . If you have a crack in your ceiling, or a worn place on your carpet, or a pimple on your countenance, thereupon he fixes his melancholy gaze. You thought that tiny scar on your horse's knee was invisible to every eye but your own: he has hardly been in the stable two minutes before you hear him exclaim, "Been down, I see," with evident satisfaction to himself. He is so absorbed in contemplating a broken pane in your library window, that you cannot induce him to look at your books. If you admire a beautiful face, he only grunts, "Awful figure!" If you praise one of your fellow-men, all you hear is, "Pity he drinks!" The weather with him is always "beastly". His cook is an idiot, and his butler is a thief. All statesmen are place-hunters, all parsons are hypocrites, all lawyers are knaves, all doctors are quacks. . . .

He is disappointed to find you in good health, and he regards any demonstration of cheerfulness with an expression which is ghastly, though it is meant for a smile. Like an owl, he blinks in the sunshine, and can only hoot in the dark. To evoke his interest, you must be in pain or sickness, and then he states, with unintentional veracity, that "no one would believe how grieved he is to see you so sadly changed, in such a serious condition. Your symptoms seem to be exactly identical with those of his uncle Robert, deceased. He earnestly hopes you have a clever doctor." "Yes, Doctor Coffin." "Oh, indeed—has not much faith in Coffin, but he has no doubt gained experience since that sad mistake at the Hall. Should recommend you to telegraph to London." . . .

As for himself, when he is in the most perfect health, he will never allow that he is well, and if the slightest ailment affects him, it is a case of *moriturus te salutat*. What a bore he is, that *malade imaginaire*! who repudiates with a solemn shake of the head your suggestion that he "looks all right", informing you that just now he may be somewhat flushed by fever or by over-exertion, but that he is a very poor creature (carried unanimously) and suffers agonies.

I remember that the elder Grossmith, a man of most delectable humour, gave an account in one of his admirable lectures of a conversation between one of these lugubrious nuisances and his next-door neighbour, whom he irritated continually with his fanciful afflictions:—

Neighbour. "Well, Dumps, how are you to-day?"

Dumps. "Oh, thanks, much worse, worse than ever. Last night, between eleven and twelve, I was at Death's door."

Neighbour. "At Death's door! Oh, Dumps, *why didn't you go in?*"

. . . The word "correspondence," . . . is richly suggestive of bores. If they cannot speak, they will write to you. Wherever you are they can reach you, and, literally, annoy you with their tongue. . . . "Will you kindly look over the enclosed" (three or four hundred pages, badly written on foolscap, your own table being covered with papers and yourself writing against time), "and will you make any alterations or additions which you think desirable, and forward the manuscript to a publisher whom we can trust? As the book is written for a charitable object" (the charitable object being, as a rule, the writer), "I shall be glad if you will make as good a bargain as possible, and remain," etc.

Sometimes they send you a bulky volume, containing the names and addresses of many hundred subscribers to some Benevolent Institution, "and will you oblige them by looking through the list, and by writing to those members with whim you have have influence, and soliciting their votes at the next election for the candidate named herewith?"

Would you obtain for the applicant, whose name you never

heard before, who is out of work and in delicate health, a clerkship, or other occupation, which would not necessitate any arduous exertion?

"Imogene" would be so awfully grateful, if you would write a few original verses, or a short story, or, if you are an artist, would contribute a drawing or a picture, in the album enclosed.

"Dean Hole would much oblige Mrs —— by forwarding letters from Charles Dickens, W. M. Thackeray, John Leech, and any other of the distinguished authors and artists which are mentioned in his *Memories*." I did not respond to this petition, being indisposed to comply, and was, therefore, perplexed to receive a second letter from Mrs —— thanking me most heartily for my great generosity." I subsequently discovered that a facetious friend, to whom I had read the application, had thought himself justified, by the impudence of the request, in manufacturing the compositions which the lady desired, and had magnanimously added contributions from Milton, Grimaldi, Byron, Blondin, Felicia Hemans, Fieschi, Adelaide Proctor, and Tom Crib.

Then there is the bore, aggravating, though in a minor degree, who sends you a huge local newspaper with a supplement, containing some reference to himself, which you are expected to find without mark or clue.

He follows you wherever you go. He comes to you on the deck of the steamer, when you are not feeling quite so well as you could wish, and he assails you with mere verbiage, until you feel like the bridegroom in Leech's sketch of "Love on the Ocean", when the bride remarks, "Oh, is there not something, dear Augustus, truly sublime in this warring of the elements?" But Augustus's heart was too full to speak.

He sits opposite to me in a waggonette, and seems to think that I have an eye in the middle of my back, or that my head revolves on its own axis, like a geographical globe, as he persists in inquiring, "What buildings are those in the far distance? Did I ever see such a lot of turkeys? What can that fellow be doing in the boat?" If this curiosity were expressed by a beautiful young lady, or by an aged, wealthy, and childless uncle, every effort should be made, but who has reached such a height of self-sacrifice as to dislocate his neck for a bore?

There is the distinguished potentate, the peer, the mayor, the rector, or the squire, who has condescended to preside at my lecture. It becomes him to introduce me to the audience with a few kind prefatory words. If he happens to be a member of the Bore family, what does he do? Ransacks dictionaries and encyclopaedias, collects all the information he can find, makes long extracts, and anticipates my favourite facts, and takes the wind out of my sails, and goes murmuring on, like Tennyson's Brook, until his hearers are weary, and the husbands are longing for a pipe, and the wives are wondering whether the dear little baby is asleep.*

There is the broad gentleman and the broad lady—I find no fault with their breadth; it is not for me to be hypercritical on the subject of size—but I refer only to those of our more extensive brothers and sisters who will stand in doorways, when supper is announced, in front of the best pictures, and at the entrance of the railway cars. That entrance suggests a pathetic story.

A gentleman travelling on the underground rail in London was addressed by a very large lady, who sat near him, as follows: "The next station at which we arrive, sir, will be Sloane Square, and I shall feel greatly obliged if you will kindly assist me to leave the carriage on our arrival. I have already been twice round London, having made unsuccessful efforts to leave the train. Being, unfortunately, very heavy and clumsy in my movements, I find it easier to descend from the doorway backwards, and I have twice been occupied in my awkward endeavour, when a porter, under the misapprehension that I was entering the compartment, has not only addressed me, 'Now, miss, be quick, train's going,' but has propelled me onwards."

But the name of the bore is Legion, and we have only time, as we pass through the crowd, to glance indignantly at the man who divides the pages of your new uncut book or magazine with his finger; who wants to know what everything costs, and where you bought it; who keeps on walking backwards and forwards, or wears a tall hat, or puts up his umbrella, at a cricket-match; who talks when your daughter is singing; who shoots pheasants running, and hares sitting, when he thinks that nobody sees; who is always disappointed, and says, when he surveys Niagara, that "any water could fall from that height;" who has a chronic laugh, with which he concludes each sentence, whether the subject be grave or gay; who will walk on the rims of rivers and the tip-ends of precipices, deriding your preference for the usual route—*et id genus omne ferarum.*

* Mr Robert Cooper of Rochester recalls a description by his father of this particular type of bore. He was at a lecture to be given by the Dean, and the Chairman began his introduction by saying that it was really quite unnecessary for him to introduce the Dean, "so well known to you all", and then went on to talk for what seemed an interminable length of time. Eventually he turned to the Dean: "And now," he said, "I will ask the Dean to give his Address." The Dean got up and said, "I will gladly give my address. It is The Deanery, Rochester, and I'm going there now." He turned and walked off the platform.

I am, of course, making many notes for "Dean Hole's American Tour" which I hope to publish about November next, and which I am told will be a much greater financial success. . . .

Another of Dean Hole's eminent acquaintances was the Baroness Burdett-Coutts. Born in 1814, Angela Burdett was the daughter of Sir Francis Burdett and Sophia, third daughter of Thomas Coutts, of the famous banking house.

The youngest of six children, she often stayed at her father's town house in St James's Place. It was here, as a young woman, that she met many of the well-known people of the day, amongst them Words-worth, the young Disraeli and the ageing Duke of Wellington. Charming, wealthy, moving in distinguished political and social circles and numbering among her intimate friends Sir Robert Peel, Wilberforce, Prince Louis Napoleon, Faraday and Hooker, it was said that every eligible bachelor in England had asked for her hand. When she attended the wedding of Queen Victoria and Prince Albert she must have been one of the most eligible ladies present.

But the fact is that she remained a spinster for another forty years. Perhaps the answer lies in a letter from the Duke of Wellington, written when he was in his seventy-eighth year, dated 8 February 1847:

My dearest Angela! I have passed every moment of the Evening and Night since I quitted you in reflecting upon our conversation of yesterday! Every word of which I have considered repeatedly! My first duty towards you is that of Friend, Guardian, Protector! You are Young! My dearest! You have before you the prospect of at least twenty years of enjoyment of Happiness in Life! I entreat you again in this way not to throw yourself away upon a Man old enough to be your Grandfather! . . . I cannot too often and too urgently entreat you to consider this well. . . . But I must add as I said frequently that my own happiness depends upon it! My last days would be embittered by the reflection that your Life was un-comfortable and hopeless. God bless you, my dearest. Believe me. Ever yours, W[n.5]

Her attention was turned to philanthropic ventures, and her wide interests, her goodness and generosity were in proportion to the size of her bank balance. She cast her net in many directions—building churches, founding missions, adopting whole areas of slums such as Bethnal Green. She aided young boys who were destitute by placing them in the Royal Navy or the merchant service, and cared for lost animals and caged birds. There was her collaboration with Charles

Dickens, whom she had met at a dinner party in 1835. It was the beginning of a close relationship in which they worked together for the public welfare and founded a home in Shepherd's Bush for "fallen young ladies". Their letters show the interest they took in each resident who came under their care and their knowledge of each special case. There is, for instance, the story of Dickens who had received a letter from an outraged contributor to their scheme on hearing that some of the funds had been "squandered" on the purchase of a piano for the young women. "I wish", he wrote to the Baroness Burdett-Coutts (she was created a peeress in her own right in 1871), "that I could have truthfully replied that we had bought not just one piano for the whole house but a piano for each individual inhabitant."[6] Unfortunately there were many times when the Baroness seemed to Dickens to introduce too many rules, and Gladstone—although writing in his diary that "he enjoyed 'going with her to a pantomime'" also found her "efforts at reforming prostitutes as well-meaning"[7] but rather inclined to severity.

In 1880, at the age of sixty-six, she married William Ashmead-Bartlett, an American who worked with her for the Turkish Compassionate Fund, and who was then but twenty-eight.

One of the most important of her interests was in gardens, open spaces and rural activities; and she encouraged the intelligent care and love of house plants amongst townspeople who had no gardens. She was also interested in flower shows, especially in large towns, and one of the best-known of these exhibitions was that held in connection with the Lansdowne Place Ragged Schools in Tabard Street, where plants were given out in the spring to be returned for competition at the end of the summer in the best possible condition.

A sketch of her public life and work, prepared by command of H.R.H. Princess Mary Adelaide, Duchess of Teck, and mother of the late Queen Mary, gives a précis of some of her activities, mentioning particularly that in connection with open spaces round London.

The preservation of commons, the provision of open spaces and parks, and, in the more densely crowded districts, of old churchyards laid out as gardens, has always had her support. She very materially assisted in the preservation of the fields and woodlands adjoining Hampstead Heath, which now affords to Londoners a recreation ground of about five hundred acres.[8]

(Her meeting with the Dean and Mrs Hole may have come about through the Duchess of Teck who was a mutual friend and sometimes came to stay at the Deanery.)

Holly Lodge, Highgate, N.   July 26th, '95.

Dear Mrs Hole, We much hope that you and the Dean propose to come to our garden party on the 30th to the members of the International Geographical Congress now in London and for which you have already or will have received an invitation but I write this letter to ask whether you and the Dean would not remain to dinner and stay the night it would be less fatiguing to you both and give Mr Burdett-Coutts* and myself such very great pleasure. Yours sincerely, With kind regards to the Dean. A. Burdett-Coutts.

If you would let us know where you would arrive and which train you come [by?] whether from London or straight from Rochester we would arrange for a carriage to meet you—the party is from 3 in the afternoon to 7.0.

Another, much younger, correspondent (Rudyard Kipling could only have been about thirty at this time) was writing a fortnight later to the Dean, almost exclusively about roses. Having travelled widely as a young man in his early twenties, Kipling arrived in London in October 1889, his work only known to a few members of the literary world. Within a matter of months he was acknowledged one of the most popular writers of the day. *Life's Handicap* 1891, *Many Inventions* 1893, and also in this year, *Barrack Room Ballads and Other Verses*, all helped to establish his reputation. In 1892 he had married the American, Caroline Starr Balestier, and settled in the United States until 1896. He had already tried his hand at a novel, *The Light that Failed* (not completely successful), but the Jungle Books of his American period, published in 1894 and 1895, must have made him many friends and added in a large degree to his establishment as a literary figure. Children all over the world have associated themselves with Mowgli ever since he made his appearance in those magical pages, and were to be still more entranced by *Kim* and the *Just So Stories* a few years later.

The Seven Seas represented a collection of his poems of this period and *Stalky & Co.* —a school story to end all others—came out in 1899. It would be impertinent to try to assess the value of his contribution as a writer, but it is good to feel that there is a place of pilgrimage for his admirers—Bateman's, his old home, near Burwash, which was acquired by the National Trust in 1940 under the will of Mrs Kipling with the furnishings and an endowment. The surroundings are described in *Puck of Pook's Hill* and *Rewards and Fairies*.

* Mr Ashmead-Bartlett, her husband.

Tisbury, Aug. 6, '95.

What can I say to so generous a letter? If I were going to be in England on the 14th wild engines should not keep me from accepting that invitation but it is my Kismet to go to Southampton on that day and wait for the *Hazel* to take me back to America. When I think of what I should learn and how I should be envied by certain rose-growing friends of mine (notably a Scotch gardener from whom I get my Roses) and how I should be entitled to say, quite quietly and without any pride:—"Excuse me, but Dean Hole whom I've had the honour of meeting says so and so"—when I think of these things I am angry with my Kismet.

But at least no one dare deny that I've been well and honourably presented to "Her Majesty" [the rose] and the thought of that will console me when I am fighting with the beasts at Ephesus under glass this winter.

I admit all you say about the American climate *but* when Providence sends us a not-too-hot summer I assure you that even austere New England can raise some fair blooms. I hate New Jersey! They can grow everything there from ginkgo-trees to mosquitoes and Philadelphia is almost as bad. When we are fighting frost on the 29th of May they are raising garden stuff in the open. Your friends would only make one burst with envy—but I only wish I could sit at their feet for a time.

What I want specially to know is the name of some book that devotes itself to telling how to tend Roses under glass and in the house. Can you help me in that matter?

With every thanks for your kindness and good thought believe me, Very sincerely yours, Rudyard Kipling.

Naulakha, Waite, Windham, Co., Vermont. 31.10.95.

Dear Dean Hole: What haven't you done for me! May of New Jersey—as who should say Smith of Asia—*the* flowering rosy May of Summit New Jersey sends me a delightful letter expressing his desire, out of love for you, to send me "some roses". I was not going to baulk his pious wishes so I said I had a very small bit of glass (10 × 10) but next spring wished to get some good H.P.s for the garden. The never-sufficiently-to-be-commended May then sends me a box of *five and forty* most lovely Teas with a La France or two thrown in, a page of valuable directions and [illegible] of the Rose! He must be a princely kind of man. The coachman and I have been neglecting our regular duties for potting and pruning and syringing and the result in the tiny greenhouse is superb. His royal present with my small stock gives me some seventy roses under glass and the hope of good blooms by Christmas. Now seeing it was your book set me on the path and your kindness that brings me May his generosity it strikes me I owe you a good deal. One can't ever say any more than "thank you" but this "thank you" of mine is a very sincere and delighted one.

My garden is put away for the winter: top-dressed and strawed over but I've been visiting up the Connecticut Valley a family who keep about an acre and a half of glass-houses: palms: ferns: peaches: grapes and roses. The gardener there was a Scot and we collogued for an hour among the hot water pipes, so I said that I had once corresponded with you. "Hole?" said the gardener amazedly, "why he's better than the professionals," and then he went on to offer me half his kingdom in the cutting-line. So you see your fame goes far among these hills. With every good wish for you and your roses believe me, Sincerely and gratefully yours, Rudyard Kipling.

In this second letter Kipling makes it plain that he has appreciated "basking in reflected glory" of the Dean's reputation as a rose-grower.

Meanwhile, the Dean had been on his tour of America. Immediately on his return he was in touch with yet another of his correspondents— Bruce Findley, Curator of the Manchester Botanical Gardens:

The Deanery, Rochester, March 9th, 1895. Dear old Friend—We only returned from America on Wednesday, but your words of congratulation were none the less welcome because they were payable in advance, before the delivery of the goods. We had more than four months in the States, and travelled as far as the Rocky Mountains, 2,000 miles from New York.

The extremes of heat and cold are very discouraging to outdoor gardening in America, but the culture of flowers under glass, especially of roses and carnations, is, owing to the continual sunshine, practical experience and profitable results, most admirable.

At one nursery I saw 9 houses, each 100 yards in length, closely packed with roses grown from cuttings, and each plant had a fine flower on its stalk. The florists welcomed me with far more enthusiasm than I have met in England . . . I have lost two very dear friends in Wm. Thompson and George Harrison—both true gentlemen in the highest meaning of the word. Please give my love to your dear ones . . .

Another letter to Mr Findley much later in the year is one of condolence on hearing of Mrs Findley's death:

. . . I do not doubt that in repeating that 23rd psalm she heard the voice and felt the Presence of the Good Shepherd, who gave His life for the sheep. I hope that you and I may remember those words and realise their beautiful truth when our time shall come. I will be with you, if I can, on the 15th July. I am heartily with you as to the allotment system, and wrote about the Nottingham gardens in my little book about roses some 35 years ago. Ever yours sincerely, S. Reynolds Hole.

Meantime, having returned from the States only at the beginning of March his book *A Little Tour in America* was listed to come out at the end of that year. (His own copy has the inscription: S. Reynolds Hole, The Deanery, Rochester, Jan. 1896.) To get the book out quickly while the tour was still in the minds of Americans—it was published by Edward Arnold simultaneously in New York and London—the script must have been almost ready to send to the publishers on his return. This meant that in addition to the fatigue of travelling, to giving lectures, interviews, preaching sermons, meeting nurserymen, taking interest in the many varying aspects of the American way of life, he also made notes in enough detail from which he was able to complete the script on his return, or else he actually wrote it, perhaps in diary form as he went along. A reporter who came to interview him for an article which came out in April 1895 in *The Christian Commonwealth*, only a few weeks after his return, describes the scene:

I am sitting in the Dean's study—a square, rather low-roofed, well-lighted, simply-furnished room, with plenty of books on the shelves, but not so many as to be oppressive. The Dean's unfinished manuscript—the size of the sheets is simply immense—is on his desk; *The Times* and *Chronicle** (the latter the only urgent note in the whole scene) lie amicably face-to-face; monthly reviews are here and there. In the broad, open fireplace a huge boulder of coal is burning. On the other side of the two small-paned, ample windows, reaching almost from the ceiling to the floor, stretches the irregular lawn, bordered and sheltered by tall trees, from which the rooks are sending forth a mild chorus of caw-caws, whilst borne on the soft, peaceful air is the sound of a distant cock-crow.
    A firm, deliberate step in the corridor, and Dean Hole enters—

---

* "If there were space, one could say a word about the *Chronicle*'s share in cheering on and steadying the new Unionism, supporting the miners in their grim, victorious struggle through the summer and autumn of 1893, pressing on factory and mining legislation, exposing the conditions in dangerous trades, and the living-in system that then prevailed in shops, . . . but the bare selection here enumerated must suffice."[8]

tall, massive, altogether powerful-looking, quite a giant of a man. "I'm a bird of passage!" the Dean cheerily remarks, in explanation of his non-appearance until some minutes after my arrival. My first thought is that I had made a mistake in supposing the Dean of Rochester to be an old man. His profusion of hair is scarcely grey, and has many quite black streaks in it; ... nor is the Dean in conversation merely garrulous, or diffuse, or remote as are most old men. I found it hard to believe that one so sturdy, so vigorous, so altogether coherent, as the Dean is, could be in his seventy-sixth year.[9]

The reporter must have been even more impressed when he read through a copy of the book a few months later. The Dean's immense interest in every aspect of American life was evident. He did not sit back, as he might have done, reserving his strength for the times of his appearance on public platforms or in the pulpit. He had taken the trouble to read beforehand "a reliable history of the country, such as Bryce's *History of the American Commonwealth*" and had carefully studied "a good modern map". He was unperturbed by warnings from friends and relatives—not uttered in his presence but repeated by "those loquacious makers of mischief who exult in repeating that which 'perhaps they ought not to tell you'," such as:

Had the amiable but slightly obtuse old gentleman forgotten that he was no chicken? ... Had he never noticed that the Atlantic beat the record for rolling and pitching, fogs, icebergs, tornadoes, collisions, and wrecks? The idea was presposterous and suggested softening of the brain ...

Notwithstanding, he explains that having obtained "the promise, 'where thou goest, I will go,' from one whom I could not leave ... I engaged [a] berth on board the *Majestic*. ..." It was from the *Majestic* that he wrote the following letter to his son, dated Wednesday, 18 October 1894:

Dear Hughie, How kind to remember the book which I shall greatly enjoy, and whatever else may decline to stay, shall inwardly digest. We had a most comfortable journey to Liverpool ... Your mother has done bravely, but could only favour the company with a narrow slit in one of her eyes after dinner last night. She is gradually acquiring a strong American accent. ...

But we are still in the preparatory chapter and must hurry ahead to the numerous events of the tour itself. He spoke to crowded halls, churches, and horticultural meetings. He found out about the running of the railways, the making of clocks and watches, the preservation of public forest reservations and the keeping of " 'Arbour Day',* for the voluntary planting of trees by the people." In New York he was complimented by an invitation to dine at the Lotos Club, established twenty-five years earlier "for the social intercourse of those who had literary or artistic inclinations". Among its guests had been Wilkie Collins, Charles Kingsley, Richard Monckton Milnes (a fellow contributor with the Dean to *The Cornhill* and a friend of Anne Thackeray), Henry Irving, Sir Edwin Arnold and Dr Conan Doyle. "At Albany I grasped the hands of the grandson and the great-grandson of Fenimore Cooper and . . . renewed the excitement which enthralled my boyhood, as I read by day and dreamed by night of 'The Spy', 'The Pioneer', 'The Pilot', and 'The Last of the Mohicans'."

But it was not only the great occasions which claimed his notice. He was interested in the food, customs and past history of the States as much as in seeing the sights and meeting the grandees. The book also included his comments on some American tourists who wanted "to do" celebrated buildings or even cities in a few hours: "We have heard", he writes, "of tourists 'knocking off St Peter's and doing the Vatican' before lunch; and I remember an elderly spinster at Cadenabbia, who informed me that she was occupied in doing Europe, and asked me how long it would take to do London. . . ."

He mentions beginning breakfast with "shaddock from Florida". ("The large roundish or pear-shaped, usually pale yellow, orange-like edible fruit of the rutaceous tree, *Citrus grandis*, grown extensively in the Orient and named after Captain Shaddock who brought the seed from the East Indies.")[10] And that he "counted some thirty preparations of corn, that is, maize, and of wheat, including hominy"; ("hominy—white corn milled and crushed or coarsely ground: prepared for use as food by boiling in water or milk.")[11] Other delicacies were prairie birds, quail, "ragout of antelope" venison, the canvas-back duck, and terrapin. The terrapin is a species of small turtle, or tortoise. . . . It is found, according to Bartlett's Dictionary, "exclusively in the salt water, and always in the neighbourhood of marshes".

He visited prisons and courts of justice and writes at some length on the law of lynching, which takes its name from Colonel Lynch, an officer of the American Revolution. He quotes four cases of lynching which occurred during January and February of 1895 and refers his reader to Bryce, *The American Commonwealth*, vol. ii, p. 507, for more detailed information.

---

* Arbour Day. A day, varying in date, observed in individual states of the United States for the planting of trees.

From The Heublein, Hartford, Connecticut, in a letter dated 16 January 1895, he again writes to Hugh:

You will be gratified by the description of "a rugged elderly gentleman, with a florid face" in whom you are interested "in knickerbockers, leggings, etc."; also with "Kentshire", . . . I hoped to have brought home £1,000 for further restoration of the Cathedral at Rochester, but I shall not achieve more than £500.

In New York he received invitations from two actors whom he knew in England to see their productions—Mr Beerbohm Tree in *Hamlet*, "splendidly supported by Mrs Tree's Ophelia"; and Mr Wilson Barrett, who was well known for his play *The Sign of the Cross* in which he also appeared in New York and London.

Flowers, florists and especially the rose naturally take up much of his time and, in view of the second letter from Mr Kipling, quoted earlier, it may be of interest to note that Mr May of New Jersey, one of the "most famous growers of chrysanthemums in the States" called to see the Dean and Mrs Hole. Mrs Hole had just come in from a shopping visit and had brought a bunch of golden-hued chrysanthemums, called Christopher Colombus. These were shown with pride to Mr May, but they received none of the expected compliments, just "the brief verdict of condemnation, 'Buncombe!'" Mr May explained that this was in reality a white flower dipped in some chemical. The term "Buncombe" had been coined many years previously in Congress when the member for Buncombe had risen with a speech so stupid and pointless that it had since always meant "bunkum, humbug, sham, rubbish".

Later the Dean paid a most enjoyable visit to Mr May's home and saw his extensive greenhouses and nursery gardens. In fact it is not surprising to find him writing that

The happiest hours which I spent in America were those in which I was entertained by my brother florists, who came not only from New York and the neighbourhood, but from distant parts of the States—the President, Mr Berry from Rochester, the Vice-President, Mr Craig from Philadelphia, at a dinner at the Savoy Hotel. The large room in which we met was a bower of roses. "The tables they groaned with the weight, not of the feast, for it was carved elsewhere, but of the flowers." The menu, supplied by Messrs Tiffany, was worthy of their artistic fame—with roses in the foreground and in the distance the old deanery of Rochester and the cathedral roofs beyond. I saw for the first time nearly all the faces which were assembled. Many of them were strangers to each other but where

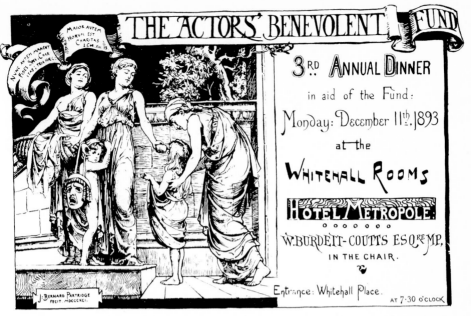

Written in blue pencil on the back of one of the invitation cards is a note from the Chairman which he must have passed down to the Dean after his speech: "Thank you for the noblest speech I ever heard—from the bottom of my heart and I *know* the heart of all the company. W.B-C."

The family at The Deanery, Rochester, about 1894: *standing*: Hugh and Geraldine Hole; *seated*: Dean Hole and Caroline; *children*: Bridget, later Lady Tallents (on the Dean's knee), and John.

yours truly
S Reynolds Hole

Left to right: Caroline, Bridget, John and the Dean.

the hands meet that have struck the cuttings . . . when the eyes meet which love to gaze with reverent admiration upon leaf and blossom and bloom . . . *the hearts meet also.*

He travelled through Detroit, Cincinnati, Virginia, Washington, Philadelphia, Chicago, and it was in this latter city that he went to see the Union Stock Yards, the great cattle market, and to Mr Armour's famous slaughter and packing houses. He writes:

I went, believing that the clergy should take a practical interest . . . as a member of the Society for the Prevention of Cruelty, and also the Society for the Promotion of Kindness to Animals, to ascertain whether the process was as free as it could be made from cruelty and unnecessary pain, and with the hope of acquiring information which might be acceptable across the Atlantic.

To take the trouble to see for himself, to spare time from a full schedule for something which could only be harrowing and unpleasant, seems typical of the Dean's outlook. He would spare himself nothing if he felt that what he was doing could be of ultimate use either to his fellowmen or, as in this case, to the welfare of animals.

A happier note is struck by his visit to Niagara where, unlike Oscar Wilde who visited the Falls two or three years earlier and is reported to have expressed his disappointment in them, the Dean writes: "If I were asked to name, according to my knowledge, the most wonderful place in the world, I should make answer, "NIAGARA FALLS". In a letter to a friend named Edward [Woodall?] 13 December 1894, from Everett House, Union Square, New York, he says: "But the one grand impression made upon me—the most sublime glory I have seen is

Niagara!"

He devotes a chapter to them giving details of seeing the Falls from both the American and Canadian sides, of walks through "groves and avenues" and of their possibilities for creating electricity, for providing power for industry as well as pure water for drinking. "When I first saw the American Falls", he writes,

a gorgeous rainbow spanned them with its arch from bank to bank, without a flaw or dimness, like a bridge made of precious stones; and solemn thoughts came to me of the waters abating, and the great flood going down, of the promise of mercy, and of the token of the covenant, and the rainbow of glory around the throne of God.

14

After many excitements, pleasurable and interesting, he ends the book first with a note of warning and then a Blessing from the Bishop of Albany. The warning is given to the young men from England who,

> in the last thirty years, have gone with brave hearts and bright hopes to invest their money in the ranch and the farm, have spent the best years of their manhood in arduous toil, and are working at this time in the daily monotonous drudgery of mean employments— cutting wood, making fires, cooking, cleaning, and mending to supply the necessaries of life. I warn young Englishmen that there is no room for them as farmers in America.

The day before I sailed from New York I received this telegram from the Bishop of Albany: "God speed you and yours home, my beloved brother. May you take with you as delightful memories as those you leave behind."

The return to the Deanery was the occasion of a practical joke—of the kind he would have enjoyed with Dean Pigou—as its recipient, the Dean's young nephew, William Francklin, remembered.

The door opened and the Dean stood on the threshold. "Hello, Bill," he said, and stayed there with his mouth open. But an extraordinary song seemed to be coming from somewhere:

> "Oh, Uncle Sam, whenever I see the Broadway,
> Oh, Uncle Sam,
> There I will remain . . .
> Life in the country's awfully dull
> And I'll never go back again."

The Dean's mouth was opening and shutting certainly, but still there was a catch somewhere. Suddenly the boy noticed that at the Dean's feet, in between them and partly concealed by his shoes, was a small box. It was one of the early types of recording box which he had brought back as a surprise for William.

The election for the new President of the Royal Academy took place on 20 February 1896, when Millais, already looking pale and ill, was unanimously elected. Many congratulations followed, but he was only going to be able to fulfil his new position for a matter of a few months. The diagnosis of a malignant growth by the throat specialist, Felix

Semon, proved to be only too sadly a true one, and he died on 13 August. Perhaps for the Dean his closest connection with Millais had been their mutual friendship with John Leech.

In 1897 the Victoria Medal of Honour was instituted by the Royal Horticultural Society, and there were sixty original medallists, of whom Dean Hole, the Rev. Honywood D'Ombrain and Canon Ellacombe were three of the recipients.

Canon H. N. Ellacombe had been a visitor to the Deanery a few years earlier, in June 1893. The canon was a genial, kindly gentleman (as the Dean would say, "in the best sense of the word"), a much-loved vicar of his parish, Bitton in Gloucestershire, of which he was made Rural Dean in 1874. In 1881 he became an honorary canon of Bristol. After his church his garden came closest to his heart and what a garden that was. It is described in William Robinson's *The English Flower Garden* as an example "of a quiet, peaceful garden of grass and trees and simple borders and every nook and corner has its appropriate flower, in a word, it is just such a garden as one would expect a scholar to possess who has sympathy for all that lives or breathes. . . ."

Miss Jekyll mentions a visit to his "most interesting garden at Bitton" in *Wood and Garden* where she first became acquainted with *Nandina domestica*, the Chinese "sacred" bamboo.

How generous, too, Canon Ellacombe was with his plants. It was once said that "his favourite doctrine was that a true gardener is known by the pleasure he takes in giving plants to his friends and judged by that standard he was a prince among gardeners". Canon Ellacombe excelled with old roses and his gingko trees seeded themselves, so that now there are quite a few tall ones in the garden. He was a close friend of E. A. Bowles and many treasures from Bitton found their way to Myddleton House, Enfield, Essex.

Other visitors during these years to the Deanery at Rochester were Alfred Parsons, the painter, in July 1894, and in October 1895, one of the several visits of the Duchess of Teck. In a letter to Henry Silver, dated 18 January 1898, the Dean remainds him that he has promised to bring his wife to stay after her convalescence "when the green leaves come again". He goes on:

Elgood came to us just when a series of sunny days had brought us a simultaneous development of beauty in our herbaceous border; and I doubt whether we shall ever see the like again. Nevertheless, there is always something pretty in our garden from May to October, the narcissus in April, the iris in May, the roses in June, the Paeonies in July, and a mixture of perennials and annuals onward. Yours ever sincerely . . . P.S. Please give my love to Tenniel when you see him.

In March 1898, the Rev. A. W. Baldwin, chaplain to H.M. Prison, Wormwood Scrubbs, visited the Deanery, and in July, Henry Silver and his wife, Blanche, fulfilled their promise to make a visit. In October came a visit from his dear and joke-loving friend, Francis Pigou. Dean Hole had written earlier to him suggesting that it was high time they met again: "I am working against time, in ecclesiastical and literary engagements, and should vastly enjoy one of our dear quiet old *talks*. I have almost forgiven the cruel sufferings which you inflicted on me when Baron Rothschild purchased 'The Times'. . . ."

In January 1899, the Dean is replying to an old parishioner from Caunton—Miss Elkington:

. . . I should delight in a conversation with your mother, but I am in my 80th year and seldom leave home. After many years of loco-motion (I have preached in 500 churches, including most of our cathedrals, and 50 sermons in St Paul's) I feel a strong desire to rest and be thankful . . .

and in March 1899, again to Henry Silver:

I appreciate your kindness in reminding me of dear Mr Richard Owen's love of his birds.* I have remembered it gratefully, ever since I heard it from you. Give my love to Tenniel. I am doing my best to catch him up, but am still eight months behind. [Sir John Tenniel had just reached eighty.] I shall be eighty in December. Yours very sincerely. . . .

The last year of the 19th century saw them back at Caunton for a holiday, and what a joy it was to be there again! He writes to Joe Birley, 21 August 1899:

Dear Joe, Come when you can and bring your gun. I don't think that the shooting here is large enough to let. We were at Thurgaton on Thursday last and, returning by Maggerdate Farm, I was re-minded of an incident which occurred some years ago when the snow was on the ground. It may interest you when we meet. We are greatly enjoying our holiday in the dear old home. Of course we miss the odour of the cement works, the music of the foghorn and the hurdy-gurdy, and the incessant ringing of the front-door bell; but we bear the trial with much patience.

* Walking with Sir Richard Owen in his garden, a lady noticed that the cherry trees, all save one, were netted. She called his attention to this, thinking it had been over-looked. "Oh, no," he answered, "it's the salary for the orchestra."

If you happen to have a cigar tube, bring it. Yours as ever,
S. Reynolds Hole.

His signature, S. Reynolds Hole, President of the National Rose
Society, November 1899, on the end paper of the "Fourth and Revized
Edition of the Descriptive Catalogue of Exhibition and Garden Roses"
is written in his usual bold hand. It shows little sign of his approaching
eightieth birthday in December. The list of roses selected for inclusion
was made by a committee of the National Rose Society and a copy of
the illustrated catalogue could be obtained, post-free for Two Shillings
[10p], "of either of the Hon. Secretaries of the Society". Perhaps the
Dean's most important recent contribution to the Society had been his
Little Tour in America.

15

Then and Now

1900—1904

THE DEAN HAD always loved going to a theatre or to the opera. It may be remembered that as a young man he went to hear Jenny Lind sing, that as a new member of the Garrick Club it was hoped that parties would be made up to go to the opera, that he attended the theatre in New York. Two amongst his many friends were Wilson Barrett—known especially for *The Sign of The Cross* and his connection with the Lyric Theatre—and Herbert Beerbohm Tree* at Her Majesty's Theatre. (*The Times* advertised the first night of "Mr Wilson Barrett's Season as beginning on Saturday, 4th January, 1896, with *The Sign of the Cross* acted by Mr Wilson Barrett, Miss Maud Jeffries and Company.") The Dean received two letters from Barrett concerning the play and the second, of 10 August, refers to a visit from Gladstone: "I have, by this post, received a most eulogistic autograph letter from Gladstone who saw the play on Saturday." And in a letter dated 21 February 1898, Beerbohm Tree writes: "It is a real pleasure to see you in the theatre, as it is a joy to have your generous encouragement."

It is a joy, too, to read the reviews of Mr Max Beerbohm, half-brother to Herbert Beerbohm Tree, for the years 1898–1903. A comment in his typically polished style comes in a review of the new play at the Lyceum in April 1899:

> Genius is a dangerous word, and one which I have not felt compelled, hitherto, to use in my dramatic criticisms. It is also an odd quality to discover suddenly in the fifth act of a play like Robespierre. Nevertheless—at the risk of turning his head—I declare that Mr Laurence Irving has it."[1]

In April and May of 1899 come further letters from Herbert

---

* Knighted in 1909, proprietor of Her (His) Majesty's Theatre from 1895 onwards, where he founded an academy for stage training which became the Royal Academy of Dramatic Art.

Beerbohm Tree, this time in connection with a matter other than a visit to the theatre. On 19 April he writes:

> I am going to ask you to do me a great service in the cause of charity. The Charing Cross Hospital, which from its proximity to the great newspapers, publishing houses and West-End theatres has especial claims upon the Press and the Playhouse, is in sore need of assistance.

But he is not asking for financial support. Mr Tree has taken on the organization of "a monster bazaar" to be held in the Albert Hall later on in June. His letter goes on:

> With the aid of my staff here I have undertaken to organize and arrange the bazaar, one of the chief features of which will be a Souvenir Album to contain contributions from all the leading artists, authors and musicians of the day. From the enclosed lists you will see who have already promised to help and I am sure you will be pleased to hear that up to now I have met with no single refusal. I should not think my book complete without it contained something from your pen. For whatever you send me I shall be grateful but I should dearly love one of your characteristic articles that the book-loving public knows so well. When the work is compiled it is to be reproduced and sold at 10/– [50p] a copy and the first editions will comprise 10,000 examples.
>
> My blocks for illustration I have received free and my paper is to be supplied and my printing done at greatly reduced prices. The originals will all be disposed of and the price realized by the sale of the same will go to reduce the cost of production. By these means I hope, from this source alone, to hand over a really substantial addition to the Hospital Funds. Will you help us? Believe me, my dear Dean, I remain, very sincerely, Herbert Beerbohm Tree.

Naturally the Dean complied; he had never been known, throughout his long life, not to give help when it was needed, however busy he might be. He received another letter addressed from Her Majesty's Theatre, again in Mr Tree's own hand and dated 25 May: "A thousand thanks for your charming contribution to our souvenir. It is delightful and so appropriate . . ."

As the Contents shows, there were many eminent names amongst the contributors, and the following short excerpts give a brief impression of a few of the writers who were asked to send in material composed especially for the occasion:

CONTENTS:

among THE ARTISTS

The President of the Royal Academy
Sir Philip Burne-Jones, Bart.
Mr Alfred Parsons, A.R.A.
Mr Bernard Partridge, R.I.
Sir John Tenniel, R.I.

(Alfred Austin)

among THE AUTHORS

The Poet Laureate . .	*The Wreck of the Stella*
Mr Max Beerbohm . .	*Carlotta Grisi in the ballet of "Giselle ou les Wilis"*
Sir Walter Besant★ . .	*Concerning Charing Cross*
Mr F. C. Burnand† . .	
Mr Hall Caine . . .	*Literary Coincidence*
Dr A. Conan Doyle . .	*A Soldier's Prayer*
W. E. Henley . . .	*Two Verses*
Dean Hole	*Flowers for the Sick*
Mr Andrew Lang . . .	*Confessions of a Pedant*
Mr Arthur W. Pinero .	*A letter to Mr Tree*
Mrs Humphrey Ward . .	*An Italian Villa in spring*
Mr William Watson . .	*The Saint and the Satyr*
Mr Algernon Ch. Swinburne .	*At a dog's grave*

among THE MUSICIANS

Mr Edward Elgar
Sir Hubert Parry
Mr Edward German
Sir Arthur Sullivan
Dr Villiers Stanford

A sigh sent wrong
A kiss that goes astray,
A sorrow the years endlong—
So they say.

So let it be!
Come the sorrow, the kiss, the sigh!
They are life, dear life, all three—
And we die.

W. E. Henley

★ The founder, in 1884, of A Society of Authors.
† Editor of *Punch* 1880–1906.

"Tell me the tale again, Mother,
  Tell me the tale again!
Of the cheery start and the joyous trip,
  And the folds of the fog, and then—
How men may be heroes in their death,
  And women as brave as men."
Alfred Austin (14 verses)

If they to whom God gives fair gardens knew
  The happy solace which sweet flowers bestow
Where pain depresses, and where friends are few,
  To cheer the heart in weariness and woe;

If they could see the smile which dries the tear,
  The new light glistening in the languid eyes . . .
. . .

I pray you to whom God gives gardens, lend
  This happy solace, which the flowers bestow,
Where pain oppresses, and where few befriend
  To cheer the suffering and to soothe their woe.
Dean Hole (7 verses)

A heart! A heart!
  Ah, give me a heart
To rise to circumstance:
  Serene and high
  And bold to try
The hazard of the chance:
  With strength to wait,
  But fixed as Fate
To plan, and dare, and do:
  The peer of all
  And only thrall,
Sweet lady mine to you.
A. Conan Doyle (3 verses)

Here for the last time together,
  Pacing down the garden slow,
Neither of us knowing whether
  We are lovers still or no. . . .

Tomorrow think no more about me:
  Day brings council with its light.

Though you mean to live without me,
You would die with me tonight!

Violet Hunt (4 verses)

The Afterword by Herbert Beerbohm Tree.

It is only fit that I should on this, the last page of our book, express
my grateful homage to the distinguished writers, painters and com-
posers who have taken part in this tribute of Art to Love. Mine has
been the modest burden of binding together the flowers which they
have brought from far and wide to lay at the feet of Charity. Under
no banner but that of Charity, indeed, could such a roll of names
have been mustered.

The contributions have been, with one unavoidable exception,
specially prepared for this volume. The originals, pictorial and other,
have been vested in the Charing Cross Hospital, and will, it is hoped,
be a perpetual source of income to that Institution in the time to
come. . . . While I am authorized by the Council of the Charing
Cross Hospital to convey their deep gratitude to the illustrious band
who have thus raised a lasting monument to this great and deserving
Institution, I cannot refrain from expressing the pride I personally
feel that this noble result should have been achieved through the
medium of the Theatre over which I have the privilege to preside.

Her Majesty's Theatre,
21 June 1899.

Despite his advancing age the Dean was still working on another
book *Then and Now*, which was published in November 1901, by
Hutchinson. It was dictated to his niece, May Burnaby-Atkins, and he
writes to her:

Dearest May, I send you some newspaper cuttings, having
reference to

OUR BOOK

By far the most gratifying and important is the review from
"Literature", a weekly paper published under the auspices and at the
Printing Offices of "The Times" . . . "The Scotsman" is canny and
puts more water in his whiskey than upon former occasions, but I
think with "Literature" notwithstanding, that "Then and Now" is
a more sterling book than "Memories". . . .

The Times of Monday, 11 November 1901, does, in fact, make this comparison:

To our mind, the charm of the Dean's view of life is its extraordinary freshness. His optimism and benevolence is indeed old-fashioned . . . but is none the worse for that; and few octogenarians are so entirely free from any of those prejudices against social innovations which have no basis except dislike of a novelty. The Dean does not cling to the very dangerous maxim, "The old is better". Another feature of his comparison of the present and the past is that, while strict enough on 'the things that matter' he is extraordinarily tolerant about things which do not essentially matter very much; . . . And a third note of the book is the Dean's wholesome contempt for pretentiousness. . . . On the whole we like this book—the ripe experience of a religious man of the world—better than the "Memories" and we warmly commend it as a "book to read".

The review from *Punch*, 13 November 1901, was almost ecstatic:

It is with the greatest pleasure that the Baron* welcomes the appearance of a volume entitled *Then and Now* (Hutchinson & Co.) written by Dean Hole, whom, as companion of Mark Lemon, Shirley Brooks, Douglas Jerrold and Thackeray, also as travelling and collaborating with John Leech in their *Little Tour in Ireland*, and as *oequalis* with Sir John Tenniel, Mr Punch is delighted to reckon amongst his staunchest friends and earliest contributors. Known to fame not only as a horticulturist specially skilled in rose-growing but also as a keen and witty observer of men and manners, the amiable Dean button-holes the reader and gives him some of his finest and freshest observations on *Then and Now*, showing how justly he appreciates every varying phase of society. . . . Not a hint of fogeyism about him, but the strong personality of a highly cultivated and as a scientific gardener, highly cultivating—genial, Christian gentleman, the best type of an English clergyman of the old school, pervades the book throughout. . . .

The Dean writes an acknowledgement dated 13 November to Sir F. C. Burnand, the editor since 1880: "My dear Burnand, I appreciate *toto corde*, with my whole heart, the kind words which I have just read in 'Punch'. The first edition of my new book was exhausted soon

---

* A pseudonym for the contributor; in much the same way as Patrick Campbell used to write under the name "Quidnunc" for *The Irish Times*.

after publication, and this genial, generous eulogium by 'The Baron'
will be most helpful to No. 2. . . ."

Then and Now seemed to be well launched on its way, but it was a
nice touch that the warmest and most appreciative review should
come from old friends on the *Punch* staff.

As its title suggests, the main theme of the book dealt largely with
comparisons, but even so, there are certain things to which a mere
matter of eighty years makes no difference at all. In his chapter on
"Babies and Children" the Dean writes:

> Some of the anachronisms and combinations suggested by children
> are remarkable; as when a small nephew of mine, roseate, with
> golden curls, came to inform me that "Mitter" (Mr.) Noah, whom
> he had taken out of the ark for a ride in his railway train, had fallen
> into the chimney of the engine head downwards, and could I get
> him out with a corkscrew?

A small domestic matter over a "new kitchen grate" reveals a similar
continuity of practice:

> When it is revealed to him (the husband) that the cook says she must
> have a new grate, he assumes such a lugubrious expression and
> heaves such a plaintive sigh as might lead you to suppose that he was
> about to order his wagonette for the conveyance of himself and
> family to the nearest workhouse. He has recently paid £300 for a
> hunter, but this £25 for a grate quite breaks him down. "It seems to
> me only the other day that I paid no end of money for the beastly
> thing now in use;" and when it is positively stated that "the other
> day" occurred eighteen years ago, and that the man who comes to
> examine the grate has said, as the man who comes to examine the
> grate always does say, that "it is completely done for" . . . he braces
> himself to the inevitable, and is finally taken from home for a fort-
> night in a state of cheerful resignation to an expensive London hotel
> until half a dozen men, leisurely working for four hours a day, have
> adjusted the new kitchen grate.

There are a good many gems which might be quoted, as the *Punch*
review said: "A few of the many good things . . . (one) is much
tempted to quote, but, on consideration, he will not make any cuttings from the rose-growing Dean's book to which, as to a garden,
he prefers to direct his readers. . . ."

Hugh Hole sums its contents up in a few words:"When my father
wrote his last book, *Then and Now*, he drew a picture of the changes

that had affected England in his lifetime: from coach to train; from the
after Napoleonic Wars poverty to the fortunes of the Roaring Forties;
sail to steam; dog-carts to Daimlers."[2] William Morris painted his own
picture in the following verse:

> Forget six counties overhung with smoke,
> Forget the snorting steam and piston stroke,
> Forget the spreading of the hideous town;
> Think rather of the pack-horse on the down,
> And dream of London, small, and white and clean,
> The clear Thames bordered by its gardens green . . .[3]

There was no disputing the facts disclosed by Dickens in his books
and by the Dean from the public platform or the pulpit. In a letter to
James Blackney, one of the Caunton choirboys who started work on
the railway after leaving the village school, he writes:

> I so much sympathize with the admirable article on "Mind and
> Labour" and the degradation of labourers, that I shall be in a state of
> anxious suspense until I know who wrote it. If it is from your head
> and heart, the confirmation of my hope will be real happiness to—
> your sincere old friend, S. Reynolds Hole. Stick to Ruskin.

Mention of Ruskin reminds one that he had died in January 1900,
after spending the last eleven years of his life in retirement near Coniston. With the death of Queen Victoria the following year came the
end of an era and the beginning of another. One of the chapters in the
book relates to "Cycling" and in it he defends the use of a bicycle on
the Sabbath. "There is ample time for public worship, early and late,
with opportunities by the way . . . We have had the nave of our
cathedral at Rochester filled with cyclists and the clergy should, I think,
have short special services in places where they 'most do congregate'."[4]
For this was the hey-day of the bicycle. Sometimes it was a means of
escape, as for W. H. Hudson from London streets to the Sussex downs,
or a convenient method of getting about, as for Tolstoy riding around
in Moscow (on a bicycle made in Coventry). Some country house
parties expected young ladies and gentlemen to include their "machine"
amongst their luggage.

Before finally closing the pages of *Then and Now* perhaps we may
turn to the Dean's selection of "Books old and new". He mentions
Mrs Radclyffe's *Mysteries of Udolpho*, of so much importance to the
heroine of *Northanger Abbey*, whose heart is more lost than ever when
Henry Tilney remarks: "The Mysteries of Udolpho, when I had once

begun it, I could not lay down again; I remember finishing it in two days, my hair standing on end the whole time." The adventures of Baron Munchausen is another favourite and one is reminded of the traveller tying his horse to a post when the snow lies thickly all around, only to find that when it has melted in the morning, the "post" turned out to be a church steeple.

But for the Dean and "his best beloved", in these few years, the garden of the Deanery must have provided some of their greatest pleasures together. Gertrude Jekyll writes of it in her book *Some English Gardens*, which was illustrated with paintings by George Elgood. The chapter is headed "The Deanery Garden, Rochester", and there is a painting of that garden by the illustrator; but Miss Jekyll begins by talking about the Dean's "fame as a rosarian" and that "his practical activity in spreading and fostering a love of Roses must have been the means of gladdening many a heart and may be reckoned as by no means the least among the many beneficent influences of his long and distinguished ministry."

Miss Jekyll talks first of visiting the Dean when he was still Vicar of Caunton. "It must have been five and twenty years ago, and it was June, the time of roses."[5] She appreciated them especially coming as she did from a garden with sandy soil, and she quotes the story of the soil being brought into the garden and pushed in heavy wheelbarrow loads. She goes on:

> The writer's experience is exactly the same. Of the quantities of garden visitors who have come . . . not one in twenty will believe that one loves a garden well enough to take a great deal of trouble about it. . . .
>
> It must have been a painful parting from the well-loved roses and the many other beauties of the Caunton garden . . . from the pure air of Nottinghamshire to that of a town, with the added reek of neighbouring lime and cement works. But even here good gardening has overcome all difficulties, and though, when the air was more than usually loaded with the foul gases given off by these industries, the Dean would remark, with a flash of his characteristic humour, that Rochester was "a beautiful place to get away from", yet the Deanery garden is now full of roses and quantities of other good garden flowers, all grandly grown and in the best of health. . . .

and then she adds significantly, "The Dean is not alone among the flowers, for Mrs Hole is also one of the best of gardeners."[6]

Coming from the "First Lady Gardener in the land" this is a comment to be valued. It also assures one of the very real partnership between the Dean and his wife. This was assuredly so from the moment that the lovely young bride came to Caunton Manor. Dame Sybil Thorndike remembers her again: "She used to ride beautifully and travelled to visit friends on her pack horse with her luggage behind her. She also drew and embroidered well and was an excellent gardener. She loved lilies especially."

Her son writes of her:

My mother was an unusually qualified countrywoman. There are not many ladies in these days who could take the harness from the saddle-room, harness four horses in their stalls, put them in a coach and drive them. Her father, John Francklin, taught her. Her mother was dead, she was the eldest child and a little housekeeper to her father, who drove a great deal.[7]

This practical ability to turn her hand to almost anything that came her way must have been invaluable to them both, and its usefulness must not be under-estimated. But the other side of her character, which would lead her out into the country lanes for a walk or a ride on her favourite horse when, as we have seen earlier, she should have been at home dispensing hospitality to guests whose existence she had forgotten, has an endearing quality about it.

When the Dean was visiting Boston, Mrs Hole was interviewed by a representative of The Women's Corner of the *Boston Journal*, on 12 December 1894. The reporter described her:

"Quite in accordance with her sensible English ideas, Mrs Hole was attired in a plain cloth gown, warm golf cape lined with bright plaid, and simple, round English felt hat, as she came into the drawing rooms of the Brunswick to greet the Corner's representative."

She must have given an impression of unruffled interest and appreciation, without any over-effusive reactions.

Regarding every question from opposite standpoints at the same time, as it were, Mrs Hole's conclusions, which determine her attitude, are moderate, for however general may be the popularity of a movement, the enthusiasm of the masses would avail but little with Mrs Hole, should she observe its plans, although she would be ready to recognize its good qualities, nevertheless. . . .

When the Corner asked if she shared her husband's admiration for flowers, Mrs Hole said, with much enthusiasm: "Yes, indeed. Perhaps I like them even better than he does. From a child I have been extremely fond of them. We are both greatly interested in growing the flowers."

"Have you extensive conservatories?" asked the Corner.

"No, we cannot have them in Rochester, you know, but before we moved into the city we had them. Even in Rochester we have a large garden where we grow all kinds of flowers in the summertime, especially roses."

"What is your favourite?"

"I think the carnation. It is very hardy, you know, being able to withstand almost any amount of frost, and we admire the blossom very much."

The interview was a lengthy one but at no time was Caroline in the least flustered or at a loss. She was asked if "women had yet appeared among the clergy of England?"

"I am thankful to say that they have not," answered Mrs Hole, emphatically, at the same time smiling very pleasantly, for while she has nothing against anyone who may approve of such things, her own opinions are firmly in the negative. . . .

"But do you not think English women will seek to enter the pulpits in time?" asked the Corner.

"Perhaps, but I am pretty sure nobody would go to hear them if they did. Besides there is plenty of church work for women. . . ."

The Corner explained that in Kansas and Denver women have full suffrage and in the latter State a woman had just been elected to the Legislature.

There was unmitigated astonishment expressed in Mrs Hole's quiet "Indeed". . . .

Calm, individual in her own ideas and not in the least afraid of opposition, she was not likely to be carried away by enthusiasms or mass reactions. And she often tempered her own opinions with a smile.

Going back to the Caunton days, James Blackney tells the story of a certain morning when it was his duty to ring the bell for a litany service. "One day", he relates,

Mrs Hole, who was at the service, asked me to stay afterwards. I was learning my notes at that time and I think it was to help me in some way. Mr Hole had left the church but before we had got well started, he came and whispered, "James, the hounds". Mrs Hole, I think, heard, and with an amused look, as if wondering what would be the result. I hardly liked to ask to be excused. She seemed to read my thoughts, and suggested that I would rather see the hounds than stop to music. She was right. The hounds and huntsmen were passing through the village and Mr Hole and I went after them . . . I did not get back to school that morning.[8]

Caroline frequently played the organ for the daily services at Caunton and on this occasion had evidently been helping James to learn his notes. She was quick to understand the longing to be off—not only of the boy but of her husband. Perhaps it was her understanding as well as their deep affection for each other that provided the key to their relationship.

In May 1901 they had their fortieth wedding anniversary. Reynolds gave her a large silver rose bowl, on it a simple inscription expressing his love and appreciation. On 5 December 1903, he made a birthday speech. "I thank you all my dear friends for your presence here tonight. Although small I can claim that our gathering is representative . . ." (He then went through the various numbers present.) "The next generation is represented by my dear grandchild, Bridget."[9]

Dean Hole died on 27 August 1904 and was buried at Caunton. Joe Birley, John Lyell and William Francklin were the Bearers at his funeral, and on his grave there are the words:

Here lies Samuel Reynolds Hole, D.D.
1850–87, Vicar of Caunton.
1887–04, Dean of Rochester.
Born, Dec. 5th, 1819, died, Aug. 27th, 1904.
"God is the Lord by Whom we escape death."
Psalm LXVIII, ver. XX.

"He believed in the democracy of the gardening art"[10]. . . Like Wellington he had "the modesty of greatness". (It is related of the Duke, that when descending the steps, having seen a model of Waterloo, he met a young lady on the way up and said to her, "Ah, you're going to see Waterloo. It's very good, very good indeed—I was there, you know.")

On the same lines Dame Sybil Thorndike loved to tell the story of the Dean's visit to Belvoir Castle. "The Duke of Rutland told the Dean that he could go over the gardens of Belvoir Castle whenever he wished. Arriving one day unannounced, the Dean asked the head gardener for permission to look round. The head gardener readily agreed and began to conduct the Dean round himself. They got on famously. After a time, realizing that his visitor was a knowledgeable gardener as well as a dignitary of the Church, the man asked the Dean to whom he might have the pleasure of showing the gardens. 'The Dean of Rochester, Dean Hole', came the reply. Upon which the gardener cupped his hands over his mouth and shouted down the gardens to various under-gardeners working there: 'Turn on the fountains! Turn on the fountains!' The Dean was surprised and delighted and said he had never felt so proud in his life."

But perhaps his friendship with Joe Birley shows even more clearly than the many eulogies of fame and distinction the true character of the man and so these extracts from the Dean's letters (especially as the last one ends on a note of comedy) are given to form his epilogue:

Dec. 5, 1887.
Dear Topper—It is very pleasant to be remembered by old friends, and I am glad to receive your kind wishes on my birthday. It will be a greater pleasure to *see* the writer . . . Caunton air will bring back the bright eyes and rosy cheeks which I can remember for a longer time than their owner. How astonished they would be at the station to see you down on the platform and to hear our old conversation:
"Gie o'er!"
"Why must I gie o'er?"
"Coz you'll catch it."
"Who'll gie it me?"
"Why *I* shall."
Well, time seems flying with swifter wings than ever, but I trust they are bearing us upward, for our dear Lord's sake. You and I shall be always true friends in this world, and shall, I trust, be together in the next. Yours ever sincerely, S.R.H.

Rochester, April 22, '93.
Dear Joe—You will know, without any words from me, the happiness which I feel in hearing of the good work which you are doing for our Divine Master in His Church; . . . I can hardly imagine that the blue-eyed boy, whose ribs I used to tickle as he struggled on the grass, is now Mr Churchwarden Birley! . . . On Tuesday last I stood over the grave of our dear Benedict. Do you remember the advice I gave you to mount him from the laundry window?

Rochester, September 30, '93.
Dear Joe—I am heartily pleased at your affectionate letter, and I can assure you that I enjoyed most happily our bright Sunday together . . . Mrs Hole was none the worse for her evening drive and we arrived here in safety, but with some regrets that our holiday in the dear old home was over. Nevertheless, as the sailor said, "Life can't

be all Beer and Skittles", and we must resume work and duty with thankfulness . . .

Coney Hill, Comrie, Perthshire. S. xiii Trinity, 1895.
Dear Joe—Your letter is written in such an excellent spirit, and I am so anxious to hear of further promotion that I have forwarded it, so far as it relates to your position on "The Midlands", to my friend Mr —— Time goes on, dear Joe, and having downed you so often in your childhood, I should like to assist in raising you in manhood, not only because of our friendship, but because you deserve an advance. . . . The Church here is about the size of the old Methodist meeting-house at Caunton, but it holds me nicely, and having put the choir on the roof, I can preach to the congregation outside from the open window—Yours always sincerely, Rennuds.

APPENDICES

APPENDIX I

ROCHESTER CATHEDRAL

Copy Resolution passed at a Special Chapter held on the 30th August 1904

Death of The
Very Reverend
Samuel Reynolds Hole, D.D.,
Dean of Rochester.

We, the Canons assembled in Chapter desire to put on record our deep sense of the loss we have sustained in the passing away of our revered Dean, Samuel Reynolds Hole. Endeared to us by his genial disposition and his kindness of heart, he was also a leader in good works both within the Cathedral and without. In particular we would keep in remembrance the earnest eloquence which drew together the Sunday evening congregations in the Nave, the efforts which brought about the restoration of the West front, the munificence which provided the vestries and the energy with which, even with failing strength, he promoted the fund for the restoration of the Organ. We desire to express our thankfulness that we have so long been blessed with the care and guidance of so true a servant of Christ, and also our deep sympathy with those who have lost a husband and father.

signed . . . R. A. ARNOLD,
Chapter Clerk.

APPENDIX II

Fulham Palace, S.W.

8, Gibson Place,
St. Andrews.
Sept. 2, 1904.

Dear Mrs Hole,

I have been away in the Highlands whither news travels slowly or I should have written before to have expressed my deep sympathy with you in the loss of your dear husband whom I have honoured for so long.

Few men were so universally loved even by many who could not claim to be intimate friends, and I have a vivid remembrance of his invariable kindness to me whenever I met him.

I shall never forget the scene at Nottingham when he addressed the working men's meeting and their great enthusiasm for him. If ever a warrior for God earned his rest, I am sure he has, and you will I know be comforted by the love and gratitude he has left behind on earth.

Please do not trouble to answer this but I could not bear the thought that you should be without one little word of sympathy.

A. F. London.

APPENDIX III

RESOLUTIONS ON THE DEATH OF THE VERY REV. DEAN HOLE

Whereas, we, the members of the New York Florists' Club, having learned with deep sorrow of the death of our much esteemed honorary member, the Very Rev. Samuel Reynolds Hole, Dean of Rochester, England, which occurred at his home there Saturday, August 27th last, be it

Resolved, that we hereby and in this manner express our appreciation of the great loss which the garden craft through the world has sustained in the passing away of one who, during his lifetime, did so much to advance its interests. His attachment to horticulture in all its branches was strong and lasting, and both by precept and example he did everything in his power to further and encourage a love for the art which he himself loved so well. His devotion to the rose in particular was one that has rarely, if ever, been surpassed. By his writings and his personal labors on behalf of this flower he gave an impetus to the cultivation of the rose, the influence of which was, and is, felt in every corner of the globe. Be it further resolved, that to his aged and dear life-partner and her sorrowing family, we tender our most sincere sympathy in their irreparable bereavement. We commend them to the care of Him who wisely orders all things well, and assure them that the memory of the beloved husband and father whom they mourn; the good and noble man whom we all loved and revered; the great example he set, will abide in our hearts as long as life lasts, fragrant and exhilarating as the breath of his own beloved flower.

> Wm. J. Stewart
> Signed: Patrick O'Mara
> Alex. Wallace

In presenting these Resolutions, your Committee would like to add a few words on the work accomplished by the late Dean Hole on behalf of horticulture generally and the rose in particular. He was the founder of the National Rose Society of England, and remained its honored president to the last. He originated the first annual rose show in that country, and always took an active part as an exhibitor. He wrote several books on gardening, among them a *Book about Roses* and *Our Gardens* replete with instructive information, and tinctured with that inimitable wit and humor of his, at once delightful and delighting. The seeker after knowledge on horticultural matters was never turned away by him empty handed. *He believed in the democracy of the gardening art*, that those who pursued and loved it, high and low, rich and poor, were on an equal footing, members of one common brotherhood, and this doctrine he promulgated by word and deed. . . .

APPENDIX IV

The Dean's Selection of the Best Roses for all Gardens

From *The Letters of Samuel Reynolds Hole*, George Allen & Sons, 1907.

Hybrid Perpetuals

Alfred Colomb, A. K. Williams, Baroness Rothschild, Captain Hayward, Charles Lefèbvre, Clio, Duke of Edinburgh, Dupuy Jamain, General Jacqueminot, Madame Gabriel Luizet, Marie Baumann, Merveille de Lyon, Mrs John Laing, Mrs Sharman-Crawford, Prince Arthur, Madame Victor Verdier, Suzanne M. Rodocanachi, Ulrich Brunner.

Hybrid Teas

Augustine Guinoisseau, Caroline Testout, Gustave Regis, Kaiserin A. Victoria, Killarney, La France, Mrs W. J. Grant, Papa Gontier, Viscountess Folkestone.

Teas

Anna Olivier, Catherine Mermet, G. Nabonnand, Gloire de Dijon (for wall), Madame Hoste, Madame Lambard, Maman Cochet, Maréchal Niel (for wall), Marie Van Houtte, Rubens, Souvenir d'un Ami, Souvenir de S. A. Prince, The Bride, White Maman Cochet, W. A. Richardson (for wall).

China Roses

Common China, Crimson China, Laurette Messimy, Madame Eugène Resal.

Polyantha Roses

Cecile Brunner, Perle d'Or.

APPENDIX V

Roses in the Deanery Garden at Rochester in 1903

From *The Letters of Samuel Reynolds Hole*, George Allen & Sons, 1907.

The Dean's List

A

Alfred Colomb
Alfred Williams
Amadis
Alice Lindsell
Anna Olivier
Augustine Guinoisseau
Austrian Yellow

B

Bardou Job
Baroness Rothschild
Belle Lyonnaise
Belle Siebricht
Ben Cant
Bessie Brown
Blairii 2
Bouquet d'Or
Bride, The

C

Camoëns
Captain Christy
Captain Hayward
Carmine Pillar
Caroline Testout
Catherine Mermet
Cecile Brunner
Celeni Forestier
Charles Lawson
Charles Lefèbvre
Climbing C. Christy
Climbing Kaiserin Victoria
Climbing Mrs Grant
Climbing Perle des Jardins

Clio
Common Moss
Common Sweet Briar
Common China
Conrad F. Meyer
Crimson China
Crimson Rambler

D

Dorothy Perkins
Duchess of Portland
Duc de Luxembourg
Duke of Edinburgh
Dupuy Jamain

E

Etienne Levet

F

Félicité Perpétue
Fisher Holmes
Flora M'Ivor
François Croupe
Frau Paul Druscki

G

General Jacqueminot
George Pernet
G. Nabonnand
Gladys Harkness
Gloire de Dijon
Gloire Lyonnaise
Grace Darling
Grüss an Teplitz
Gustave Regis

H

Her Majesty
Honble. Edith Gifford

I

Innocente Pirola
Irish Beauty

J

Jeannie Deans

K

Kaiserin Augusta Victoria
Killarney

L

Lady Bathence
Lady Moyse Beauclerc
Lady Penzance
La France
La Tosca
Laurette Messimy
Liberty
L'Ideal
Lord Penzance
Longworth Rambler
Louis Van Houtte

M

Madame Abel Chatenay
Madame Alfred Carrière
Madame Berard
Madame Chédane Guinoisseau
Madame de Watteville
Madame Eugène Resal
Madame Gabriel Luizet
Madame Hoste
Madame Jules Grolez
Madame Lambard
Madame Isaac Percine
Madame Pernet Ducher

Madame Ravany
Madame Victor Verdier
Maman Cochet
Maréchal Niel
Marguerite Dickson
Marie Baumann
Marie Van Houtte
Marquise de Salisbury
Marquise Litta
Merveille de Lyon
Mildred Grant
Mrs Bosanquet
Mrs B. R. Cant
Mrs John Laing
Mrs Reynolds Hole
Mrs Sharman-Crawford
Mrs W. J. Grant

N

Niphetos

P

Papa Gontier
Papa Lambert
Paul Lergon
Perle d'Or
Perle des Jardins
Perle des Rouges
Persian Yellow
Prince Arthur

Q

Queen Alexandra

R

Rev. Alan Hicks
Reve d'Or
Reynolds Hole
Reine Marie Henriette
Rosa Lucida
Rose Macrantha
Rosa Mundi

Rosa Linica
Rubens

S

Senator Varpe
Soleil d'Or
Souvenir de Catherine Guillot
Souvenir de Pierre Notting
Sunrise
Suzanne M. Rodocanachi

U

Ulrich Brunner

V

Village Maid
Viscountess Folkestone

W

White Maman Cochet
William Allan Richardson

REFERENCES

The principal published sources are listed in the Bibliography on p. 246. Thus, for the sake of brevity, it has been decided to abbreviate these in the References, as follows:

Brown Dr John	*Horae Subsecivae*	= HS
Frith W. P.	*John Leech: His Life and Work*	= Leech
Fuller Hester T.		
Hammersley V.	*Thackeray's Daughter*	= TD
Hole S. Reynolds	*A Book About Roses*	= Roses
	The Memories of Dean Hole	= Memories
	More Memories	= MM
	Then And Now	= Then
	A Book About The Garden	
	And The Gardener	= Garden
	A Little Tour in Ireland	= Ireland
	Our Gardens	= OG
	A Little Tour In America	= America
Ritchie Hester	*Letters of Anne Thackeray Ritchie*	= Ritchie Letters

The principal unpublished source is the diaries of Henry Silver to which reference is made by the initials HSD.

Chapter 1

1 Memories
2 ibid
3 ibid
4 Trevelyan G. M. *Illustrated English Social History*, vol. 4
5 Booth General William *In Darkest England And The Way Out*, Salvation Army, London, 1890
6 Maurois André *Byron*, Cape, London, 1930
7 Article on "Nottingham Lace" from *Blackwood's Magazine*, vol. 132, October 1882
8 Children's Employment Commissioners' Report 1843
9 Then
10 ibid
11 Memories
12 ibid
13 ibid
14 Then

15 ibid
16 MM
17 MM
18 Dewar George *The Letters of Dean Hole*, George Allen, London, 1907
19 *Rochester, Chatham & Gillingham Journal*, 2 September 1904
20 ibid
21 Dewar George op. cit.
22 *Rochester, Chatham & Gillingham Journal*, 2 September 1904
23 ibid
24 Robbins A. F. *The Early Public Life of William Ewart Gladstone*, Methuen, London, 1894
25 ibid
26 *Rochester, Chatham & Gillingham Journal*, op. cit.
27 Memories
28 ibid
29 ibid
30 ibid
31 ibid
32 ibid
33 ibid
34 Briscoe John Potter (ed.) *Old Nottinghamshire*, Hamilton Adams, London, 1884
35 Mitton G. E. *Jane Austen and Her Times*, Methuen, London, 1905
36 Jane Austen, *Emma*
37 Memories
38 ibid

Chapter 2
1 John Raymond (ed.) *Queen Victoria's Early Letters*, Batsford, London, 1963
2 Austen Jane *Sense and Sensibility*
3 Austen Jane *Mansfield Park*
4 ibid
5 Memories
6 Eliot George "The Sad Fortunes of the Rev. Amos Barton" from *Scenes of Clerical Life*, Macmillan, London, 1909
7 Eliot George "Janet's Repentance" from *Scenes of Clerical Life*
8 Memories
9 Shairp J. C. "John Keble" taken from *The Oxford Movement 1833-45* by R. W. Church, Macmillan, London, 1891
10 Memories
11 ibid
12 ibid
13 Church R. W. *The Oxford Movement 1833-45*, Macmillan, London, 1891
14 MM
15 McCormick G. D. K. *The Private Life of Mr Gladstone*, Muller, London, 1965
16 Church R. W. op. cit.
17 Austen Jane *Sense and Sensibility*
18 Austen Jane *Mansfield Park*
19 Austen Jane *Sense and Sensibility*
20 Austen Jane *Pride and Prejudice*
21 ibid

22 Austen Jane *Emma*
23 Austen Jane *Pride and Prejudice*
24 ibid

Chapter 3

All references in this chapter, unless stated otherwise, are taken from Roses.

1 Garden
2 Dewar George op. cit.
3 Rivers Thomas *The Rose Amateur's Guide*, 1837
4 Garden
5 ibid
6 MM
7 Then
8 ibid
9 ibid
10 ibid
11 Loudon J. C. *Encyclopaedia of Gardening*, Longmans, London, 1878
12 Memories
13 Rivers op. cit.

Chapter 4

All references in this chapter, unless stated otherwise, are taken from Ireland.

1 Roses and Memories
2 Leech
3 Memories
4 Leech
5 Adrian Arthur *Mark Lemon—First Editor of Punch*, OUP, London, 1966
6 Leech
7 Leech
8 Leech
9 Millais J. G. *Life and Letters of J. E. Millais*, vol. 1, Methuen, London, 1899
10 Leech
11 Steel Anthony *Jorrocks's England*, Methuen, London, 1932
12 Hole Hugh *Looking Life Over*, Nicholson & Watson, London, 1934
13 ibid
14 ibid
15 O'Connor Frank *A Book of Ireland*, Collins, London, 1959
16 Bozman E. F. (ed.) *Everyman's Encyclopaedia*, 5th edition, Dent, London
17 HS
18 *The Times* 26 September 1859

Chapter 5

All references in this chapter, unless stated otherwise, are taken from HS.

1 Sime J. G. "In a Canadian Shack" taken from the anthology *Love* compiled by Walter de la Mare, Faber, London, 1943
2 Sitwell Osbert (ed.) *A Free House. The Writings of Walter Richard Sickert*, Macmillan, London, 1947

3 ibid
4 ibid
5 Leech
6 ibid
7 ibid
8 Redgrave *A Century of British Painters*, Phaidon, London
9 Leech
10 ibid
11 ibid
12 Gill Eric *Essays*, Cape, London, 1947
13 Leech

Chapter 6

All references in this chapter, unless stated otherwise, are taken from HSD.

1 Spielman M. H. *The History of Punch*, Cassell, London, 1895
2 Adrian Arthur op. cit.
3 ibid
4 Spielman M. H. op. cit.
5 Memories
6 ibid
7 ibid
8 ibid
9 ibid
10 ibid
11 ibid
12 ibid
13 ibid
14 TD
15 Ritchie Letters
16 TD
17 ibid
18 ibid
19 ibid
20 ibid
21 ibid
22 Ritchie Letters
23 TD
24 TD
25 TD
26 TD

Chapter 7

All references in this chapter, unless stated otherwise, are taken from Memories.

1 Leech
2 HS
3 ibid
4 Ireland
5 Tout, T. F. *An Advanced History of Great Britain*, Longmans, London, 1923
6 Barry F. V. *Maria Edgeworth: Chosen Letters*, Cape, London, 1931
7 Roses

16

8 Dewar George op. cit.
9 Hole Hugh op. cit.
10 Spielman M. H. op. cit.

Chapter 8

1 Millais J. G. op. cit.
2 TD
3 ibid
4 ibid
5 ibid
6 ibid
7 ibid
8 ibid
9 ibid
10 ibid
11 HSD
12 Memories
13 ibid
14 HSD
15 Brown John and Forrest D. W. (eds) *The Letters of Dr John Brown*, Nelson, London, 1912
16 ibid
17 ibid
18 ibid
19 HS
20 Peddie Alexander *Recollections of Dr John Brown*, Percival, London, 1893
21 HS
22 Adrian Arthur op. cit.
23 HS
24 ibid
25 ibid
26 Millais J. G. op. cit.
27 Layard G. S. *A Great Punch Editor: A Life of Shirley Brooks*, Pitman, London, 1907
28 ibid
29 Leech
30 ibid
31 ibid
32 ibid

Chapter 9
All references in this chapter, unless stated otherwise, are taken from Ritchie Letters.

1 HSD
2 TD
3 Trollope Anthony *An Autobiography*, Williams & Norgate, London, 1883
4 TD
5 ibid
6 ibid
7 Maitland F. Wm. (ed.) *The Life and Letters of Leslie Stephen*, Duckworth, London, 1906

8 TD
9 ibid
10 OG
11 TD
12 ibid
13 ibid
14 ibid
15 Hind C. Lewis *Hercules Brabazon Brabazon—His Art and Life*, published privately
16 ibid
17 Leslie George D. *Our River*, Bardbury Agnew, London, 1888
18 ibid
19 ibid
20 Robinson William *The Garden Beautiful*, Murray, London, 1907
21 Frederick Warne, London, 1868

Chapter 10

All references in this chapter, unless stated otherwise, are taken from Roses.

1 Garden
2 ibid
3 ibid
4 ibid
5 ibid
6 Rohde E. Sinclair *The Scented Garden*, Medici Society, London, 1935
7 Nicolson Philippa (ed.) *V. Sackville-West's Garden Book*, Joseph, London, 1968
8 Sitwell Sacheverell *Old Fashioned Flowers*, Country Life, London, 1939
9 Taylor Geoffrey, *The Victorian Flower Garden*, Skeffington, London, 1952
10 Bunyard Edward *Old Garden Roses*, Country Life, London, 1936
11 Jekyll Gertrude and Mawley Edward *Roses for English Gardens*, Country Life, London, 1903
12 ibid
13 Garden
14 ibid
15 ibid
16 ibid

Chapter 11

1 Printed for T. Garthwait by T. Maxey at the little North door of St Paul's 1652. (Dated, inside, in the Introduction, 1632.)
2 Printed for Bernard Lintott between the Temple-Gates in Fleet Street, London, 1714
3 OG
4 Memories
5 ibid
6 Naylor Major-General R. F. B. "The History, Development and Growth of the National Rose Society", R.H.S. Journal, September 1964, vol. LXXXIX, part 9
7 ibid
8 ibid
9 Then
10 Arnold Dr Sermons, vol. 1, ch. vii, 1829

11 McGuigan Dorothy G. *The Habsburgs*, W. H. Allen, London, 1966
12 Hussey Christopher *The Life of Sir Edwin Lutyens*, Country Life, London, 1953
13 ibid
14 ibid
15 Hole S. Reynolds *Addresses Spoken To Working Men from Pulpit and Platform*, Arnold, London, 1894

Chapter 12
1 Hole S. Reynolds *Nice and Her Neighbours*, Sampson Low, London, 1881
2 Hole S. Reynolds *Hints to Preachers with Sermons and Addresses*, Parker, London, 1880
3 ibid
4 ibid
5 Hole S. Reynolds *Buch von der Rose*, Verlag von Wiegandi, Berlin, 1880
6 Noakes Vivien *Edward Lear—The Life of a Wanderer*, Collins, London, 1968
7 Robinson William *The Parks, Promenades and Gardens of Paris*, Murray, London, 1869
8 Hill W. T. *Octavia Hill*, Hutchinson, London, 1956
9 Fedden Robin *The Continuing Purpose*, Longmans, London, 1968 (to be published by Jonathan Cape, London, 1974 in paperback)
10 This and subsequent extracts on pp. 169–170 from newspaper reports are taken from Dean Hole's book of cuttings from *The Chatham & Rochester News* (Military and Naval Chronicle, Strood, Brompton and Gillingham News, Maidstone Gravesend and North Kent Spectator) and *The Rochester & Chatham Journal* (Mid-Kent Advertiser)
11 Dewar George, op. cit.
12 ibid
13 ibid

Chapter 13
1 Dutton Ralph *The English Garden*, Batsford, London, 1937
2 Robinson William *Gleanings from French Gardens*, Warne, London, 1868
3 Memories
4 Published by John Murray, London, 1883
5 Jekyll Gertrude, *Wood and Garden*, Longmans, London, 1899
6 Jekyll Francis *Gertrude Jekyll A Memoir*, Cape, London, 1934
7 Hussey Christopher op. cit.
8 Jekyll Gertrude *Home and Garden*, Longmans, London, 1900
9 Jekyll Gertrude *Colour Schemes for the Flower Garden*, Country Life, London, 1914
10 Jekyll Gertrude *Children and Gardens*, Country Life, London, 1908
11 Jekyll Gertrude *Flower Decoration in the House*, Country Life, London, 1907
12 Jekyll Gertrude *Lilies for English Gardens*, Country Life, London, 1903
13 Jekyll Gertrude *Wall and Water Gardens*, Country Life, London, 1901
14 Jekyll Gertrude *Old West Surrey*, Longmans, London, 1904
15 OG
16 ibid
17 ibid
18 ibid
19 Memories
20 Hibberd Shirley *The Fern Garden*, Groombridge, London, 1875

21 Hibberd Shirley *The Amateur's Kitchen Garden*, Groombridge, London, 1877
22 Humphris *Garden Glory*, Collins, London, 1965
23 Hibberd Shirley *The Ivy*, Groombridge, London, 1872
24 Hibberd Shirley *The Rose Book*, Groombridge, London, 1864
25 Hibberd Shirley *Field Flowers*, Groombridge, London, 1870
26 Memories
27 Hibberd Shirley *The Amateur's Greenhouse*, Groombridge, London, 1883
28 ibid
29 Hibberd Shirley *The Fern Garden*, op. cit.
30 Hibberd Shirley *Garden Favourites*, Groombridge, London, 1858
31 Fairchild Thomas *The City Gardener*, London, 1722
32 Hibberd Shirley *Rustic Adornments for Homes of Taste*, Groombridge, London, 1856
33 ibid
34 Jekyll Gertrude *Home and Garden*, op. cit.

Chapter 14

All references in this chapter, unless stated otherwise, are taken from America.

1 Shorthouse J. H. *John Inglesant*, Macmillan, London, 1880
2 Memories
3 MM
4 ibid
5 Patterson Clara Burdett *Angela Burdett-Coutts and the Victorians*, Murray, London, 1953
6 Osborne Charles C. (ed.) *Letters of Charles Dickens to the Baroness Burdett-Coutts*, Murray, London, 1931
7 McCormick G. D. K. *The Private Life of Mr Gladstone*, Muller, London, 1965
8 Nash Vaughan *A Selection from the Writings of H. W. Massingham*, Cape, London, 1925
9 *The Christian Commonwealth*, 11 April 1895
10 *The American College Dictionary*, Random House, New York
11 ibid

Chapter 15

1 Beerbohm Max *More Theatres*, Hart-Davis, London, 1969
2 Hole Hugh *Looking Life Over*, Nicholson & Watson, London, 1934
3 Morris William Prologue to *The Earthly Paradise*, 1868
4 Hole S. Reynolds *Then And Now*, Hutchinson, London, 1901
5 Jekyll Gertrude *Some English Gardens* op. cit.
6 ibid
7 Hole Hugh *Looking Life Over* op. cit.
8 Dewar George op. cit.
9 ibid
10 "Resolution on the Death of the Very Rev. Dean Hole", see appendix III

BIBLIOGRAPHY

Works by S. Reynolds Hole

A Little Tour in Ireland Bradbury Agnew, London, 1858
A Book About Roses (2nd edtn) Blackwood, Edinburgh, 1870
Hints to Preachers with Sermons and Addresses Parker, Oxford, 1880
Nice and Her Neighbours Sampson Low, London, 1881
The Memories of Dean Hole Arnold, London, 1892
More Memories (being thoughts about England spoken in America) Arnold, London, 1894
A Little Tour In America Arnold, London, 1894
Our Gardens Dent, London, 1899
Then And Now Hutchinson, London, 1901
A Book About The Garden Arnold, London, 1904
Addresses Spoken to Working Men from Pulpit and Platform Arnold, London, 1894

Related Works

Adrian, Arthur A. *Mark Lemon—First Editor of Punch*, OUP, Oxford, 1966
Beerbohm, Max *More Theatres 1898–1903*, Hart-Davis, London, 1969
Briscoe John Potter (ed.) *Old Nottinghamshire* (2nd series), Hamilton Adams, London, 1884
Brown Dr John *Horae Subsecivae*, (3rd series) Black, London, 1900
Brown John and Forrest D. W. *Letters of Dr John Brown*, Nelson, London, 1912
Bunyard Edward A. *Old Garden Roses*, Country Life, London, 1936
Casson John *Lewis and Sybil—A Memoir*, Collins, London, 1972
Church R. A. *Economic and Social Change in a Midland Town*, Cass, London, 1966
Church R. W. *The Oxford Movement 1833–45*, Macmillan, London, 1891
Dewar George (ed.) *The Letters of Dean Hole*, George Allen, London, 1907
Dickens Mamie and Howarth Georgina (eds.) *The Letters of Charles Dickens*, Macmillan, London, 1893
Eliot George *Scenes of Clerical Life*, Macmillan, London, 1909
Ellacombe Henry N. *In a Gloucestershire Garden*, Arnold, London, 1896
Farrar Frederic W. *Eric; Or, Little by Little*, Hamilton, London, 1971
Fedden Henry R. *The Continuing Purpose—A History of the National Trust, its Aims and Work*, Longmans, London, 1968
Frith William P. *John Leech, His Life and Work*, Bentley, London, 1891
Fuller Hester Thackeray and Hammersley Violet (eds.) *Thackeray's Daughter—Some Recollections*, Euphorian Books, Dublin, 1951
Green John Richard *A Short History of the English People*, Macmillan, London, 1907

Herbert George *A Priest to the Temple or The Country Parson*, printed by T. Maxey for
   T. Garthwait at the Little North Door of St Paul's, 1652 (dated inside in the
   Introduction, 1632)
Hibberd Shirley *The Rose Book*, Groombridge, London, 1854
                  Rustic Adornments for Homes of Taste, Groombridge, London, 1856
                  Garden Favourites, Groombridge, London, 1858
                  The Fern Garden, Groombridge, London, 1875
                  The Amateur's Kitchen Garden, Groombridge, London, 1877
                  The Amateur's Flower Garden, Groombridge, London, 1878
                  The Amateur's Greenhouse, Groombridge, London, 1883
Hill A. W. *Henry Nicholson Ellacombe*, Country Life, London, 1919
Hill William T. *Octavia Hill*, Hutchinson, London, 1956
Hole Hugh *Looking Life Over*, Nicholson & Watson, London, 1934
Humphris Ted *Garden Glory*, Collins, London, 1965
Hussey Christopher *The Life of Sir Edwin Lutyens*, Country Life, London, 1953
Jekyll Gertrude *Wood and Garden*, Longmans, London, 1899
                  Home and Garden, Longmans, London, 1900
                  Some English Gardens, Longmans, London, 1906
                  Wall and Water Gardens, Country Life, London, 1901
                  Colour Schemes for the Flower Garden (first published as *Colour in the
                  Flower Garden* in 1908), Country Life, London, 1914
Jekyll Gertrude and Mawley Edward *Roses for English Gardens*, Country Life, London,
   1902
Johnson Edgar *Letters from Charles Dickens to Angela Burdett-Coutts 1841–1865*, Cape,
   London, 1953
Lawrence John *The Gentleman's Recreation*, London, 1716
Layard G. S. *A Great Punch Editor: A Life of Shirley Brooks*, Pitman, London, 1907
Lutyens Mary *Millais and the Ruskins*, Murray, London, 1967
Maitland F. W. *The Life and Letters of Leslie Stephen*, Duckworth, London, 1906
Mare Walter de la *Love*, Faber, London, 1943
Maurois André *Byron*, translated from the French by Hamish Miles, Cape, London,
   1930
McCormick G. D. K. *The Private Life of Mr Gladstone*, Muller, London, 1965
Meller Helen E. (ed.) *Nottingham in the Eighteen Nineties—A Study in Social Change*,
   Dept. of Adult Education, University of Nottingham, 1971
Millais J. G. *The Life and Letters of J. E. Millais*, vols I and II, Methuen, London, 1899
Mitton G. E. *Jane Austen and Her Times*, Methuen, London, 1917
Noakes Vivien *Edward Lear—The Life of a Wanderer*, Collins, London, 1968
O'Connor Frank (ed.) *A Book of Ireland*, Collins, London, 1959
Osborne Charles C. (ed.) *Letters of Charles Dickens to the Baroness Burdett-Coutts*,
   Murray, London, 1931
Patterson Clara Burdett *Angela Burdett-Coutts and the Victorians*, Murray, London, 1953
Paul William *The Rose Garden*, Shirwood Gilbert & Piper, London, 1848
Peddie Alexander *Recollections of Dr John Brown*, Percival, London, 1893
Raymond John (ed.) *Queen Victoria's Early Letters*, Batsford, London, 1963
Redgrave *A Century of British Painters*, Phaidon, London, 1947
Ritchie Hester (ed.) *Letters of Anne Thackeray Ritchie*, Murray, London, 1924
Ritchie Lady *From Friend To Friend*, Murray, London, 1920
Robbins Alfred F. *The Early Public Life of William Ewart Gladstone*, Methuen, London,
   1894

Robinson William *Gleanings from French Gardens,* Warne, London, 1868
                 The Parks, Promenades and Gardens of Paris, Murray, London, 1869
                 The Wild Garden, Murray, London, 1870
                 Garden Design, Murray, London, 1892
                 The English Flower Garden, Murray, London, 1897 (reprinted in
                 1956)
Ruskin John *Praeterita 2,* George Allen, Orpington, 1887
            Praeterita 3, George Allen, Orpington, 1888
            Unto this Last & Other Essays on Art and Political Economy, Dent, London,
            1907
Shorthouse J. H. *John Inglesant,* Macmillan, London, 1930
Sitwell Osbert *Free House. The Writings of Walter Richard Sickert,* Macmillan, London,
1947
Spielman M. H. *The History of Punch,* Cassell, London, 1895
Steel Anthony *Jorrock's England,* Methuen, London, 1932
Thackeray William Makepeace *The Newcomes,* OUP, Oxford, 1864
Tout T. F. *An Advanced History of Great Britain,* Longmans, London, 1923
Trevelyan G. M. *Illustrated English Social History,* vol. 4, Longmans, London, 1967
Vidler Alec R. *The Church in an Age of Revolution,* Penguin, Harmondsworth, 1961

Miscellaneous Publications

American College Dictionary, Random House, New York
Rochester, Chatham & Gillingham Journal, 2 September 1904
"Children's Employment Commissioners' Report", 1843
The Chatham & Rochester News, 1888–1904
The Rochester & Chatham Journal, 1888–1904
The Rose Amateur's Guide Thomas Rivers, 1837

INDEX

by

F. T. DUNN

NOTE: Dean Hole's writings are indexed
under the entry for Hole himself